DATE DUE

PRESIDENTIAL
COMMISSIONS
&
NATIONAL
SECURITY

PRESIDENTIAL COMMISSIONS

&

NATIONAL SECURITY

The Politics of Damage Control

KENNETH KITTS

LYNNE
RIENNER
PUBLISHERS

BOULDER
LONDON

Published in the United States of America in 2006 by
Lynne Rienner Publishers, Inc.
1800 30th Street, Boulder, Colorado 80301
www.rienner.com

and in the United Kingdom by
Lynne Rienner Publishers, Inc.
3 Henrietta Street, Covent Garden, London WC2E 8LU

Library of Congress Cataloging-in-Publication Data
Kitts, Kenneth, 1964–
Presidential commissions and national security : the politics of damage
    control / by Kenneth Kitts.
    Includes bibliographical references and index.
    ISBN 1-58826-404-1 (hardcover : alk. paper)
    1. Executive advisory bodies—United States—Case studies. 2. National
security—United States—Decision making—Case studies. I. Title.
JK468.C7K58 2006
355'.033073—dc22   2005029420

British Cataloguing in Publication Data
A Cataloguing in Publication record for this book
is available from the British Library.

Printed and bound in the United States of America

The paper used in this publication meets the requirements
of the American National Standard for Permanence of
Paper for Printed Library Materials Z39.48-1992.

5   4   3   2   1

In loving memory of
Dr. Warren Hugh Kitts

Contents

Tables

Acknowledgments

The idea for this book began over a decade ago with a conversation in the office of Betty Glad at the University of South Carolina. Then a doctoral student, I mentioned to Betty that I was interested in the work of blue-ribbon commissions. She urged me to pursue the idea, and with that I was off and running. Betty agreed to sign on as my dissertation director and major professor. Our association continues to this day, and I could not have asked for a better mentor.

More recently, my good fortune continued when I contacted Lynne Rienner Publishers to pitch this project. Leanne Anderson, Steve Barr, and the rest of the staff have been wonderful to work with, and I appreciate their guidance and professionalism.

Many experts helped me uncover the secrets of commissions past. Among those who went above and beyond the call of duty were Evelyn Cherpak of the Naval Historical Collection, Naval War College; Robert Clark of the Roosevelt Presidential Library; Geir Gundersen of the Ford Presidential Library; Edwin N. Probert II of Germantown Academy (Owen Roberts's alma mater); Kathryn Stallard of the John Tower Papers, Southwestern University; and numerous archivists at the Manuscript Division of the Library of Congress and at the National Archives.

More than twenty commission insiders also took the time to talk with me regarding their experiences. All were and are busy, important people. Their insight gives the book an authority and richness it otherwise would not have. With few exceptions, they were willing to talk candidly and for attribution. None requested prepublication review of my work. I suspect some will agree with my conclusions and others will not. In either case, I am grateful to them all.

At Francis Marion University, special thanks go to the staff of Rogers Library, as well as to the Professional Development Committee for providing the travel grants that underwrote much of my off-site research. Along the way I have also benefited from the encouragement of my faculty colleagues. I owe a special debt of gratitude to Neal Thigpen for sharing so freely his wit, wisdom, books, and encyclopedic political knowledge.

On a more personal level, I am lucky to have a wonderful network of family and friends who have helped me stay on task. At the center of this universe are two remarkable women, Betty Kitts and June Strickland. To the rest of the gang in Waynesville, Latta, Richmond, Houston, Florence, and Lumberton, you know who you are and what you mean to me. Finally, this book would never have seen the light of day without the love and support of my amazing wife, Dena. Thank you for believing in me.

Despite this army of support, I am ultimately the one responsible for the content that follows. Any errors of fact or interpretation are mine.

PRESIDENTIAL COMMISSIONS

&

NATIONAL SECURITY

1

Presidents and the Blue-Ribbon Option

Commissions are a kind of national narcotic, a prescription that has worked brilliantly for some of the most high-achieving presidents.
—William Powers in *The New Republic*

B lue-ribbon commissions are the ghosts of US politics. Like apparitions, they materialize from time to time and wade into the middle of public debate—for example, the Kennedy assassination, Social Security reform, 11 September 2001 ("9/11")—then disappear in the blink of an eye. Left behind are the dusty accounts of tragedy and scandal, the well-intended recommendations, and the warnings that so often go unheeded. This ephemeral quality makes commissions notoriously difficult to study. And to make matters worse, no two commissions are alike. They differ tremendously in size, scope, mandate, membership, and power.

National security commissions, the focus of this study, are a special type of blue-ribbon panel. These bodies usually have some degree of presidential backing. Their investigations take them into the dangerous world of the soldier, the secret world of the spy, and the pressure-filled world of the policymaker. Consequently, they attract more attention than their less glamorous counterparts in the realm of domestic policy. But attention does not come cheap in Washington, DC. National security commissions have paid a heavy price for visibility, and that price has come in the form of political pressure.

This book is devoted to illuminating the role and function of presidential commissions in the context of US national security policy. Special attention is given to the politics that lead to the appointment of these panels, their organizational dynamics, and their recommendations. Significantly, the evidence suggests that the use of security commissions is linked to executive–legislative clashes over control of foreign and defense policy. When challenged, presidents have used these panels to defuse crises, deflect criticism, and maintain the initiative in national security decisionmaking.

Ad Hoc Advisory Groups in US Politics

Decisionmakers in the United States have long recognized the need to occasionally reach outside normal bureaucratic channels for advice on difficult issues. As early as 1794, George Washington deemed it necessary to send a group of respected men to the scene of the Whiskey Rebellion in western Pennsylvania. The three commissioners were to "repair to the scene of the insurrection ... to confer with any bodies of men or individuals" in an attempt to peacefully resolve the crisis.[1] Washington's decision set a precedent that opened the door for his successors to create specialized investigatory bodies when necessary.

The early appearance of these bodies in the new United States owed much to the British tradition of the royal commission. Created by warrants of appointment issued by the British crown, these commissions had been in use for centuries before the Revolutionary War. They proved their usefulness by contributing to the development of the civil service system and other progressive reform measures.[2] In the twentieth century, they examined issues ranging from consumer credit to spy scandals. British Commonwealth states, most notably Australia and Canada, have also used these panels for investigation and exploration.

Royal commissions have long enjoyed greater stature than government commissions in the United States.[3] The prestige gap is attributable to differences between British and US political systems. The Madisonian system of separated powers contrasts sharply with the parliamentary principle of majority-party control. In the United States this means that a certain level of tension will necessarily exist between the executive and legislative branches of government.

For this reason there is, politically speaking, no real equivalent to the British royal commission in the US system of government. Lawmakers hold that "Congress has the right, and need, to make its own investigations and that the best advice comes from its own members."[4] Conversely, presidents have been reluctant to endorse or cooperate with congressional investigations of executive branch activities. One early student of the ad hoc advisory system framed the issue succinctly.

> No royal commission operates without the actual or implied consent of Parliament; no royal commission would be suggested by the Cabinet unless Parliament would approve. In the United States, Congress is free to have its own commissions but lacks both the tradition and the perspective for great success. The President can, within limits, engineer his own investigations but proposals for legislation which may grow out of such investigations may be met by an indifferent Congress—made so perhaps by reason of feeling that the President has encroached on a legislative prerogative.[5]

Despite these challenges blue-ribbon commissions have proven to be durable fixtures in US politics, and they experienced something of a boom in the twentieth century. "With presidents and lawmakers turning to commissions to solve everything from Social Security and Medicare to elections and intelligence," joked one wag, "Washington has amassed more panels than a 1950s basement."[6] Much of this expansion can be traced to the growth of the administrative state in the years following the Great Depression and World War II. Historian Hugh Davis Graham notes that executive advisory commissions have been broadly reflective of the presidency itself, enjoying "growth and power" in the immediate postwar period, but also suffering from the "electoral disruptions" and partisan attacks of later years.[7]

Presidential commissions, the focus of this book, are only one type of advisory committee. Other bodies created within the executive branch are actually departmental committees, reporting not to the president but to a cabinet secretary or agency supervisor. These bodies tend to deal with mundane, procedural questions far removed from matters of grand strategy or constitutional design. Still others are interagency groups created to enhance policy coordination between two or more bureaucratic entities. Though the interagency groups operate above the departmental level, they are composed entirely of executive branch officials and thus lack the public quality that is the hallmark of true blue-ribbon inquiries.

The complexity of the system is compounded by legislative involvement in the advisory process. Congress has occasionally appointed its own blue-ribbon commissions.[8] Perhaps the best-known examples of this type of group were the two Hoover Commissions on the Organization of the Executive Branch (1947–1949 and 1953–1955). Both of these panels were created by the US Congress and composed of members selected by leaders in the House and Senate. Their reports, though shared with presidents Truman and Eisenhower, were tailored specifically for congressional consumption.

In an effort to streamline the system, Congress passed the Federal Advisory Committee Act (FACA) in October 1972.[9] The act defined advisory committee as any group established "in the interest of obtaining advice or recommendations for the President or officers of the Federal Government." There are two key exceptions to FACA coverage. The act does not apply to (1) those advisory committees composed entirely of government officials; and (2) those committees deemed to have "operational" functions that go beyond an advisory mandate. The passage of FACA has injected some order into the advisory system and enhanced accountability. In 1972, the government reported 1,436 advisory committees in existence. Three decades later, that figure was below 900.[10]

Despite these improvements, it remains exceedingly difficult to classify or even count federal advisory committees with scientific precision. "No one knows," states a report by the Government Accounting Office (GAO), "exactly how many miscellaneous boards, committees, and commissions exist at any given time."[11] Nor does the GAO offer much hope that greater clarity will be forthcoming:

> It is always helpful at the outset to define your universe. In this instance, however, we have been unable to discover or devise a satisfactory definition.... Advisory committees are only one type of these miscellaneous bodies, albeit the largest. The impossibility of crafting a useful definition becomes apparent upon considering the key elements of function, creation, membership, and duration.[12]

President Bill Clinton's Task Force on National Health Care Reform provides an excellent example of how difficult it can be to classify panels. The task force found itself at the center of a federal court case in 1993.[13] At issue was the legal status of committee chair Hillary Rodham Clinton. The duties of a first lady, the court decided, made her a de facto government employee. That decision, coupled with the fact that all other members of the panel were also executive branch officers, meant that the panel did not qualify as a "public" advisory committee under FACA guidelines.

Presidential Commissions

When the departmental, interagency, and congressional panels are pared from the list of federal advisory bodies, there remain a small number—generally less than 5 percent of the total—that may be loosely classified as presidential commissions.[14] And *loosely* is indeed the operative word! Some groups (e.g., the Warren Commission) are easy to classify as presidential, being created by executive order, comprising members chosen by the president, and reporting only to the White House. Other panels (e.g., the 9/11 Commission) present more of an analytical challenge.

To aid in the process of classification, scholars have crafted a number of definitions to help identify the essential ingredients of a "true" presidential commission.[15] Some widely accepted attributes are that the panel must be clearly temporary, with three years normally specified as the maximum duration; and that the panel must have at least one member from outside the executive branch (or the federal rolls generally, depending on the definition).

Defining criteria for membership selection has proven more difficult. Thomas Wolanin wrote in 1975 that a commission could not be considered presidential unless *all the members* were appointed directly by the president.[16] But that degree of White House control over commissions has become increasingly rare. By the end of the 1980s it was clear that Congress did not intend to sit on the sidelines and watch the president pack important panels with his own appointees. The 1994 Commission on the Roles and Capabilities of the US Intelligence Community (Aspin-Brown Commission) is indicative of the change. Of the seventeen members appointed to that panel, President Clinton selected only nine.[17] Still more recently, President George W. Bush appointed only one member, albeit the chair, to serve on the commission investigating the terrorist attacks of 11 September 2001. Table 1.1 illustrates the range of presidential involvement in blue-ribbon investigations of national security issues.

This study follows the lead of Stephen Zink, Amy Zegart, and others who argue for a more inclusive view of presidential commissions.[18] Modern definitions account for the growing number of "national" or "presidential-congressional" panels that feature varying degrees of legislative input. But inclusiveness does not mean that *any* blue-ribbon panel qualifies as presidential in nature. Certain minimal criteria must be satisfied. The president must endorse the panel's creation by proclamation, executive

Table 1.1   The Presidential Role in National Security Commissions

Type	Characteristics	Example
Strongly Presidential	• Created by executive order or other presidential act • All members appointed by president • President designated as sole recipient of final report	1975 Commission on CIA Activities Within the United States (Rockefeller)
Moderately Presidential	• Created by executive order or public law • Membership is shared responsibility; president appoints a majority of members • President and Congress designated as co-recipients of final report	1994 Commission on the Roles and Capabilities of the U.S. Intelligence Community (Aspin-Brown)
Loosely Presidential	• Created by public law with presidential consent • Membership is shared responsibility; president appoints a minority of members • President and Congress designated as co-recipients of final report	2002 National Commission on Terrorist Attacks Upon the United States (Kean)
Non-Presidential	• Created by public law with or without presidential consent • President excluded from membership selection • Congress designated as sole recipient of final report	1998 Commission to Assess the Ballistic Missile Threat to the United States (Rumsfeld)

order, or bill signing; the president must play a role in membership selection; and the president must be formally designated as a recipient of the final report.

The five panels featured in this book meet these criteria. Even so, variety remains the order of the day when it comes to commissions, and it is likely that scholars will continue to grapple with these definitional issues for years to come. The diversity of titles helps to underscore the point. Some presidential commissions actually carry that label. Others bear the "blue-ribbon" modifier, while still others are formally designated as a "board of inquiry," "task force," or "review board."

Whatever label they bear, presidential commissions hold a special place in the universe of federal advisory bodies. The president alone can grant a commission instant prestige by lending the sanction of the Oval Office to an inquiry. The participation of well-known personalities from government, big business, labor organizations, academia, and the arts guarantees significant media coverage. The panel's leader, if not already a national figure, will likely become so during the course of the investigation. Most presidential commissions become so familiar to the public that they quickly shed their official title and take on the name of the chairperson. Even today, reference to the Tower, Grace, or Warren commissions serves as a ready point of reference for students of political history.

Commission Scholarship

The body of literature on presidential commissions is small. An initial work, Carl Marcy's *Presidential Commissions* (1945), has been followed by only a handful of books and journal articles. Of these, two stand out as particularly noteworthy: Thomas Wolanin's *Presidential Advisory Commissions* (1975) and Terrence Tutchings's *Rhetoric and Reality: Presidential Commissions and the Making of Public Policy* (1979).[19] Wolanin and Tutchings were the first to make extensive use of primary-source materials in their analyses. Their research produced a wealth of data on the organizational and structural characteristics of the panels appointed in the post–World War II era. Commissions have received sporadic attention since the 1970s. The 1980s gave rise to only one book-length study, David Flitner's *The Politics of Presidential Commissions*.[20] David Linowes's *Creating Public Policy: The Chairman's Memoirs of Four Presidential Commissions* appeared in 1998 and provided the detail one would expect of an insider.[21]

Significantly, most of the mainstream scholarship on commissions presents a positive, even enthusiastic, view of blue-ribbon activity. Wolanin's assessment is typical of this perspective:

Commission reports usually ... received presidential support and were very often an important contribution to proposed or implemented changes in federal policy. Commissions also had a broad and significant impact as educators of the general public, government officials, the professional community, and their own members.[22]

Similarly, Linowes views commissions as consistent with the American egalitarian tradition:

I see the blue-ribbon panel to be one of the best manifestations of the citizen as "governor." It truly is government in action. More precisely, it is America's governed in action. The ad hoc commission brings together a cross-section of private citizens—businessmen and women, attorneys, educators, legislators and other professionals—with no political responsibility to institutionalized government.... It is truly democratic.[23]

Authors who share this orientation are quick to emphasize the twin advantages of analytical objectivity and blue-ribbon prestige. Conversely, they de-emphasize the role of political pressure in generating and shaping commission-based inquiries. When the issue is raised at all, it is accompanied by the claim that the blue-ribbon option plays a *useful* function in defusing crises and deflecting calls for drastic policy reform. George Sulzner termed this the "conflict-management aspect of study commissions." He counseled that such a role "should not be ignored or viewed despairingly," lest we gain an "inaccurate impression" of what commissions can bring to the political process.[24] Flitner echoed the sentiment: "Commission appointments permit delay. They may provide a 'cooling off' period during which tensions may be reduced. The evidence does not support the criticism that commissions are appointed out of some cynical desire to avoid a more substantive response."[25]

Journalists, pundits, and political hacks have tended to adopt a very different view of blue-ribbon activity. This view from the street holds that presidential commissions must be understood as political creatures. They are used by presidents to deflect criticism, delay action, preempt Congress, and in the words of commentator Chris Matthews, "take the heat for controversial decisions."[26] In short, commissions serve virtually every purpose *except* fact finding and analysis.

Elizabeth Drew's 1968 commentary, "On Giving Oneself a Hotfoot: Government by Commission," still rates as the purest example of this alternative view.[27] With tongue in cheek she described the eight reasons why presidents appoint commissions, including the goal of obtaining "the blessing of distinguished men for something you want to do anyway," and "to postpone action, yet be justified in insisting that you are at work on the problem." Of the commissioners themselves, Drew advised that they be chosen for their caution and reliability. Similarly, the panel's chair should "be able, but safe, but better safe than able." Three decades later, William Powers of the *New Republic* weighed in with this assessment:

> Blue-ribbon bodies have always worked this way. Each begins with some Really Bad Thing (crime, poverty, disease, Oliver North) that, it is generally agreed, we want to be rid of. The president, in lieu of action, appoints a board of deeply accomplished types—reverends, doctors, honorables—to make the problem go away. After many months, the worthies issue their report, a thick document so packed with abstraction, difference-splitting and pretzeled syntax that they must include a one-page Cliff's Notes for the media, called the "executive summary." Reporters read this page and rush to press with the commission's "policy recommendations." And, in a perverse way, the problem has been solved: the Really Bad Thing has been rendered so boring that nobody cares anymore.[28]

Few scholars have been equally harsh in their assessment of commissions. Some, however, have produced studies that provide insight into the political pressures that surround blue-ribbon inquiry.

An appreciation of the political pressure on commissions began to grow in the years following the release of the twenty-six volume *Report of the President's Commission on the Assassination of President Kennedy* (Warren Commission). A number of books appeared during the latter half of the 1960s that took issue with the conduct of the Warren panel's investigation. The most important of these was Edward Jay Epstein's *Inquest: The Warren Commission and the Establishment of Truth* (1966).[29] Noting that "a government inquiry does not take place in a vacuum," Epstein detailed how external pressures bear heavily on blue-ribbon investigations, often subverting the goal of fact finding and analysis to the more acceptable quest for "political truth."[30] For the Warren panel, these pressures resulted in curious personnel selections, inexplicable administrative decisions, and an investigation that "was by no means exhaustive or even thorough."[31]

Michael Lipsky and David Olson took aim at the National Advisory Commission on Civil Disorders (Kerner Commission) in "Riot Commission Politics" (1969).[32] The authors pointed out that the pressure on commissions is often subtle.

> We think there is a built-in tendency toward the whitewash, to the extent that riot commissions minimize criticism of the public official to whom they must look for primary implementation of the report. Further, for the sake of commission solidarity and to avoid diminishing the report's impact by the airing of dissension, riot commissions minimize criticisms of institutions with which individual commissioners are intimately associated.[33]

Lipsky and Olson also noted the peculiar challenges that accompany ad hoc investigation. Time constraints, they argued, are among the more serious obstacles a commission must overcome.

These critical studies offer an unflattering portrait of blue-ribbon politics that cannot be reconciled with the sanguine conclusions of the mainstream literature on commissions. Some of the difference is attributable to method. Studies based on large data sets emphasize breadth over depth and claim the advantage of generalizability. Case studies, on the other hand, are more apt to uncover subtle, contextual political dynamics. In this sense, it comes as little surprise that the thickly descriptive efforts of Epstein and Lipsky and Olson have done the most to advance our understanding of commission politics.

Commissions and National Security

Almost all previous studies of commissions have focused heavily on domestic-policy questions. Partly this is a function of age. Most of the early works were written in an era when commissions were created to deal with issues like campus unrest, urban disturbances, and pornography. Writing in 1970, Frank Popper explained the absence of national security commissions by noting that such questions were considered "too sensitive to entrust to a group as public and as independent as a commission."[34] A 1975 congressional report was similarly dismissive.

> There is little problem of overlapping or duplication of advisory committees in the crucial area of the overall substance of U.S. foreign policy, its direction and major goals, and its relationship to national security. The principal problem may actually be whether there are significant gaps that need filling. Few advisory committees deal with the central political issues of foreign policy and national security.[35]

By the 1970s and 1980s, however, issues such as the Strategic Arms Limitation Talks (SALT) II, the Strategic Defense Initiative ("star wars"), and Iran-Contra loomed large on the public agenda. These issues also generated bitter policy struggles between the president and Congress. As a by-product of the times, presidential commissions began to play a more visible-role in national security debates. Gerald Ford appointed a commission in 1975 to examine the Central Intelligence Agency. Jimmy Carter and Ronald Reagan followed suit, creating panels to study issues ranging from Americans missing in Vietnam to nuclear deterrence. Hugh Graham was the first to recognize the significance of this development.

> It has been with major policy commissions that Reagan has moved most dramatically—witness the Greenspan Commission on Social Security, the

Scowcroft Commission on the MX missile, and the Kissinger Commission on Central America. Not only has President Reagan boldly reasserted the presidential initiative in commission inquiries, but he has exercised it in the crucial and sensitive areas of national defense and foreign policy which previously had been out of bounds for national commissions.[36]

Graham believed this expansion was a positive step. Noting that security matters had long been the focus of attention by royal commissions in Great Britain, he speculated that US panels could enhance their prestige by tackling these high-profile issues.[37]

For the sake of historical accuracy, it should be noted that Popper, Graham, and others overstate the newness of national security commissions. In fact, blue-ribbon commissions had been used on defense and foreign policy issues prior to the 1970s. As discussed in Chapter 2, President Franklin Roosevelt's use of the blue-ribbon option after Pearl Harbor set a precedent that continues to resonate to this day. Even so, most of the panels established in the first three decades after World War II were low-profile affairs. Some operated in complete secrecy.[38] Others disbanded without issuing a final report.[39] None achieved the degree of fame or political prominence of the commissions profiled in this book. It is in this sense that national security commissions can be said to have "emerged" in the past three decades.

As a topic of scholarly inquiry, national security commissions have only recently begun to draw attention from political scientists and historians. Loch Johnson's analysis of the Aspin-Brown Commission stands as a good example of this new focus. Johnson notes the problem of conducting research in a policy area so shrouded in secrecy. "Commission doors," he writes, "have been locked tight against scholars and reporters."[40]

There is considerable justification for suspecting that security panels might differ from their domestic policy counterparts. In 1966 Aaron Wildavsky famously observed that presidents possess greater resources, have more latitude to act, and are challenged less frequently on national security than on matters of domestic policy.[41] As a result, the former "have consistently higher priority for Presidents."[42] This belief, formalized as the "two presidencies" thesis, has proved enormously influential in the discipline of political science. Even today it remains the clearest statement on the relationship between executive power and national security.

The importance of national security was also a central theme of *The Imperial Presidency* by Arthur Schlesinger Jr. (1972).[43] According to Schlesinger, presidential preoccupation with foreign affairs and defense has given rise to an expanded view of executive power—a view that has weakened the role of Congress and accorded the president more authority than the founding fathers intended. In *The Personal President* (1985), Theodore

Lowi suggests that a key characteristic of the "plebiscitary presidency" is a desire to limit congressional intrusion into national security decisionmaking. "If the president is already under some kind of compulsion to maintain the initiative in the White House, he is *least* willing to share initiatives in the foreign policy field. No star was ever more jealous of the light."[44]

Though each of these works approaches the topic from a different perspective, there is a unifying theme: national security holds a special place in executive-power prescriptions, and as a result presidents behave differently when these issues are in play.

The early 1990s gave rise to an academic debate on the continuing relevance of the two-presidencies thesis.[45] The end of the Cold War and the realities of interdependence had combined to blur the line that separates domestic and nondomestic issues. As a result, critics argued that national security issues were losing their unique status. But while conceding to some modification of his original thesis, Wildavsky continued to make the case that the fundamental basis for distinguishing between the two types of policy remains intact. "The fact that foreign policy has become more like domestic policy does not mean that presidents cannot win," he argued, "they simply must win differently."[46]

Objectives

This book is based on the proposition that national security commissions are interesting enough and important enough to warrant more attention than they have received. Much of the initial spadework on this subject is yet to be done. As with any political phenomena, description is a precondition of explanation. Yet our knowledge of these entities is limited. All we really know is that they represent a distinct type of advisory body, that they have become more common in recent decades, and that they deal with policies that have close ties to executive power.

Armed with that understanding, the chapters that follow feature case studies of five national security commissions. By order of appearance, they include the Commission to Investigate the Japanese Attack on Pearl Harbor (Roberts Commission), the Commission on CIA Activities Within the United States (Rockefeller Commission), the President's Commission on Strategic Forces (Scowcroft Commission), the President's Special Review Board (Tower Commission), and the National Commission on Terrorist Attacks Upon the United States (9/11 Commission). Table 1.2 provides a comparative overview of the panels.

Why these five commissions? First, each ranks among the most important national security panels ever appointed. Second, the commissions are scattered throughout the period from World War II to the present. This chronological spread makes it easier to detect changes over time in the way

Table 1.2 Five National Security Commissions

Commission Name	Administration	Method and Date of Creation	Number of Members	Duration[a]
Commission to Investigate the Japanese Attack of December 7, 1941 *(aka Roberts Commission, Pearl Harbor Commission)*	F. Roosevelt	Executive Order 8983 12/18/41	5	37 Days
Commission on CIA Activities Within the United States *(aka Rockefeller Commission)*	Ford	Executive Order 11828 01/04/75	8	153 Days
President's Commission on Strategic Forces *(aka Scowcroft Commission, MX Panel)*	Reagan	Executive Order 12400 01/03/83	12	98 Days
President's Special Review Board *(aka Tower Commission, Iran-Contra Panel)*	Reagan	Executive Order 12575 12/01/86	3	87 Days
National Commission on Terrorist Attacks Upon the United States *(aka 9/11 Commission, Kean Commission)*	G. W. Bush	Public Law 107-306 11/27/02	10	603 Days

Note: a. Date of creation to issuance of final report.

commissions operate. Third, each of the commissions dealt with issues in which the specter of scandal, gridlock, or public outrage loomed large. This last point is important in light of Lowi's argument that the president will act decisively to guard his prerogative in matters of national security, especially when he perceives that prerogative to be threatened.

One objective of this book is simply to provide an enriched understanding ("thick description" in academic jargon) of some of the most important blue-ribbon investigations ever undertaken in the field of national security.[47] Although these five panels appear in the historical literature, few have received more than cursory treatment and none has ever been examined from the standpoint of presidential politics. To help fill in the blanks, this analysis draws from interviews with commission insiders, government documents, contemporaneous press reports, memoirs, and the archival record.[48] As a result, the case studies provide substantial detail on the inner workings of national security commissions.

Chapters 2 through 6 feature a common format. The analysis proceeds sequentially through the life cycle of each commission. Seven key stops along the way include (1) the precipitating crisis or event; (2) the political situation confronting the president; (3) the decision to create a commission; (4) the process of determining the commission's mandate and membership; (5) the mechanics and politics of the investigation; (6) the drafting, issuance, and impact of the final report; and (7) the political aftermath. As a result each case is both a story unto itself as well as one piece of the larger puzzle.

A second objective is to identify and explain the political forces that shape blue-ribbon inquiry. Each of the five cases sits directly astride the intersection of presidential power and national security. Throw in personal conflict, partisan rivalry, and Washington, DC, politics inside the Beltway, and it becomes clear that these commissions constitute what Harry Eckstein calls "most likely cases"—that is, cases that so closely fit a theoretical construct that the expected outcome must necessarily be present.[49] Simply put, if there is anything to the notion of commission politics, this is the place to look.

This focus on blue-ribbon politics brings with it a certain analytical emphasis. Personalities loom large. The people in and around the commission are assumed to be important, not only as numbers (e.g., size of the commission and its staff) but also as individuals. They bring with them all the wonder and frailties of the human condition. They are honorable and shady, hard-working and lazy, selfish and altruistic, partisan and patriotic. Institutions are also important. Presidents and Congress lock horns in a way that would make Madison proud. The media are a constant presence, as are bureaucratic actors from deep within the executive branch. Even interest groups make an occasional guest appearance.

Chapter 7 identifies the common threads that link the five cases together. As the title of the book indicates, the overarching theme is that national security commissions must be understood as political creatures buffeted by a range of pressures. Many of those pressures flow from the executive. For the president, the blue-ribbon option is attractive because it represents a mechanism of control. The temptation to choose that option becomes all the greater when the chips are down and the political winds are blowing away from the White House. This is the story of how presidents respond to that challenge. This is the story of damage control.

Notes

1. J. C. Fitzpatrick, ed., *Writings of George Washington,* Vol. 34 (Washington, D.C.: US Government Printing Office, 1938), p. 31. Wolanin makes the point that the group Washington dispatched was more of a peace delegation than a fact-finding commission, and thus may not qualify as the first true presidential advisory commission. Nevertheless, Washington's mandate makes it clear that the group was given some investigatory responsibilities. More important, it set a prece-

dent by which future presidents could justify the creation of ad hoc groups whenever political circumstances dictated the need. See Thomas R. Wolanin, *Presidential Advisory Commissions* (Madison: University of Wisconsin Press, 1975), p. 5.

2. The better-known works on royal commissions include Charles J. Hanser, *Guide to Decision: The Royal Commission* (Totowa, NJ: The Bedminster Press, 1965); Richard A. Chapman, ed., *The Role of Commissions in Policy-Making* (London: George Allen and Unwin, 1973); Gerald Rhodes, *Committees of Inquiry* (London: George Allen and Unwin, 1975); and T. J. Cartwright, *Royal Commissions and Departmental Committees in Britain* (London: Hodder and Stoughton, 1975).

3. The use of the term "national" in reference to the US commissions is intentional. Because the United States is a federal system, the states also make use of ad hoc advisory bodies.

4. Hanser, *Guide to Decision*, p. 229.

5. Carl Marcy, *Presidential Commissions* (New York: King's Crown Press, 1945), p. 5.

6. Dana Milbank, "The Small Bundle of Names Tied up with Blue Ribbons," *Washington Post*, 4 February 2004, p. C1.

7. Hugh Davis Graham, "The Ambiguous Legacy of American Presidential Commissions," *Public Historian* 7 (Spring 1985), 8.

8. See Colton C. Campbell, *Discharging Congress: Government by Commission* (Westport, CT: Praeger, 2002).

9. For an overview of the FACA, see U.S. Congress, Senate, Committee on Governmental Affairs, *The Federal Advisory Committee Act: A Source Book*. 95th Congress, 2nd session, 1978.

10. *Annual Report of the President on Federal Advisory Committees* (Washington, DC: General Services Administration, 1972–2005).

11. *Principles of Federal Appropriations Law*, 2nd ed., Vol. 1 (Washington, DC: Office of the General Counsel, US General Accounting Office, July 1991), 17–6.

12. *Principles of Federal Appropriations Law*, 17–5.

13. *Association of American Physicians and Surgeons v. Clinton*, 997 F.2d 898 (Washington, DC, ca. 1993).

14. The figure hovered around 5 percent throughout most of the 1990s. *Annual Report of the President on Federal Advisory Committees*.

15. See, for example, Wolanin, *Presidential Advisory Commissions*, pp. 7–9, Terrence R. Tutchings, *Rhetoric and Reality: Presidential Commissions and the Making of Public Policy* (Boulder, CO: Westview, 1979), pp. 11–12; Stephen D. Zink, *Guide to the Presidential Advisory Commissions, 1973–1984* (Alexandria, VA: Chawyck-Healey, 1987), xiii; and Amy B. Zegart, "Blue Ribbons, Black Boxes: Toward a Better Understanding of Presidential Commissions," *Presidential Studies Quarterly* 34:2 (June 2004), 369–370.

16. Wolanin, *Presidential Advisory Commissions*, p. 7.

17. "Statement on Appointments to the Commission on the Roles and Capabilities of the United States Intelligence Community," *Weekly Compilation of Presidential Documents* 31 (6 February 1995), 182.

18. Zink, *Guide to the Presidential Advisory Commissions, 1973–1984*, xiii; and Zegart, "Blue Ribbons, Black Boxes," 369–370.

19. Wolanin, *Presidential Advisory Commissions*; Terrence R. Tutchings, *Rhetoric and Reality*.

20. See David P. Flitner, *The Politics of Presidential Commissions* (New York: Transnational Publishers, 1986).

21. David E. Linowes, *Creating Public Policy: The Chairman's Memoirs of Four Presidential Commissions* (Westport, CT: Praeger, 1998).

22. Wolanin, *Presidential Advisory Commissions*, p. 193.

23. Linowes, *Creating Public Policy*, p. 1.

24. George T. Sulzner, "The Policy Process and the Uses of National Government Study Commissions," *Western Political Quarterly* 24 (September 1971), 448.

25. Flitner, *The Politics of Presidential Commissions*, p. 180.

26. Chris Matthews, *Hardball: How Politics Is Played—Told by One Who Knows the Game*, revised edition (New York: Simon and Schuster/Touchstone, 1999), p. 205.

27. Elizabeth Drew, "On Giving Oneself a Hotfoot: Government by Commission," *Atlantic Monthly* 221 (May 1968), 45–49.

28. William Powers, "Oh My!" *New Republic* 216 (11 August 1997), 9.

29. Edward Jay Epstein, *Inquest: The Warren Commission and the Establishment of Truth* (New York: Viking Press, 1966).

30. Ibid., xvi.

31. Ibid., 153.

32. Michael Lipsky and David J. Olson, "Riot Commission Politics," *Transaction* 6 (July/August 1969), 9–21. Lipsky and Olson later developed the theme of commission politics into a book-length manuscript titled *Commission Politics: The Processing of Racial Crisis in America* (New Brunswick, NJ: Transaction Publishers, 1977). Over thirty years later, these two authors continue to press the case for a politically sensitive understanding of commission work. See Lipsky and Olson, "Sins of Commission," *The American Prospect Online*, 17 June 2001.

33. Lipsky and Olson, "Riot Commission Politics," 21.

34. Frank Popper, *The President's Commissions* (New York: Twentieth Century Fund, 1970), p. 10.

35. US Congress, Senate, Committee on Foreign Relations, *The Role of Advisory Committees in U.S. Foreign Policy.* 94th Congress, 1st session, 1975, p. 16.

36. Graham, "The Ambiguous Legacy of American Presidential Commissions," 25.

37. Ibid., 8.

38. One of the more secretive groups was the four-member Special Study Group on Covert Activities (Doolittle Commission) created by President Eisenhower in July 1954.

39. President Truman created the nine-member President's Commission on Internal Security and Individual Rights (Nimitz Commission) in January 1951. The commission dissolved under congressional pressure in October 1951 without issuing a final report.

40. Loch K. Johnson, "The Aspin-Brown Intelligence Inquiry: Behind the Closed Doors of a Blue Ribbon Commission," *Studies in Intelligence* 48:3 (2004) < http://www.cia.gov/csi/studies/vol48no3/article01.html>.

41. Aaron Wildavsky, "The Two Presidencies," *Transaction* 4 (December 1966), 7–14.

42. Ibid., 9.

43. Arthur Schlesinger Jr., *The Imperial Presidency* (New York: Popular Library, 1974).

44. Theodore J. Lowi, *The Personal President: Power Invested; Promise Unfulfilled* (Ithaca, NY: Cornell University Press, 1985), p. 165.

45. Critics typically argue that Wildavsky's thesis was contextually bound in the tightly bipolar world of the early Cold War. For an early statement of this revisionism, see Donald Pepper's "The Two Presidencies: Eight Years Later" in Steven A. Shull, ed., *The Two Presidencies: A Quarter Century Assessment* (Chicago: Nelson-Hall, 1991).

46. D. M. Oldfield and Aaron Wildavsky, "Reconsidering the Two Presidencies" in *The Two Presidencies: A Quarter Century Assessment*, p. 189.

47. The goal of "thick description" is discussed in Daniel Little, *Varieties of Social Explanation* (Boulder, CO: Westview Press, 1991), pp. 70–74.

48. Wolanin's 1975 work on commissions has proven durable in part because he undertook the extensive interviewing necessary to understand the goals of presidents in appointing blue-ribbon panels, the commissioners' understanding of their roles, and the activity of the panel's staff.

49. Harry Eckstein, "Case Study and Theory in Political Science," in *Regarding Politics: Essays on Political Theory, Stability, and Change* (Berkeley: University of California Press, 1992), p. 157.

2

The Politics of Infamy:
The Roberts Commission
and Pearl Harbor

We did our damndest, and no one can do more.
—Major General Frank Ross McCoy,
member of the Roberts Commission

*Of all the difficult and onerous duties in a long career of public service,
my membership on that Presidential Commission was beyond comparison
the most unpleasant.*
—Admiral William Harrison Standley,
member of the Roberts Commission

Few dates in US history are as instantly recognizable, as politically significant, and as laden with emotion as 7 December 1941. President
Franklin Roosevelt's prediction that the date would "live in infamy" proved
to be prophetic. Over six decades later, it stands as the defining moment
that marked the US entry onto the stage of world power and the coming of
the Pax Americana.

None of that, of course, mattered in December 1941, for in the wake of
the attack the American people were plainly and simply furious. Everything
about the Japanese raid—the deception, the decision to strike on a Sunday
morning, and the catastrophic loss of life and materiel—combined to
ensure that this country would be galvanized to see the conflict through to
its end. But fury was not the only emotion beginning to grow in the United
States. Shock gave way to finger pointing and a search for answers to help
explain away the success of the Japanese attack. Someone must have been
asleep at the switch. But who?

President Roosevelt's first attempt to address these questions resulted in the creation of a special board of inquiry headed by Supreme
Court Justice Owen Roberts. Roosevelt's action set a precedent that
would help launch future blue-ribbon probes of high-profile national
security issues. The Roberts panel is the oldest of the commissions featured in this book. It is also embedded in the larger historical drama of
Pearl Harbor. Consequently, it has been the subject of considerable
analysis as scholars have debated the nine investigations of the attack

and the extent to which each contributes to an understanding of what actually happened on 7 December 1941.[1] The goal here is not to reinvent that particular wheel. Instead, this study presents a fresh look at the commission as an ad hoc advisory body appointed by and answering to the president of the United States. The work of the Roberts Commission is the focus of this chapter.

A Formal Investigation

From the start, it was clear that some type of investigation into the circumstances of the 7 December attack was inevitable. Secretary of the Navy Frank Knox was the first to act: on 9 December he flew to Oahu in his private plane to survey the damage; and survey is the appropriate word. For although the trip is often styled as the first Pearl Harbor investigation, Knox himself avoided using that word to characterize his effort. His comments upon returning to Washington help illustrate the point:

> That trip of mine to Hawaii was an inspiration that came to me just as I heard the President read his message [to Congress]. Immediately the air was filled with rumors. There was a prospect ahead of a nasty congressional investigation, and I made up my mind in a flash to go out there and get the actual facts, and if the facts warranted it, to initiate the investigation myself.[2]

Thus Knox believed that his fact-finding tour simply paved the way for a formal investigation. He hardly could have argued otherwise. After all, how could the head of the US Navy be expected to investigate the country's worst naval disaster? An editorialist for the *Washington Times-Herald* noted wryly that cynics had already compared the secretary's trip "with an order to a man to go and investigate himself."[3]

Knox returned to Washington on the night of 14 December 1941 and reported directly to the president. He told Roosevelt that Adm. Husband E. Kimmel and Lt. Gen. Walter C. Short, the two top military commanders in Hawaii, had admitted to a "lack of a state of readiness against such an air attack." Neither officer had regarded such an attack as likely, due to "the preponderance of the American Naval strength in Hawaiian waters."[4] He met again with Roosevelt the following morning. The president's notes from the meeting are more elaborate than one might expect, and indicate that Roosevelt used the two discussions with Knox to help outline a strategy for dealing with the unfolding crisis. Under point four Roosevelt wrote:

> The U.S. services were not on the alert against the surprise air attack on Hawaii. This calls for a formal investigation, which will be initiated immediately by the President. Further action is of course dependent on the

facts and recommendations made by the investigating board. We are all entitled to know if (a) There was any error of judgment which contributed to the surprise (b) There was any dereliction of duty prior to the attack.[5]

When Knox left the meeting, he immediately contacted Secretary of War Henry L. Stimson to notify him of the president's decision to initiate an investigation.[6]

It is clear that Knox played an important role in getting the commission under way. But it is equally clear that he had a receptive audience in President Roosevelt. For by the time Knox returned to Washington, two political pressures were beginning to build that would have forced the president to initiate some type of investigation even without Knox's input. First, there was already talk of a legislative inquiry into the attack. During a late-night briefing on 7 December Senator Thomas Connally (Democrat-Texas) had grilled Knox relentlessly. What had happened to the earlier assurances of preparedness? Why had Knox permitted the ships to be "crowded" at Pearl Harbor? What steps had been taken once the attack began?[7]

Roosevelt and his aides knew that such questions could easily take on a life of their own. Supreme Court Justice Felix Frankfurter was particularly concerned.[8] A staunch supporter of the New Deal, Frankfurter functioned as an informal adviser to Roosevelt. He was also a student of history who knew the folly of the Civil War–era Committee on the Conduct of the War. In the days after Pearl Harbor he worried that an investigation by Congress might open the door to even broader legislative intrusions into defense policy. Although the archival record provides few details regarding Frankfurter's role in getting the commission under way, at least one well-positioned admiral caught wind of his influence through Washington gossip.[9] Whatever the extent of his involvement, Roosevelt shared Frankfurter's concerns and wanted to make it clear that no "back seat drivers" were needed in the war effort.[10]

The second pressure stemmed from interservice rivalry. When the fleet was at anchor in Pearl Harbor, as had been the case on 7 December, the US Army and Navy shared responsibility for defense. Consequently, there was great fear that reverberations from the attack could, if unchecked, grow into a full-blown bureaucratic war that would divert time and attention from the very real war with the Axis powers. "We are doing our best to keep from having a row with the Navy," Stimson wrote in his diary on 11 December 1941. "Knox agrees with me that there has been remissness in both branches … and we are both very anxious not to get into any inter-departmental scrap."[11] This concern was not limited to Washington officials. Edwin T. Layton, a navy captain at Pearl Harbor, also worried about "the danger of a major inter-service fight in the offing."[12]

The Commission Takes Shape

By the morning of 15 December 1941, the decision to form a blue-ribbon panel had been taken. The next round of discussion focused on possible members. Roosevelt told Knox that he envisioned a committee of five composed of two army officers, two navy officers, and a civilian head.[13] He asked Knox and Stimson to recommend individuals for service. Knox quickly identified the naval representatives: retired Adm. William Standley and retired Rear Adm. Joseph Reeves.

It fell to Stimson to nominate the army members. He brought Chief of Staff General George C. Marshall into the discussion, and the two men agreed that one seat would go to retired Maj. Gen. Frank McCoy. For the other slot, Stimson toyed briefly with the idea of nominating Gen. Malin Craig, Marshall's immediate predecessor as head of the army. However, the two determined that it would be more appropriate to name an air officer, given the nature of the Japanese attack. On the morning of 16 December, Marshall asked Stimson to consider Brig. Gen. Joseph T. McNarney, deputy chief of staff and an airman by training. Stimson accepted the recommendation, and with that the four uniformed members of the panel were set.[14]

Still remaining was the question of the panel's chair. There were false starts and rumors before the final decision was taken. Knox weighed in first, contacting Stimson on 15 December to lobby for Judge Philip Sullivan of Chicago. But Sullivan's candidacy turned out to be short-lived. Stimson knew nothing about the judge and "couldn't find that he had quite guns enough in the way of reputation to swing such a position as this."[15] Instead, he offered the name of Supreme Court Justice Owen J. Roberts. Stimson remembered Roberts's service as prosecutor during the Teapot Dome scandal and, based on that experience, deemed him the "outstanding man" who should lead the investigation.[16] Knox agreed that Roberts would make an admirable selection and agreed to drop Sullivan's name in order to join Stimson in presenting the recommendation.[17]

On the morning of 16 December Stimson formalized these recommendations in a memorandum to the president. Roosevelt accepted each of the names without comment, and by that afternoon word of the commission and its membership had begun to circulate in Washington.[18]

What Manner of Men?

As with any ad hoc board of inquiry, personnel selection is of paramount importance. A closer examination of the appointments to the Pearl Harbor commission reveals an interesting mix of professional experience, personal ties, and political affiliations.

At age sixty-nine, Adm. William Harrison Standley was the oldest member to serve on the panel. A former chief of naval operations, Standley had left active service in 1937 but had continued to serve as a naval adviser to President Roosevelt; in June 1940, he had advocated a US declaration of war against Nazi Germany. The president brought the admiral out of retirement in March 1941 as a member of the Production Planning Board. Upon his appointment to the commission, he told a *New York Times* reporter that he "didn't know a thing about it [the attack], but I expect to find out a hell of a lot."[19] Although he would later clash with Roberts over the commission's findings, the justice nonetheless declared Standley "one of the keenest and ablest men I have ever known and one of the fairest."[20]

Rear Admiral Joseph Mason Reeves had retired from active naval service in 1936 after rising to the position of fleet commander. Nicknamed "Bull," he had returned to active duty in 1940 when Knox appointed him as the navy's representative on the Lend Lease board. Reeves emerged as one of Kimmel's fiercest critics during the Pearl Harbor inquiry. Kimmel in turn described him as a "fast talker ... a Roosevelt man body and soul if indeed he had a soul."[21] Nor was Reeves held in high regard by Standley. The older man had clashed with Reeves in 1935–1936, and the animosity surfaced during commission proceedings.[22] Even so, Roberts was impressed at the obvious respect accorded Reeves by many of the naval personnel who appeared before the commission. "Navy men just flocked to him," reported the chairman, "as if to a father, and with respect to many of the witnesses who were admirals who came before us, Reeves would turn to me and say, 'He is one of my boys.'"[23]

Major General Frank Ross McCoy was the senior of the two army officers appointed to the Roberts Commission. A decorated combat veteran, he had been wounded in the Spanish-American War during the assault on San Juan Hill. McCoy's rise to national prominence came as a member of the court martial that found Col. William ("Billy") Mitchell guilty of insubordination. McCoy was also something of a blue-ribbon fixture, having served as head of the Nicaraguan election commission in 1927 and as a member of the 1932 Lytton Commission, a League of Nations undertaking that examined Japanese aggression in Manchuria. A Washington insider, McCoy had enjoyed a close personal friendship with Stimson for thirty years. Because of these ties, he had more persistent and extensive contact with administration officials during the Pearl Harbor investigation than any other member of the commission. McCoy had left active service in 1938 but was returned to active duty at the beginning of his service on the commission.[24] The day after the Pearl Harbor attack he told a friend that responsibility for the tragedy was "not even a debatable question, that the Navy [had] failed to make good and must shoulder the blame."[25]

Brigadier General Joseph Taggart McNarney, at forty-eight years of

age, was the youngest member of the commission. As an active-duty officer, he answered directly to General Marshall—a curious arrangement
given that his boss would be questioned during the course of the investigation. From May to December 1941, McNarney had been involved in a
secretive mission to Great Britain as part of a special US Army observer
group. Admiral Kimmel viewed him as "a hatchet man" who was "primarily concerned with ... protecting Marshall and his precious air service."[26]
General Short, Kimmel's more subdued army counterpart, agreed that
"McNarney seemed to be the SOB of the Commission."[27] McNarney was
promoted to major general while the investigation was under way, receiving the good news just as the commissioners began work on the final
report, and remained a prominent figure throughout the war.[28] In 1944 he
served as Marshall's liaison with an investigation conducted by the army's
Pearl Harbor board.

As chairman, Justice Roberts occupied the most important position on
the commission. Known as the "Fighting Welshman," he had acquired a
national reputation, first as a special prosecutor for espionage cases during
World War I and later as the lead prosecutor in the Teapot Dome scandal
during the Harding administration.[29] Roberts was regarded as a tireless
investigator and relentless prosecutor.

Roberts's ascent to the high court was born of controversy. In 1930
President Herbert Hoover had nominated John J. Parker, a circuit court
judge from North Carolina, for the Supreme Court. But the Senate rejected
Parker due to concerns about his record on race and labor issues. Hoover
went back to the drawing board and returned with Roberts's name. This
time there was no hesitation. The Senate confirmed the Pennsylvanian by
acclamation only one minute after the Judiciary Committee sent his name
to the floor. One court historian characterized Roberts as "to the manner
born" and "an eagerly sought out practitioner of the law ... his nomination
was broadly applauded—support came from all parts of the political spectrum."[30] Once on the court, Roberts established a reputation as a judicial
moderate. In the early days of the New Deal, he tended to vote with conservative justices who took a dim view of the expansion of federal government
powers. But all that changed when, in 1937, Roberts began to vote in favor
of Roosevelt's programs and thus acquired the label of the famous "switch
in time that saved nine."

By the time of Pearl Harbor, it was easy to see why the president and
his advisers considered Roberts an attractive choice to head the panel. First,
he was a justice on the highest court in the land. Second, he was a lifelong
Republican—an important concern if the panel was to have bipartisan
appeal. And, third, he had proven himself sympathetic to Roosevelt, his
policies, and the war effort.

Roosevelt invited Roberts to the White House on the afternoon of 16

December to make the pitch. The meeting took place at 5 p.m. in the president's executive office; present were Knox, Stimson, Adm. Harold "Betty" Stark, chief of naval operations, and admirals William Leahy and Ernest King. Roberts tentatively agreed to accept Roosevelt's invitation to chair the panel. (One of his former law partners reported that Roberts felt like it "was his patriotic duty to do it.")[31] Roberts's chief concern was time away from the court. Before making final his commitment, he told the president he would need to secure a leave of absence from Chief Justice Harlan Fiske Stone. That turned out to be more of an obstacle than anyone contemplated. Stone was not enamored of extrajudicial assignments and thought that the court "might have been left alone" as Roosevelt cast about for trustworthy individuals to appoint to this and other panels.[32] "There are some important cases coming up here," Stone complained to Roberts, "and I do not want a court of eight to hear them."[33] But in the end he acquiesced. Roberts phoned the president later that same evening to report for duty.[34]

Preliminaries

By the close of business on 16 December the commission's membership was fixed. The public learned of the board's composition the following day.[35] In an editorial, the *New York Times* opined that the board "could scarcely have been better picked."[36] The *Washington Post* offered a similar endorsement, with an especially strong vote of confidence in the leadership of Roberts.[37] The *New York Daily News* weighed in as well, applauding the selections with one small reservation:

> There is this criticism to be made of the board, though, we think: It contains only one fighting air man, Gen. McNarney. Gen. McCoy and Admirals Standley and Reeves are old time land and sea fighters respectively—fine fighters in their time, but times have changed. Doesn't this board need heavier representation from the air fighting element of the armed services? We think it does.... We would therefore like to see two associate members added to the Roberts committee. One of these would be an experienced man, and a young man, from the naval air arm.[38]

The reaction from Washington officials divided along party lines. Representative Carl Vinson, the Georgia Democrat who headed the House Naval Affairs Committee, declared that his committee would not launch an independent inquiry into Pearl Harbor "since the President has named such an outstanding board to conduct the investigation." Senator David I. Walsh (Democrat-Massachusetts) agreed that the panel was "in every way commendable."[39] Republicans, however, were concerned that a group handpicked by the president would drive the investigation. In a speech on 19 December Senator Robert Taft of Ohio warned that the "surprise at Hawaii should ... be investigated by committees of Congress, and not left entirely to the Executive Department."[40]

The commission got off to a rocky start, due in no small part to the chaos of the times and the pressures of trying to get the investigation up and running as soon as possible. Lost in the shuffle was any discussion of blue-ribbon basics like mandate, time frame, subpoena power, and staff resources.

The only administrative guidance came from Stimson. He invited Roberts and three of his fellow commissioners (Standley was en route from the West Coast) to his office for a 10 a.m. meeting on 17 December to "get instructions."[41] Stimson talked about the inquiry and advised the members that they "should not limit themselves to merely the question of individual delinquency and responsibility, but that they should go further into the whole situation of the defense of the Islands with a view to ascertaining whether the system which has been in effect is adequate."[42] Stimson added that the army and navy wanted to cooperate with the investigation. Knox agreed and once again took the opportunity to warn against pitting the two branches against one another. "It is not a question," he told the commissioners, "of Army against the Navy or the Navy against the Army."[43]

Roberts realized the need for administrative support and began to pull together a small staff to assist in the work. His longtime law clerk, Albert J. Schneider, agreed to sign on as secretary.[44] Lieutenant Colonel Lee Brown of the Marine Corps joined as legal assistant. And in the most important move with regard to staffing, Roberts accepted the recommendation of Commissioner McCoy that Washington attorney Walter Bruce Howe, a civilian, be appointed as the panel's recorder.[45] Howe's official title was deceptive, for in this capacity he would have a critically important role as the commission's chief of staff and liaison with most external actors. At least one of the commissioners felt that Howe became a de facto judge advocate during the proceedings.[46] For help with transcription, Roberts contracted with the Washington firm of Hart and Dice for the service of three professional stenographers.

The single most important day in the brief history of the Roberts Commission was 18 December 1941. On that day two decisions were taken that continue to reverberate. First, the commission opted to commence a series of informal interviews with high-ranking military officers in Washington, and, second, the commission sought to formalize its own mandate by means of an executive order.

Among those interviewed on 18 December were General Marshall, Admiral Stark, Rear Adm. Richmond "Kelly" Turner, chief of the navy's War Plans Division, and Maj. Gen. Leonard T. Gerow, chief of the army's War Plans Division. Roberts recalled that "General Marshall and Admiral

Stark ... gave us an outline of the whole transaction from their points of view."[47] In a crucial decision, Roberts decided that the men would not have to take oaths, nor would their testimony be recorded. He employed the same format the following day with five other officers, including the intelligence chiefs for the army and navy.

The reasons for this decision are unclear. Roberts noted that "at that time we had not decided how we would take testimony, and we had no stenographer."[48] But he also admitted that, even if the stenographers had been available, "we had been warned that nobody outside of the Commission was to be there."[49] This warning was tied to security concerns over fears that someone would leak word of US code-breaking activities. Yet another possible explanation is found in the official minutes of the commission:

> Owing to the tentative and preliminary nature of the hearings on December 18 and 19, 1941, *the Commission decided that it was unnecessary to have the statements of the above mentioned officers noted stenographically and verbatim.* The foregoing condensed statements have been prepared by the Recorder and the Secretary to the Commission from stenographic notes taken by him at the time, showing mainly topics taken up in several statements [emphasis added].[50]

When asked to comment on the matter in 1946, Roberts told congressional investigators that the men "were not under oath but were upon honor."[51] But his faith in human nature apparently waned as the investigation progressed. After the interviews in Washington, Roberts moved to formalize procedures. Henceforth all witnesses appearing before the commission would be sworn and testimony duly transcribed.

Roberts's statement is also curious for what it reveals about his own personality. Some of his fellow jurists noted that he had an almost childlike tendency to take the word of others at face value. Justice Hugo Black considered Roberts "the most naïve man I have ever known in my life—a fine character but as innocent as a child."[52] In fairness it should be noted that Black had different judicial leanings than did Roberts. But even Justice Robert Jackson, a more sympathetic associate, found himself exasperated. "Roberts is just beyond me," he once confessed. "He's a complete sap so far as understanding men is concerned."[53]

The second decision taken on 18 December was to draft an executive order that would give the commission official status and, more important, formalize the panel's investigative responsibility. At the time of Knox's return from Hawaii there was some discussion of the purpose of the "formal investigation." Stimson had offered his own "instructions" on the matter during his initial meeting with the commissioners. Moreover, a White House spokesman had told the press on 17 December that the "board will determine whether there was negligence on the part of Army, Navy or Air Corps officials which resulted in undue loss of life or damage to American forces. If it finds that negligence contributed to the losses it will fix responsibility for them."[54] But the historical record makes it clear that while all of these ideas were under discussion the exact parameters of the commission's mandate were still a work in progress.

The issuing of an executive order appears to be an afterthought. When Admiral Standley finally arrived in Washington on 18 December, he walked into the middle of a commission meeting and was shocked by the informality of the proceedings.

> I tried to satisfy my curiosity as to just what I had gotten into. What was the nature of this Commission—was it an Army or Navy board, a joint commission or what? What rules governed its procedures: Army, Navy or civil? Had we power to summon witnesses and enforce their attendance and to administer oaths and take testimony thereunder? The answers I got were not reassuring.
>
> It was a "mixed"— and a very mixed up—Presidential Commission with civilian, naval and military members, for which there was no precedent in law, custom, or jurisprudence.... Witnesses were being examined on their own conscience, that is, without swearing.
>
> To express it in an extremely kindly fashion, the make-up of the Commission and the conduct of its proceedings were most unusual.[55]

Standley requested that a written charge be drafted to guide the commission in its investigation. Roberts consented. He notified the White House that the commission was "organizing this morning and I will send over to the President a little later on, an executive order which, after it is signed, should be lodged in the State Department."[56] Roberts also bowed to Standley on the issue of subpoena power. He informed Roosevelt that he had "asked the Chairman of the Judiciary Committee to pass a short joint resolution reciting our appointment and giving us that power."[57] But Roberts was not willing to bend on everything. He refused to budge when Standley suggested that the panel request a formal interview with President Roosevelt. That idea, the admiral recalled, was "quickly squelched."[58]

Roosevelt signed Executive Order 8983 on 18 December just eleven days after the attack. The order provided an official title, the "Commission to Investigate the Japanese Attack of December 7, 1941," and specified the panel's membership. Then came the mandate:

> The purposes of the required inquiry and report are to provide bases for sound decisions whether any derelictions of duty or errors of judgment on the part of United States Army or Navy personnel contributed to such successes as were achieved by the enemy on the occasion mentioned, and if

so, what these derelictions or errors were, and who were responsible thereof.[59]

The narrow construction of the charge came as a shock to Standley. "Such instructions," he realized, "precluded any investigation into the activities of high civilian officials in Washington."[60]

Roosevelt's executive order did not specify how long the investigation would last. For future blue-ribbon panels a deadline for completion of the investigation would be routine. But things were less formal in 1941, and the question of time was handled as loosely as the question of mandate. Even so, the archival record provides evidence that the members expected the investigation to be short-lived. In a 19 December letter staff director Howe noted that he "expects to return [from Hawaii] about two to three weeks from now."[61] On 20 December, Roberts also signed life insurance policies for the contracted stenographers providing them with protection against accidental death for one month from the date of the contract.[62]

The Investigation

Chronologically, the activity of the Roberts Commission can be broken down into three segments. The first phase ran from 15 December to 20 December 1941 and involved activities related to the panel's creation, personnel assignments, and investigation schedule. The second phase ran from 20 December 1941 to 9 January 1942 and was wholly devoted to hearings and collection of evidence in Hawaii. The third phase ran from 10 January to 24 January 1942 and covered the return to Washington, a few last-minute interviews in the capital, and the drafting of the findings and the presentation of the final report.

Given its mandate, the commission decided that a trip to Hawaii was in order: an on-site visit was the only way to get a feel for the command environment and to assess the overall state of army and navy activity. Roberts also reported that the Washington interviews on 18–19 December 1941 helped to convince the commissioners of the need for the trip.[63]

Roberts spent the day before his departure attending to last-minute business. First he stopped by the office of Secretary of State Cordell Hull. That visit took place at the urging of former President Hoover, who had written a letter to his good friend and commission member Frank McCoy on 17 December. Hoover's letter asked:

Did the State Department apprise the Army and Navy of the ultimatum and its serious impact? If so, did the Washington heads of these departments transmit it to the forces in the field? Now the only reason why I write this is the feeling that perhaps some Admiral or some General in the Pacific may be made a goat for action or lack of action higher up, and thus a great injustice done.[64]

Roberts reported that he spent "an entire day" in Hull's office discussing these questions.[65] Hull's responses were summarized in a letter to the commission dated 30 December. In that communication, he made the case that he was well aware of the war threat, that high officers in the war and navy departments shared his view, and that Washington officials had taken all necessary steps to communicate the seriousness of the threat to the appropriate field commanders.[66]

Also on 19 December Roberts asked Walter Howe to write to Lt. Col. William "Wild Bill" Donovan with a curious request. Donovan, soon to gain fame as the wartime spy chief, had worked since summer as Roosevelt's coordinator of information. The chairman asked Donovan to prepare a "resume of public opinion about the Commission ... which could be gathered from editorial and other comment in the Press," and to deliver the report upon the board's return from Hawaii.[67] That deadline meant that Donovan and his staff would have to limit the survey to press comment about the creation of the commission, its purpose, and its membership. They complied with a polished report dated 16 January 1942 that was "based upon almost a thousand newspaper clippings" from both the American and foreign press.[68] The report demonstrated that press coverage of the board was overwhelmingly positive—an appropriate finding for one of the oddest vanity searches in US history.

The commission departed for Hawaii on 20 December 1941. Arriving after a one-night stopover in San Francisco, the commission began taking testimony on 22 December. While in Hawaii, the commission met at three different locations: from 22 to 26 December the panel received testimony at US Army headquarters, Fort Shafter. From 27 December 1941 until 3 January 1942, the panel convened in the wardroom of the submarine base at Pearl Harbor. And from 5 through 9 January of 1942 the commission met in room 300 of the Royal Hawaiian Hotel.

There was little down time during the commission's three-week stay in Hawaii. Admiral Standley, however, did find time to visit with Cmdr. Joseph J. Rochefort, chief of naval combat intelligence and a future hero of the Battle of Midway. He showed Standley around the navy's code-breaking facility and then took him down to the harbor to view the extensive battle damage. The old admiral's comments must have come as a shock. "Well, after all," he told Rochefort, "this was a small price for uniting the country."[69]

As the interviews in Hawaii got under way, it was clear that Roberts was still struggling to find his cadence as chair. The first witness, Lt. Col.

William E. Donegan, appeared before the commission at 10:45 on the morning of 22 December. Roberts greeted the officer warmly and initiated what was to be a friendly exchange before being cut off by General McCoy:

> The Chairman: What have you there, Colonel?
> Colonel Donegan: I have here....
> General McCoy: Let us get the colonel's name, rank, and position.
> The Chairman: Your name?
> Colonel Donegan: William B. Donegan, Lieutenant Colonel, General
>   Staff Corps.[70]

Roberts's luck did not improve with the second witness. This time it was General McNarney who interrupted the questioning to complain: "Unless I know what the standing orders and procedures were, I cannot really ask an intelligent question. I can get a lot of details and a mass of data, but I cannot apply them. I would like to study these documents before we go ahead."[71] These administrative missteps might have been simple human errors attributable to the whirl of events around the commission. Admiral Standley, however, was not inclined to give Roberts the benefit of the doubt. Years later he told an interviewer that the justice "expected the Commission to be a brief whitewashing adventure that would not require much formal reporting."[72]

The commission interviewed 127 individuals in Hawaii. Of that total, 41 percent came from the army, 29 percent from the navy, and 30 percent from the civilian population.[73] Because he was confronted by a steady stream of gossip and rumors, Roberts decided to run an advertisement in the Honolulu press inviting "any persons who have personal knowledge of facts which relate to the objects of its inquiry" to present in person before the commission.[74] Those accepting the invitation ran the gamut from the serious to the downright peculiar. For example, Paul Waterhouse, president of the Temperance League of Hawaii, appeared before the commission to argue that drunkenness in the US military ranks had contributed to the success of the Japanese raid.[75]

The star witnesses in Hawaii were Admiral Kimmel and General Short. Kimmel appeared four times: 27 December 1941 and 6, 7, and 9 January 1942. Short's testimony came on 23 December and 8 January. The pressure on the two commanders was tremendous. At one point Kimmel confronted an aide in the hallway. "What are they trying to do," he asked, "crucify me?"[76] Short was more fatalistic about the whole affair: he told a subordinate before his appearance that he knew he would be relieved of command and that he also would probably lose at least one or two stars in rank.[77] Admiral Standley noted that Kimmel's performance compared unfavorably with Short's, possibly due to the fact that the admiral had to prepare his presentation with minimal staff assistance—most of his subordinates being either at sea or otherwise engaged in meeting the Japanese threat.[78]

Admiral Reeves was particularly tough on the two commanders. During Short's testimony he "raked the general over the coals" with questions about the Hawaiian air defense system.[79] But as a navy man himself, Reeves reserved his harshest judgment for the fleet commander. He fell ill shortly after Kimmel's opening statement and had to be hospitalized. Reeves's biographer speculates that "the thought of listening to Kimmel's testimony was so unsettling ... that it made him physically ill."[80] Reeves rejoined the commission on 2 January 1942 and continued to serve without further incident. But his contempt for Kimmel and Short never diminished. "I used to say that a man had to be both a fighter and to know how to fight," he said upon returning to the mainland. "Now all I want is a man who fights."[81] Once back in Washington he squared off with Standley over the degree to which the report would fix blame on the two commanders.

Rear Admiral Robert A. Theobald, one of the officers permitted to accompany Kimmel during his appearances before the commission, was surprised at the sharp tone of the questioning: "Associate Justice Roberts for a considerable period of time forgot his status as a presiding officer of an impartial commission and questioned Admiral Kimmel in a loud tone of voice; in fact, in a manner more to be expected of a trial lawyer in a lower court."[82]

As testimony wound down, Roberts began to think about securing the documentary evidence assembled by the commission. The United States was at war, after all, and there was no guarantee of an easy return trip to the West Coast. He took the unusual step of asking army officer Louis Truman, a second cousin of the future president, to take a copy of the minutes and testimony back to Washington. Roberts instructed Truman to have the briefcase "handcuffed to [his] wrist, and take it up to General Marshall's office and give it to him personally." Truman recalled that the chairman was particularly interested in seeing that Marshall "get it to the President as soon as possible."[83]

The commission departed Honolulu on 10 January 1942 and began the long trek back to Washington. Once in San Francisco, the commissioners boarded a train that became their home for the next three days. They met in the drawing room daily to "discuss facts ... and to start to prepare findings" that would become the centerpiece of their report to the president.[84]

The train pulled into Washington on 15 January, by which point the commission was ready to begin work on putting the findings into a final report. All five members were active in this stage of the deliberations. As the final report began to take shape, each received a rough draft to review for content, organization, and wording.[85] Roberts recalled that the group started with a master list of over seventy findings that were eventually condensed into a more manageable set of nineteen.[86]

The task of assembling the final report was not an easy one. McCoy wrote to a friend regarding the experience:

> I spent all of last week in Washington, but didn't see much of anyone but the Board, as we sat night and day until midnight Friday in order to send the report to the President the next day. It was a tragic mission for me for all the reasons that you suspect, but we all finished up with a clear conscience—in other words, we did our damndest, and no one can do more.[87]

Clear conscience or not, Standley recalled a "number of acrimonious arguments" regarding the extent to which the report should focus blame on Kimmel and Short. At one point Roberts dared the admiral to issue a minority report. Standley called his bluff. "If I do have to make a minority report on this matter," he warned the chairman, " I shall state that the report you are making is false. The evidence we have taken will certainly bear me out."[88]

In the end, the commission was able to reach a consensus. The commission's report was a model of efficiency—tightly organized into an introduction, nineteen findings of fact, a summary of the "most important facts," and twenty-one itemized conclusions.[89] The report concluded that Knox and Stimson had "fulfilled their obligations," just as Knox and Stark had "fulfilled their command responsibilities." Conclusion 9 contained the first hint of what was to come, stating that the "responsible commanders" in Hawaii had "failed to confer with respect to the warnings and orders issued on and after November 27." These commanders suffered (conclusion 16) from a "sense of security due to the opinion ... that any attack by Japan would be in the Far East." But damning as they were, none of these observations could match conclusion 17 for sheer dramatic effect: "In the light of the warnings and directions to take appropriate action ... it was a dereliction of duty on the part of each of them [Kimmel and Short] not to consult and confer with the other respecting the meaning and intent of the warnings, and the appropriate measures of defense required by the imminence of hostilities."[90]

To say that the report landed heavily on the Hawaiian command is an understatement. For proud career officers like Kimmel and Short, the determination of "dereliction of duty" was both a personal and professional rebuke of the highest order. Washington officials, on the other hand, survived the report almost unscathed. With one very small exception—a vague complaint that the War Department should have offered better guidance on antisabotage measures—the report did not hold any administration official, uniformed or civilian, responsible for the disaster at Pearl Harbor.[91]

Roberts phoned the White House on 23 January to inform presidential secretary Grace Tully that the report was complete and that he would await instructions. Tully soon phoned back to report that the president wished to meet alone with the chairman the following morning. Roberts did as he was told:

> So I called at the White House on the morning of January 24 at 11 o'clock, saw the President in his study on the second floor. He was at his desk. I handed him an envelope containing these two duplicate reports. He opened it, and then started to read it. I sat there and he read it line by line, and so far as I could make out he read every word of it, carried his finger on the pages. I was there over 2 hours.[92]

As he read the report, Roosevelt would periodically stop and question Roberts. Did the commission report on the nature of the damage at Pearl Harbor? Was the commission satisfied that the army, navy, and FBI had cooperated fully in the investigation? "Two or three times," Roberts recalled, "he would shake his head and say, 'Tsk, Tsk,' or something of that sort."[93]

As the meeting wound down, Roosevelt asked if Justice Roberts knew of any reason why the report should not be made public. Roberts could think of none. With that, the president summoned his assistant, Marvin H. McIntryre, and "threw this whole thing across the desk and said, 'Mac, give that to the Sunday papers in full.'"[94] This move was not anticipated by the president's inner circle. White House Press Secretary Steve Early had previously warned reporters that the report would have to pass muster with government censors before being made public.[95]

The Roberts report appeared in the national press the following day. Many of the largest dailies ran the full text of the report, just as Roosevelt had hoped. In Honolulu, the *Star-Bulletin* carried the story in a special extra edition. Street sales were unusually heavy.[96] An Associated Press report from Oahu noted that the "bite" in the report represented "stronger medicine" than many had anticipated.[97]

The reaction from Washington officialdom was predictably generous. Chief Justice Stone, no doubt relieved to know that Roberts would soon be returning to the Supreme Court, deemed the report "a thorough document, ably dealing with one of the most unhappy episodes in our history."[98] Secretary Stimson agreed that it was an "admirable report, candid and fair," laid out with "merciless thoroughness."[99] Justice Frankfurter wrote to Roberts to praise the "thoroughness, clarity and courage of the document ... no one who knew you expected anything else from you."[100]

Controversy

Gordon Prange, the dean of Pearl Harbor historians, once deemed the Roberts Commission the "most controversial" of all the investigations into the attack.[101] The past six decades have validated that judgment. Critics have had ample time to scour the historical record for evidence of individual bias, procedural errors, and questionable conclusions.

Much of the criticism centers on the issue of inadequate information. The members of the Roberts Commission had a general understanding that US policymakers had access to secret Japanese communications—the "Magic" intelligence—but they did not seek nor see specifics of this activity. There has also been a corollary suspicion that administration officials, especially secretaries Knox and Stimson and their uniformed subordinates, were purposely evasive on the subject. Roberts himself noted that "the Navy was rather chary about even telling us about the thing [code breaking] for fear there might be some leak from our commission."[102] Some revisionists suspect that had the commission known the degree to which relations with Japan had deteriorated, it would have been more aggressive in determining how clearly the threats were disseminated to the Hawaiian command. Historian John Costello points out that Magic messages were disseminated to British commanders in Hong Kong and Singapore but were not provided to the Pearl Harbor commanders since the wisdom then prevalent held that Hawaii was safe from attack.[103]

Another set of concerns has focused on the issue of investigative competence. To be sure, the early days of the inquiry were marked by confusion and a lack of guidelines. Even after the investigation moved to Hawaii, there were persistent questions about the quality of the staff support, especially in the area of transcription. Dispute over the official transcript became an issue with Admiral Kimmel:

> The practice in the Navy at that time was to permit a witness to correct his testimony after it had been typed. I waited a few days until I noted a naval officer just outside the hearing room working on some papers. When I inquired he stated he was correcting the testimony he had presented to the Commission. I thereupon requested permission to correct my testimony.
>
> There was a hullabaloo and I was finally told if I would come to the hotel where the commission was by then making its headquarters I would be permitted to correct my testimony. I found it in such a complete mess that I requested permission to bring my former stenographer (Chief Yeoman Drew) and Admiral Theobald to assist me in reconstructing what I had said.[104]

Roberts also caught considerable flak for failing to articulate the nature of the investigation. He would later tell congressional investigators that some of his critics misunderstood the role of the commission.

> This seemed to me a preliminary investigation, like a grand jury investigation, and I did not think, for our report, that was to be taken as precluding every one of the men mentioned in it from a defense before his peers. In other words, you could not conduct a proceeding without cross-examination and without publicity and call it a trial. It was not a trial.[105]

This distinction was less obvious to others. Chief of Staff Marshall asked the judge advocate general to explore possible actions that the army might take against General Short as a result of the finding of dereliction of duty by the Roberts Commission.[106] Roberts's assurances also failed to comfort Admiral Kimmel. "In the eyes of the American people," he told the chairman, "I am on trial and nothing you can say will alter that."[107]

But the strongest and broadest criticism comes from those who believe the Roberts Commission was monumentally unfair to Kimmel and Short. These critics charge that, in focusing so heavily on missteps by the Hawaiian command, the board de-emphasized or even ignored equally serious mistakes by Washington officials. This charge has had a remarkably long shelf life, thanks in no small part to the visceral reaction of Kimmel and Short to the accusation of dereliction of duty. Neither man was the sort to accept the finding without a fight. Short termed the proceedings a "Star Chamber."[108] Kimmel was even more direct, referring to Roberts as "that son of a bitch."[109]

Others in the high command were similarly dissatisfied. Admiral Ernest King, who had been present at the creation of the Roberts Commission, agreed that the two commanders had been "sold down the river" because of the report.[110] "You and Short," wrote Adm. William Halsey to Kimmel, "were the greatest military martyrs this country has ever produced."[111] Admiral Raymond Spruance took a more pragmatic position, arguing that the assignment of blame to Kimmel and Short was understandable "in order that the American people might have no reason to lose confidence in their government." Even so, he warned against "forever damning these two fine officers."[112]

In recent decades the defense of Kimmel and Short has become a cottage industry of sorts, driven in large part by the efforts of Kimmel's descendants. These family members have labored tirelessly to remove what they see as an unfair stigma from the late admiral. They argue that in relieving the two commanders on 16 December Roosevelt had effectively condemned the two men before his own fact-finding body could get under way.[113] The issue returned to national headlines in 1995 when Under Secretary of Defense Edwin Dorn conducted a review of the actions taken with regard to Kimmel and Short. Dorn concluded that while blame for Pearl Harbor should be widely shared, the "official treatment of Admiral Kimmel and General Short was substantively temperate and procedurally proper."[114] Three years later, Senator William Roth of Delaware introduced a resolution designed to symbolically clear Kimmel and Short's name by returning them to their highest wartime ranks.[115]

In academic circles, a growing number of scholars have concluded that the commission was unduly harsh in its condemnation of Kimmel and Short. Prange himself disagreed with the charge of dereliction of duty and argued that "errors of judgment" more accurately captured the commanders' performance.[116] More recently, historian Michael Gannon has offered a comprehensive assessment of the evidence against Kimmel and Short. With regard to the "contrived censure" produced by the Roberts Commission, he notes that none of the subsequent Pearl Harbor investigations repeated the charge of dereliction of duty.[117]

Political Interference

Of the five blue-ribbon panels presented in this book, none feature the degree of political interference in the case of the Roberts Commission. Secretary Knox handpicked two of the commission's five members and advised Roosevelt on the panel's organization and mandate. But his role paled in comparison to that of his counterpart at the War Department. Henry Stimson had served as secretary of war under President Taft, followed by four years as secretary of state under President Hoover. Thus, as Prange notes, by the time Roosevelt brought him back into cabinet circles as secretary of war, Stimson already had a reputation as "a hardy perennial in the garden of American statecraft."[118]

Stimson took a keen interest in the creation and work of the Roberts Commission. He selected McCoy and McNarney as members and lobbied successfully to have Roberts installed as chair. He also had direct contact with commission members on at least seven separate occasions—contact that could be viewed as questionable *ex parte* communication, given his position as a party of interest in the investigation.[119]

- *16 December* – Stimson is present at White House meeting when Roosevelt asks Roberts to chair commission.
- *17 December* – Stimson hosts meeting with four commission members; provides "instructions" regarding investigation.
- *18 December* – Stimson meets with McCoy prior to first official meeting of the commission.
- *19 December* – Stimson meets with McCoy to talk about "situation that he is confronting as a member of the Roberts Board."
- *15 January* – Stimson hosts dinner party for McCoy and wife upon commission's return from Hawaii.
- *20 January* – Stimson, Roberts, and McCoy attend dinner party at home of Justice Felix Frankfurter.

- • *21 January* – Stimson meets with McCoy and McNarney for "long discussion over the situation."

Prange is inclined to give Stimson the benefit of the doubt on this point, arguing that "frenzy, not clear thinking" drove his decisionmaking in the days after the attack.[120] But it is difficult to reconcile that judgment with the clear, deliberate thinking evidenced by Stimson in his diary and external correspondence during this period.

Stimson's influence also manifested itself through the actions of Justice Felix Frankfurter. As district attorney for southern New York under President Theodore Roosevelt, Stimson had brought Frankfurter onto his staff as an assistant, thus launching the latter's legal career. Frankfurter returned the favor by lobbying Franklin Roosevelt to give him the top post at the War Department. As noted earlier, Frankfurter was rumored to have played a role in encouraging Roosevelt to create a special board of inquiry on the attack. Although the historical record does not provide conclusive evidence of his involvement at that stage, it is not difficult to believe that he did so. He was a close friend of Roberts and, even more important, he was a trusted confidant of the president. Stimson himself marveled at the justice's "unimaginable gift of wiggling in wherever he wants to."[121]

Frankfurter's biographer wrote that the justice was always "quite impenitent about his part in arranging for Mr. Justice Roberts to make a personal report to the President on the immediate events that led to Pearl Harbor, and what happened after the attack began. He was afraid of a vindictive search for scapegoats."[122] Frankfurter's interest in the probe only increased over time. On 17 January 1942 he wrote to President Roosevelt:

> Owen Roberts is, as you well know, the most forthright of men. But he is not only—thank God!—very modest. He is also truly shy. And so I venture to suggest that you get him alone, and not with the other members of his Board, to tell you of things that have no proper place in their report—particularly on matters of personnel pertaining not to the past but to what lies ahead.[123]

Three days later Frankfurter hosted a dinner party attended by Stimson, Roberts, and McCoy. At this point the commission was entering the final phase of its deliberations. Stimson used the opportunity to learn of Roberts's views on "the general situation in Hawaii." It was, he wrote in his diary, a "fruitful evening."[124]

A Desperately Bad Thing

The release of the Roberts Report was soon overshadowed by news from the war's front lines and by the seven subsequent investigations into Pearl

Harbor. The members of the commission returned to their jobs and families, Roosevelt got on with the business of governing a wartime nation, and the citizenry became less interested in revisiting the defeat at Pearl Harbor than in anticipating victories against the Axis powers.

Owen Roberts's life followed a curious trajectory in the years after the investigation. His return to the Supreme Court was marked by feuds with his fellow justices and by a perceptible turn back to the political right. "Although he was considerably more able than 'average,'" wrote one court historian, "Justice Roberts' performance makes any other categorization difficult to sustain."[125] Roberts grew disillusioned with life at the high court and resigned from the bench in 1945. As an indicator of the friction that had developed among the brethren, a disagreement arose over the customary farewell letter sent upon a justice's retirement, and none was sent to Roberts.[126]

But even after retiring from public life, Roberts found it difficult to separate himself from the Pearl Harbor inquiry. In January 1946 he was called to testify before the congressional joint committee looking into the circumstances of the Pearl Harbor attack. He described his work as chair of the investigating commission and defended the group's findings. It was clear that Roberts was irritated at having to explain his actions before a group of elected officials. He clashed repeatedly with Republican senators Owen Brewster and Homer Ferguson, and objected to the insinuation that the commission had itself been derelict in its duty to uncover all the pertinent facts about the attack.[127]

Following his appearance before Congress Roberts gradually faded from public view. In 1948, he resurfaced to speak before a special committee of the City Bar Association of New York and addressed the question of whether judges should be tapped for service on blue-ribbon panels:

> It would be a good thing to prevent the justices from taking outside duties. The President in the last war took Federal judges and put them in all sorts of administrative jobs, the nature of which would make enemies and create hard feeling. That put a judge's judicial position in the future in all sorts of jeopardy. If the Federal judges have the time to do that, then there are too many judges.... I believe that was a desperately bad thing for the court.[128]

Then Roberts personalized the issue: "I had another unpleasant experience as a result of the Pearl Harbor Commission report, when a Congressional investigating committee sought to comb over what was done, and there might have been rather an unfortunate reflection on the Justice who was a member of that commission."[129] But his most interesting ruminations appeared in an undated note written to Frankfurter some time after the investigation:

> War makes many exactions, and one of them is suspending judgment on
> matters which in the nature of things can not be fully made clear until
> after the war. Every person entrusted with any responsibility during the
> war is under duty fully to discharge it. The members of the Pearl Harbor
> board and myself were under the duty of ascertaining the truth and report-
> ing it. It is the simple fact to say that we did so. It is good Christian as
> well as American doctrine to assume, until the contrary is shown, that
> other people have likewise acted in good conscience.[130]

It is difficult to know what to make of these cryptic remarks. Unfortunately,
Roberts never chose to expound on the nature of the "many exactions" he
referred to.

But the mystery of Owen J. Roberts does not stop there. For after a
brief stint as dean of the University of Pennsylvania School of Law, he
retired once again to Bryn Coed, his working farm outside Philadelphia.
There he lived until his death on 17 May 1955, and there he made the decision to burn his personal papers, including those that would have shed light
on the commission that bore his name.[131] In so doing, he established himself as the most enigmatic of the commission chairs covered in this book.
Without access to a diary, letters, or contemporaneous notes, we are left
with precious little Roberts in the story of the Roberts Commission. Felix
Frankfurter once lamented his friend's "unconcern for his own record" and
concluded that "more needs to be said for Roberts than he cared to say for
himself."[132] Although Frankfurter was referring to Roberts's record on the
Supreme Court, his observation can be applied to the Pearl Harbor investigation as well. Roberts's destruction of his papers produced a documentary
vacuum that has made it easier for critics of the investigation to question
his conduct.

Evaluation

The long-term significance of the Roberts Commission rests on four factors. First, the creation of the commission helped extend blue-ribbon
inquiry into the area of national security. As noted in Chapter 1, presidential commissions were primarily associated with domestic policy concerns
until World War II. The Roberts Commission had much to do with changing
that. Richard Ben-Veniste, a member of the 9/11 investigation, recognized
the link. "From an historical perspective," he noted, "it would seem that the
closest precedent to our assignment was the Roberts Commission."[133]

Second, the Roberts Commission must be given credit for beginning
the move to standardize commission inquiry. The probe began, like so
many before it, as a highly informal affair, loose in organization and looser
still in operating procedure. Administration insiders expected the investigation to be quick, low key, and informal. Roberts himself appeared uncertain

about the nature of his task. Staff resources were minimal, and little thought was given to the disposition of sensitive materials or the question of how to handle the final report. Roberts did not anticipate the logistical challenge of trying to ensure that an accurate record was kept of the voluminous testimony offered before the panel. Nor did he expect that those who appeared would be sworn in, questioned in an adversarial manner, and that his fellow commissioners would demand access to a range of supporting documentation.

Ironically, much of the impetus to create a more formal operating environment stemmed from the military background of most of the commission's members. The two generals and two admirals were men who had made careers out of doing things by the book. They had little patience for poor planning or slipshod administrative work. In Washington, for example, it was Standley who pressed for clarification of the mandate and subpoena power. And once in Hawaii, commissioners McCoy and McNarney insisted that the panel formalize the interview process.

Roosevelt and Roberts eventually responded to these concerns with a series of moves that had the net effect of making the inquiry more professional. And so an executive order was drafted and signed to specify the commission's mandate, and Congress acted to arm the commission with subpoena power. The commissioners charged military aides with acquiring reports and memoranda for use in the investigation, and a small staff of stenographers was hired to accompany the commission to Hawaii. Henceforth, all witnesses would be sworn and all testimony would be transcribed and made a matter of the record (although not without controversy, as in the case of Admiral Kimmel). These steps set a precedent for future commissions. By the time of the Kennedy assassination, for example, it was simply assumed that basic organizational matters—an executive order, subpoena power, and reporting authority—would be settled before the Warren Commission got underway.

Third, the Roberts Commission demonstrates that political interference can, at times, be quite overt. Commission politics was in its infancy in 1941, and there was a clumsy quality to the administration's handling of the investigation. Because presidential commissions are creatures of the executive, there will always be the suspicion of inappropriate contact and influence between the governing administration and the members of the panel. This suspicion is not unfounded. Each of the case studies that follow—the Rockefeller, Scowcroft, Tower, and Kean Commissions—reveal the politics behind the scenes and attempts by administration loyalists to interfere with the work of the commission. So the fact that such efforts took place during the work of the Roberts Commission is not remarkable. What is remarkable is the nature and extent of the political pressure that was brought to bear. Nowhere was this more evident than in the conduct of secretaries Knox and

Stimson. These two men headed the very departments that were at the center of the investigation. Consequently, the fact that they enjoyed the level of access and involvement they did is a telling commentary on the state of commission politics in 1941.

Finally, the Roberts Commission demonstrates the political utility of the blue-ribbon option for presidents. None of the commission's rough edges—that it was conceived on the fly, created in haste, poorly organized, or heavily politicized—kept Roosevelt from using the panel to his advantage. When pressed to defend the administration's posture on Pearl Harbor, he and his lieutenants could refrain from comment by simply pointing out that an investigation was under way. And when the final report came in, it gave the president an official set of findings to wave as proof that his administration was on top of the issue. The strategy worked. A poll taken four years after the Japanese attack revealed that fewer than one in ten Americans held Roosevelt personally responsible for the disaster.[134] That underscores an important dynamic that will be seen with some of the later commissions. When commissions are created on the front end of a crisis, their findings, however flawed, tend to set the tone for subsequent discussion of the issue.

Conclusion

By the standards of blue-ribbon inquiry, the Roberts Commission has had a remarkably long life as a topic of discussion. Much of the longevity is due to its association with an event that had no parallel in US history—that is, until 11 September 2001 ("9/11"). In the wake of the 9/11 terrorist attacks, Americans went through the classic range of emotions that occur in the wake of a tragedy: denial turned to shock, and shock turned to anger. And as with Pearl Harbor, that anger soon gave rise to questions regarding culpability. The Bush administration's attempt to deal with those questions is the subject of an extended analysis in Chapter 6. At this point it is sufficient to note that Roosevelt's creation of the Roberts Commission to investigate the Pearl Harbor attack loomed large in the national discussion over 9/11. And remarkably, no one really seemed to care that Roberts had presided over an investigation that was far from perfect. What mattered from the perspective of 2001 was that Roosevelt had done something.

No one was as quick to refer to the Roberts Commission as Democratic Senator Joseph Lieberman of Connecticut. A frequent guest on the talk-show circuit in the fall of 2001, Lieberman kept the pressure on the Bush White House to get to the bottom of things. In an interview with newsman Tim Russert, Lieberman took the opportunity to suggest a blue-ribbon commission. He specifically invoked the example of the Pearl Harbor investigation and expressed his hope that Bush would establish "something just like

The Roberts Commission and Pearl Harbor   41

that real soon." Then Lieberman offered his closing comment. "We need another Roberts Commission," he said. "We need to know the truth."[135]

Notes

1. Although the Roberts Commission turns up frequently in the literature, it has not been the subject of a specialized analysis. Other investigations of Pearl Harbor have been written about in more detail. For example, see Henry Dozier Russell, *Pearl Harbor Story* (Macon, GA: Mercer University Press, 2001), and Henry C. Clausen and Bruce Lee, *Pearl Harbor: Final Judgement* (New York: HarperCollins, 2001).

2. Letter, Frank Knox to Paul Scott Mowrer, 18 December 1941, Folder General Correspondence 1941, Container 4, Papers of Frank Knox, Library of Congress.

3. Editorial, "An Honest Board of Inquiry," *Washington Times-Herald*, 18 December 1941, in Newspaper Clippings Folio, Papers of Walter Bruce Howe, MS Collection 122, Naval Historical Collection, Naval War College, Newport, RI (hereafter NWC).

4. *Pearl Harbor Attack: Hearings before the Joint Committee on the Investigation of the Pearl Harbor Attack*, 79th Congress, 1st session, 1946 (hereafter PHA), Part 24: 1,749–1,755.

5. Elliott Roosevelt, ed., *F.D.R.: His Personal Letters 1928–1945*, Vol. 4 (New York: Duell, Sloan and Pearce, 1947), p. 1,254.

6. Entry for 15 December 1941, *Diaries of Henry Lewis Stimson*, Reel 7, Yale University Collection (hereafter *Stimson Diaries*).

7. Gordon W. Prange, *At Dawn We Slept: The Untold Story of Pearl Harbor* (New York: Penguin Books, 1981), p. 559.

8. Max Freedman, ed., *Roosevelt and Frankfurter: Their Correspondence, 1928–1945* (Boston: Little, Brown and Co., 1967), p. 644.

9. James O. Richardson and George C. Dyer, *On the Treadmill to Pearl Harbor: The Memoirs of Admiral James O. Richardson* (Washington, DC: Department of the Navy–Naval History Division, 1973), p. 453.

10. Memorandum, President Roosevelt to Stephen T. Early, 23 December 1941, Folder Pearl Harbor Inquiry 1941–1942, Box 7, Official File 400, Franklin D. Roosevelt Library, Hyde Park, NY (hereafter FDRL).

11. *Stimson Diaries*, 11 December 1941.

12. Edwin T. Layton, Roger Pineau, and John Costello, *And I Was There: Pearl Harbor and Midway—Breaking the Secrets* (New York: William Morrow and Co., 1985), p. 33.

13. *Stimson Diaries,* 15 December 1941.

14. Ibid.

15. Ibid., 16 December 1941.

16. Ibid.

17. Admiral Richardson, former fleet commander, reported hearing rumors that Chief Justice Harlan F. Stone had been asked to serve as chair. Richardson and Dyer, *On the Treadmill to Pearl Harbor*, p. 453.

18. Larry I. Bland, ed., *The Papers of George Catlett Marshall*, Vol. 3 (Baltimore: The Johns Hopkins University Press, 1991), p. 22.

19. "Board of Inquiry Meets Again," *New York Times*, 19 December 1941, p. 3.

20. PHA 7: 3,300.

21. Letter, Husband E. Kimmel to Harry Elmer Barnes, 12 July 1962, Folder

Roberts Commission (1), Box 127—Roberts Commission, John Toland Papers, Series V—Infamy, FDRL.

22. Thomas Wildenberg, *All the Factors of Victory: Admiral Joseph Mason Reeves and the Origins of Carrier Airpower* (Washington, DC: Brassey's Inc., 2003), p. 257.

23. PHA 7: 3,300.

24. Orders, 20 December 1941, Folder Roberts Commission, Container 84, Papers of Frank Ross McCoy, Library of Congress.

25. A. J. Bacevich, *Diplomat in Khaki: Major General Frank Ross McCoy and American Foreign Policy, 1898–1949* (Lawrence: University Press of Kansas, 1989), p. 182.

26. Letter, Kimmel to Barnes, 12 July 1962, Folder Roberts Commission (1), Box 127—Roberts Commission, John Toland Papers, Series V—Infamy, FDRL.

27. Prange, *At Dawn We Slept*, p. 592.

28. Adjutant general's file on Joseph Taggart McNarney, Folder Roberts Commission (1), Box 127—Roberts Commission, John Toland Papers, Series V—Infamy, FDRL.

29. M. R. Werner and John Starr, *Teapot Dome* (New York: Viking Press, 1959), pp. 155–156.

30. Henry J. Abraham, *Justices and Presidents: A Political History of Appointments to the Supreme Court*, 2d ed. (New York: Oxford University Press, 1985), p. 200.

31. Donald Grey Brownlow, *The Accused: The Ordeal of Rear Admiral Husband Edward Kimmel, U.S.N.* (New York: Vantage Press, 1968), p. 144.

32. Alpheus Thomas Mason, *Harlan Fiske Stone: Pillar of the Law* (Hamden, CT: Archon Books, 1968), p. 707.

33. Owen J. Roberts, "Now is the Time: Fortifying the Supreme Court's Independence," *ABAJ* 35:1 (January 1949), 1.

34. PHA 7: 3,273.

35. "Board of Inquiry Set up on Hawaii," *New York Times*, 17 December 1941, p. 9.

36. Hanson W. Baldwin, "The Events at Hawaii," *New York Times*, 18 December 1941, p. 4.

37. "Justice Roberts Heads Pearl Harbor Inquiry Board," *Washington Post*, 17 December 1941, p. 1.

38. "An Honest Board of Inquiry," *New York Daily News,* 18 December 1941, in Newspaper Clippings Folio, Papers of Walter Bruce Howe, NWC.

39. "Justice Roberts Heads Pearl Harbor Inquiry Board," *Washington Post*, 17 December 1941, p. 1.

40. Clarence E. Wunderlin, ed., *Papers of Robert A. Taft 1939–1944,*, Vol. 2 (Kent, OH: Kent State University Press, 2001).

41. *Stimson Diaries,* 16 December 1941.

42. Ibid.,17 December 1941.

43. PHA 7: 3,283.

44. Schneider had served as law clerk to Roberts from 1931 to 1945. Fellow Justice William O. Douglas noted that this was at odds with Supreme Court custom that law clerks would work for only one year. William O. Douglas, *The Court Years, 1939–1975* (New York: Random House, 1980), p. 169.

45. Telephone interview with Bruce Howe, 6 August 2004.

46. Harry Elmer Barnes, Interview with Admiral William H. Standley, Folder Roberts Commission (1), Box 127, John Toland Papers, Series V—Infamy, FDRL.

47. PHA 7: 3,262.

48. Ibid.

49. Ibid, 7: 3,273.

50. Ibid., 22: 3.

51. Ibid., 7: 3,262.

52. Joseph P. Lash, *From the Diaries of Felix Frankfurter* (New York: W.W. Norton and Co., 1974), p. 174.

53. 3 February 1943, Diaries of Felix Frankfurter, Reel 1, Box 1, Library of Congress.

54. "Board of Inquiry Set up on Hawaii," *New York Times*, 17 December 1941, p. 9.

55. William H. Standley and Arthur A. Ageton, *Admiral Ambassador to Russia* (Chicago: Henry Regnery Company, 1955), p. 81.

56. Memorandum, Owen Roberts to President Roosevelt, 18 December 1941, Folder Pearl Harbor Inquiry 1941–1942, Box 7, Official File 400, FDRL.

57. Ibid.

58. Harry Elmer Barnes, Interview with Admiral William H. Standley, Folder Roberts Commission (1), Box 127, John Toland Papers, Series V—Infamy, FDRL.

59. Samuel I. Rosenman, ed.. *The Public Papers and Addresses of Franklin D. Roosevelt*, Vol. 1941 (New York: Harper and Brothers, 1950), p. 136.

60. Standley, *Admiral Ambassador*, p. 88.

61. Letter, Walter Bruce Howe to William Donovan, 19 December 1941, Folder 36: Roberts Commission Correspondence, Papers of Walter Bruce Howe, NWC.

62. PHA 23: 1,249.

63. Ibid., 7: 3,262.

64. Letter, Herbert Hoover to Frank McCoy, 17 December 1941, Folder Roberts Commission (1), Box 126, John Toland Papers, Series V—Infamy, FDRL.

65. Prange, *At Dawn We Slept*, p. 595.

66. Letter, Cordell Hull to Justice Roberts, 30 December 1941, Entry 167J, Box 64, Exhibits 1941–1942, Pearl Harbor Liaison Office: The Roberts Commission, RG 80 General Records of the Department of the Navy, 1798–1947, National Archives.

67. Letter, Walter Bruce Howe to William J. Donovan, 19 December 1941, Folder 36: Roberts Commission Correspondence, Box 4, Papers of Walter Bruce Howe, NWC.

68. PHA 24: 1,287–1,304.

69. Harry Elmer Barnes, Interview with Captain Joseph J. Rochefort, Folder Roberts Commission (1), Box 127, John Toland Papers, Series V—Infamy, FDRL.

70. PHA 22: 7.

71. Ibid., 22: 21.

72. Harry Elmer Barnes, Interview with Admiral Standley, Folder Roberts Commission (1), Box 127, John Toland Papers, Series V—Infamy, FDRL.

73. Martin V. Melosi, *The Shadow of Pearl Harbor: Political Controversy over the Surprise Attack, 1941–1946* (College Station: Texas A&M Press, 1977), p. 36.

74. PHA 27: 1,266.

75. Ibid., 27: 1,304–1,305.

76. Prange, *At Dawn We Slept*, p. 596.

77. Transcript, Oral History Interview with Gen. Louis W. Truman, 7

December 1991, Harry S. Truman Presidential Library, 33 <www.trumanlibrary.org/oralhist/truman1.htm>.

78. Standley, *Admiral Ambassador*, p. 84.
79. Thomas Wildenberg, *All the Factors of Victory*, p. 263.
80. Ibid.
81. Ibid., 264.
82. "Statement of Rear Admiral Robert A. Theobald," in Husband E. Kimmel, *Admiral Kimmel's Story* (Chicago: Henry Regnery Company, 1955), p. 154.
83. Truman Oral History, p. 33.
84. PHA 7: 3,263.
85. Draft of Findings of Fact, Folder Reports: Roberts Commission, Box 12, Papers of William Harrison Standley, Library of Congress.
86. PHA 7: 3,263.
87. Letter, General Frank McCoy to Lieutenant Colonel William Biddle, 28 January 1942, Folder General Correspondence 1942, Box 49, Papers of Frank Ross McCoy, Library of Congress.
88. Standley, *Admiral Ambassador,* p. 87.
89. PHA 7: 3,299.
90. Ibid.
91. Ibid.
92. Ibid., 7: 3,265.
93. Ibid., 7: 3,282.
94. Ibid., 7: 3,266.
95. "Roberts Report," *Sunday Star* (Washington, DC), 25 January 1942, Newspaper Clippings Folio, Papers of Walter Bruce Howe, NWC.
96. "Roberts Report Amazes Hawaii," *Washington Times-Herald*, 26 January 1942, Newspaper Clippings Folio, Papers of Walter Bruce Howe, NWC.
97. Associated Press Report, "Bite in Report on Pearl Harbor Stirs Honolulu," 25 January 1942, Newspaper Clippings Folio, Papers of Walter Bruce Howe, NWC.
98. Mason, *Harlan Fiske Stone,* p. 581.
99. *Stimson Diaries,* 25 January 1942.
100. Frankfurter to Roberts, 25 January 1942, Reel 59, Box 96, Papers of Felix Frankfurter, Library of Congress.
101. Prange, *At Dawn We Slept,* p. 602.
102. PHA 7: 3,262.
103. "Remarks at the Meeting of the Office of the Secretary of Defense and Members of the Kimmel Family," 27 April 1995, transcription by Patricia A. LaMonica (Riverton, NJ: LBS, Inc., 1995).
104. Letter, Husband E. Kimmel to Harry Elmer Barnes, 12 July 1962, Folder Roberts Commission (1), Box 127—Roberts Commission, John Toland Papers, Series V—Infamy, FDRL.
105. PHA 7: 3,267.
106. Bland, *The Papers of George Catlett Marshall*, Vol. 3 , p. 84.
107. Letter, Kimmel to Barnes, 12 July 1962, Folder Roberts Commission (1), Box 127—Roberts Commission, John Toland Papers, Series V—Infamy, FDRL.
108. John Toland, *Infamy: Pearl Harbor and Its Aftermath* (New York: Berkley Books, 1982), p. 195.
109. Ibid., 54.
110. Layton, Pineau, and Costello, *And I Was There,* p. 351.
111. Kimmel, *Admiral Kimmel's Story*, p. 168.

112. Michael Gannon, *Pearl Harbor Betrayed: The True Story of a Man and a Nation Under Attack* (New York: Owl Books, 2001), p. 260.

113. Layton, Pineau, and Costello, *And I Was There*, p. 337.

114. Report of Under Secretary of Defense Edwin Dorn, 15 December 1995, <http://www.ibiblio.org/pha/pha/dorn/dornmemo.html>.

115. S.J. Res. 55, 105th Congress, 2d session, 1 September 1998 [THOMAS Legislative Information System].

116. Prange, *At Dawn We Slept*, p. 601.

117. Gannon, *Pearl Harbor Betrayed*, p. 278.

118. Gordon W. Prange, *Pearl Harbor: The Verdict of History* (New York: Penguin Books, 1986), p. 204.

119. *Stimson Diaries,* 16 December 1941 to 21 January 1942.

120. Prange, *At Dawn We Slept*, p. 593.

121. Lash, *From the Diaries of Felix Frankfurter*, p. 74.

122. Freedman, *Roosevelt and Frankfurter: Their Correspondence, 1928–1945*, p. 644.

123. Ibid.

124. *Stimson Diaries,* 20 January 1942.

125. Abraham, *Justices and Presidents*, p. 201.

126. Charles A. Leonard, "A Revolution Runs Wild: Mr. Justice Roberts' Last Four Years on the Supreme Court," *Supreme Court Historical Society 1980 Yearbook*, p. 3.

127. PHA 7: 3,273, 3,278, 3,280.

128. Roberts, "Now is the Time," *ABAJ* 35:1, 1–2.

129. Ibid.

130. Roberts to Frankfurter, undated correspondence ca. 1942–1944, Reel 59, Box 96, Papers of Felix Frankfurter, Library of Congress.

131. On Roberts's destruction of his papers, see Charles A. Leonard, *A Search for a Judicial Philosophy: Mr. Justice Roberts and the Constitutional Revolution of 1937* (Port Washington, NY: Kennikat Press, 1971), pp. 184–185; Edwin N. Probert II, "Owen Josephus Roberts: A Short Retrospective on a Favorite Son," *The Patriot,* 1990–2000 edition, Germantown Academy, PA, <http://www.germantownacademy.org/aboutga/ history_traditions/profiles/Roberts/portrait.shtml>; Edwin N. Probert II, e-mail correspondence with author, May–June 2004.

132. Leonard, *A Search for a Judicial Philosophy,* p. 185.

133. Public Hearing, 31 March 2003, National Commission on Terrorist Attacks Upon the United States <http://www.9-11commission.gov/hearings/hearing1.htm>.

134. "The Quarter's Polls," *Public Opinion Quarterly* 9:4 (1945), 511.

135. Transcript, "Meet the Press," *Washington Post*, 21 October 2001 [Lexis-Nexis Academic].

3

The Politics of Spying:
The Rockefeller Commission
and the CIA

It's become a government all of its own and all secret. They don't have to account to anybody. That's a very dangerous thing in a democratic society, and it's got to be put a stop to. The people have got a right to know what those birds are up to.
—President Harry Truman, on the CIA, 1961

If you knew what they were doing, it would curl your hair.
—President Gerald Ford, on the CIA, 1975

In late 1974, the postwar US intelligence community came under the sharpest attack of its thirty-year existence. The accusations against the community included spying at home, questionable activities abroad, and misconduct at high levels. As the most visible organization in the community, the Central Intelligence Agency was singled out for specific condemnation. Some critics even suggested that the time had come to abolish the agency.[1] A popular book of the period warned that an "invisible government," controlled by shadowy figures in the intelligence underworld, existed behind the facade of US democracy.[2]

The growing controversy threatened to disrupt President Gerald Ford's effort to heal the wounds left by Watergate and restore faith in the government. In response, he created a blue-ribbon panel, headed by Vice President Nelson Rockefeller, and gave it the task of examining the various charges leveled against the spy agencies. Once under way, the panel secured a place in history as one of the most important investigations into the means and ends of US intelligence. The work of the Commission on CIA Activities Within the United States is the focus of this chapter.

Political Context

The origins of the intelligence crisis date to the spring of 1973. At that time, Director of Central Intelligence (DCI) James Schlesinger circulated an internal memorandum within the CIA soliciting information on questionable activities from the agency's past. The responses were compiled in a summary of almost 700 pages that became known as the "family jewels." An insider at the agency told the Pulitzer Prize–winning journalist Seymour Hersh that Schlesinger had been "extremely concerned and disturbed by what he discovered." CIA officials also sensed that Schlesinger's actions were causing considerable resentment within the ranks; they took steps to increase the number of personal bodyguards charged with protecting the director.[3] As agency morale declined in the wake of Vietnam and Watergate, internal security suffered and portions of the jewels began to leak.

On 18 December 1974, Hersh informed William Colby, who had replaced Schlesinger as DCI the previous year, that he had discovered evidence of domestic spying by the CIA and would soon publish the story. Colby alerted Brent Scowcroft, Ford's deputy assistant for national security affairs, of the conversation: Though Scowcroft passed the information on to the president, it appears that the matter received little attention initially and was not widely discussed. Phil Buchen, Ford's close friend and White House counsel, later denied having heard "any reference before the Hersh article appeared that there were problems out there."[4]

Hersh's story appeared on the front page of the *New York Times* on 22 December. The banner headline demanded attention: "Huge CIA Operation Reported in U.S. Against Antiwar Forces, Other Dissidents in Nixon Years." The article that followed was over a page long. Hersh detailed a "massive, illegal domestic intelligence operation" that had involved everything from mail intercepts to the surveillance of members of Congress. Some of the activities were the work of overzealous intelligence officers; others appeared to have been coordinated by those higher up the chain of command. The article identified Nixon aide Tom Charles Huston as the author of a plan to use the CIA to combat student unrest and other disturbances "fomented by black extremists." Hersh also hinted darkly of future revelations that would connect the agency to a series of "mysterious burglaries and incidents" that had occurred in recent years.[5]

The story continued to grow in the days that followed. On 29 December the newspaper revealed the existence of a domestic operations division at the CIA. While many of the division's activities were directly tied to foreign intelligence operations, others had been undertaken for the sole purpose of disrupting the work of dissident groups within the United States. "Intelligence," said one agent, "is where you find it."[6] Even the conservative *Wall Street Journal* acknowledged "ferment" at the CIA and predicted that Congress would promptly impose new legal restraints on the agency.[7]

Key lawmakers began to join the issue. In a 30 December appearance on the news program "Issues and Answers," Senator William Proxmire (Democrat-Wisconsin) reported that material in his possession confirmed the accuracy of Hersh's article.[8] Senator Lowell Weicker (Republican-Connecticut) voiced his belief that the allegations could not be "dismissed as isolated instances of individual excesses."[9] In the House, newly elected Watergate babies had swelled the Democratic ranks and were vowing to gain an equal footing with the executive in exercising control over the intelligence agencies.

The public outcry wrought by the revelations presented an unwelcome challenge to Ford. He found himself at the center of a political storm that directly challenged his authority over a significant part of the national security apparatus. Questions regarding the politicization of the CIA, the shaping of national security policy, and the proper mechanism for intelligence oversight were all soon involved. Ford realized that his capacity to act was seriously hampered by his status as the nation's first unelected president. His pardon of Richard Nixon the previous September had further eroded his base of popular support and placed de facto limits on the constitutional power he did have. Even worse, the sins of Johnson and Nixon had convinced many that the presidency itself was dysfunctional and that presidential power was not to be trusted.

On 22 December, the day Hersh's initial story appeared, Ford spoke with Colby by phone from Air Force One as he traveled to Vail, Colorado, for the Christmas holiday. He would remain there until 3 January 1975, consulting with his closest aides and devising a strategy to deal with the unfolding crisis. While at Vail, Ford solicited advice from Buchen, Scowcroft, de facto chief of staff Donald Rumsfeld, Deputy White House Assistant Richard Cheney, Press Secretary Ron Nessen, and Counselor Jack Marsh, a Virginia Democrat responsible for congressional liaison. The key figure missing from the entourage was Henry Kissinger, who at that time was wearing two hats as national security advisor and as secretary of state. Though Kissinger remained in Washington for the holiday, he spoke with Ford daily and played a major role in fashioning the administration's response to the disclosures.[10] In fact, his presence in Washington actually served a purpose, enabling him to meet with Colby and function as informal liaison between the CIA and Ford during the early days of the crisis.

Creating the Commission

The decision to establish a blue-ribbon commission to investigate the charges was taken early. On 24 December 1974, a scant two days after the Hersh story appeared, Marsh and Buchen recommended to Ford that a presidential commission be appointed to "look at the present complaint."[11] Kissinger joined in the following day, calling for a blue-ribbon panel to be established early in the new year.[12] In a closed meeting with the president on 27 December Cheney had discussed a number of different options for dealing with the crisis, but ultimately advised Ford that setting up a "mechanism to investigate" was the best possible response.[13]

Ford was receptive to the idea. Privately he had already sought advice from Washington "superlawyer" Edward Bennett Williams. Although serving as treasurer of the Democratic National Committee, Williams had recently grown disenchanted with the direction of his party. Ford detected a strategic opening and used the CIA scandal as an opportunity to court Williams. In response to Ford's confidential inquiry, Williams recommended a special commission to help the White House stay in front of the issue. Ford thought it a "great idea" and praised Williams's "intuitive ability to analyze public and press reaction."[14] By 30 December 1974 the decision had been made final. On that day Ford again met with Cheney—this time to discuss commission membership.[15]

In the case at hand, there is ample evidence to suggest that the desire to preempt congressional action was a powerful force in the decision to appoint the commission. Ford himself acknowledges as much in his memoirs, arguing that "unnecessary disclosures" would have resulted from an investigation dominated by Congress.[16] "What we are trying to do," he explained to former DCI Richard Helms, "is look into the charges and protect the functions of the Agency with a Blue Ribbon group which will operate responsibly."[17]

Each of the key aides that recommended a commission-based investigation to Ford also cited preemption as a key consideration. Marsh's memo of 24 December was the most direct, arguing that "the panel's efforts would take the initiative rather than finding ourselves whipsawed by prolonged congressional hearings."[18] Director Colby, however, was kept in the dark even as the plan began to take shape. Only after Ford's return was he told that a panel would be created "hopefully to still the outcry and thus prevent a full investigation of intelligence from getting started."[19]

This idea of using an ad hoc group to protect the intelligence community from congressional action was not without precedent. In 1954, President Eisenhower established a committee under the leadership of Lt. Gen. James Doolittle to ward off an investigation by Senator Joseph McCarthy. Lyndon Johnson also shielded the agency in this fashion when he established a panel in 1967 to deal with charges that the CIA was funding the National Students Association.[20] Though both of these attempts succeeded in protecting the community from outside scrutiny, the issues involved were minor compared with those of the mid-1970s, and an earlier, more forgiving political climate afforded those presidents much greater latitude. Even so, the similarities were not lost on everyone. William Pawley, a member of the Doolittle probe, wrote to Ford praising his appointment of the commission and warning of the dangers involved should Congress become more involved.[21] Nicholas Katzenbach, chairman of the 1967 panel, likewise opined in early January 1975 that extended congressional hearings could end up "destroying the CIA's intelligence integrity."[22]

Even though preemption was clearly the primary consideration in these early decisions, the White House strategy was more sophisticated than it appeared. Ford realized that, given the highly charged post-Watergate environment and the debate generated by the Hersh article, some form of congressional investigation was likely. He acknowledged as much on the day he announced the formation of the Rockefeller Commission, remarking on the "current plans of various committees of the Congress to hold hearings."[23] What Ford sought to prevent, however, was a special congressional probe that would be singularly aggressive and receive extensive publicity. This was not an idle fear. On 29 December 1974, Senator William Proxmire (Democrat-Wisconsin) went public with a call for Congress to establish "an independent special prosecutor with subpoena powers who will prosecute every illegal action by CIA agents, past or present."[24]

Ford told Nessen that he [Ford] "would be held accountable if he allowed the intelligence services to be crippled by excessive exposure."[25] Kissinger also seemed particularly worried by this possibility. The day after the Hersh story appeared, he wrote to Rumsfeld that the administration should act decisively to "head off, if possible, a full-blown congressional investigation outside of the normal legislative channels."[26]

The presidential entourage returned from Vail on 3 January 1975 and immediately began to make final plans for the commission. On that day, Ford had his first face-to-face meeting with DCI Colby since the publication of the *New York Times* article. Also present were Kissinger, Rumsfeld, and Buchen. At this session Ford received his first full briefing on the family jewels. Later that evening Ford personally called the individuals selected to serve on the panel. In selling the idea of commission service, Ford first mentioned the importance of protecting the public from illegal CIA activity and then stressed the need to protect the agency's ability to operate. He also told the individuals that a staffer would soon be in contact to discuss "any public positions on CIA activities that might be troublesome."[27]

The Commission to Investigate CIA Activities Within the United States was officially created the following day by Executive Order 11828. Ford empowered the panel to investigate "activities conducted within the United States by the Central Intelligence Agency which give rise to questions of compliance with the provisions of [the U.S. Code]."[28] Using technical compliance with the law as the yardstick by which actions would be judged obviously limited the scope of the commission's inquiry. As John Oseth notes in his careful study of intelligence oversight, the narrowness of the mandate signaled that Ford "hardly intended to launch a 'zero-based' review of the CIA and its operations."[29] Ford also asked the commission to look at the existing safeguards against such domestic activity and to make recommendations for strengthening the system.

Commission Structure and Personnel

Ford's executive order of 4 January 1975 granted the panel a life span of only three months. This represented less than half the time normally allotted for a blue-ribbon probe.[30] But Ford and his advisers must have realized that a short inquiry would be far less likely to uncover material that might prove embarrassing to the administration. Equally important, the three-month mandate guaranteed that the White House would have an official finding in hand even as the congressional committees were beginning their investigations in the spring.

Ford's decisionmaking team also exercised great care in making personnel decisions. The eight individuals selected to serve on the commission included Vice President Nelson Rockefeller, chairman; John T. Connor, secretary of commerce 1965–1967 and CEO of the Allied Chemical Corporation; C. Douglas Dillon, secretary of the treasury 1960–1965 and chairman of Dillon, Read & Company, a Wall Street banking house; Erwin Griswold, solicitor general 1967–1972 and partner in the Washington law firm of Jones, Day, Reavis and Pogue; Ronald Reagan, governor of California 1966–1974 and soon to be a presidential aspirant; Lyman Lemnitzer, (USA ret.) chairman of the Joint Chiefs of Staff 1960–1963; Edgar Shannon, president of the University of Virginia 1959–1974; and Lane Kirkland, secretary and treasurer of the AFL-CIO.

Behind-the-scenes politics significantly affected the final composition of the panel. Ron Nessen recalls that the eight names were selected from a list of more than two dozen.[31] Cheney's notes from Vail indicate that both Supreme Court Justice Lewis Powell and former Secretary of State Dean Rusk were considered for commission membership before being dropped for unknown reasons.[32] Federal Circuit Court Judge Henry Friendly turned down an offer to serve, citing his "belief that federal judges should confine themselves to their judicial function."[33]

There was also significant discussion regarding the selection of the commission's chairman. Ford writes in his memoirs that he simply regarded Rockefeller as the "best candidate" for the position.[34] But the decision was less certain than that. As late as 3 January 1975, the day before the commission was officially created, Cheney was still operating under the assumption that Erwin Griswold would be chairman. Why this never came about is the subject of some dispute. Nessen suggests that Ford decided to drop Griswold as chairman when he learned that the Watergate special prosecutor had investigated the former US solicitor general.[35] Griswold, however, had contacted the White House after the initial phone call from

Ford and asked to be removed from consideration as chairman. He cited the damaging perception of "too many Nixon people" and argued that such a visible panel would need a "more political" figure at the helm.[36] Griswold was also committed to teach at the University of Florida during that spring semester, an obligation that placed serious constraints on his time and would have made it difficult for him to serve in an administrative capacity.[37]

At first glance, the commission appointments appear to be quite conventional. The academic (Shannon), labor (Kirkland), business (Dillon, Connor), and legal (Griswold) communities were all well represented on the panel. As is typical with presidential commissions, there was also some degree of partisan balance. Three of the eight members (Shannon, Kirkland, and Connor) had strong ties to the Democratic Party.

In other ways, however, the selections were less typical. First, even by the standards of the early 1970s, there was remarkably little cultural diversity among the members. All were white, all were male, and all were over fifty years old. The 1967 National Advisory Commission on Civil Disorders (the Kerner Commission), by contrast, had included two African Americans and a woman among its eleven members. There was also no congressional representation on the panel, a remarkable fact, given Ford's own experience, as a member of the House, on the 1963 President's Commission on the Assassination of President Kennedy (the Warren Commission). That particular analogy was not lost on everyone. When Ford asked Congress to grant the panel subpoena power, Representative Peter Rodino (Democrat-New Jersey), chairman of the House Judiciary Committee, cited the lack of congressional input as a point of friction and noted the unfavorable comparison with Ford's service on the Warren Commission.[38] As a result the CIA panel was never granted that authority.[39]

With the exception of Commissioner Shannon, all the members had experience in government, including some strong ties to the intelligence community itself. Rockefeller had served on the President's Foreign Intelligence Advisory Board since 1969 and was considered an expert on psychological warfare. His principal speechwriter would later note that Rockefeller "enjoyed an intimate knowledge of and developed a lasting taste for CIA covert operations. His sympathies did not pass unnoticed at CIA."[40] General Lemnitzer presided over the Joint Chiefs of Staff during the Bay of Pigs invasion, and later called the release of the Pentagon Papers "a traitorous act."[41] Douglas Dillon had helped form the Office of Strategic Services (OSS) during World War II and, as undersecretary of state in the Eisenhower administration, helped construct the cover story during the U-2 crisis in 1960. Ronald Reagan's conservative predilections were well known, as was the hard stance he had assumed against the student protest movement in California while governor. In the AFL-CIO, Lane Kirkland answered only to George Meany. It was Meany, in fact, who Ford initially called the night he contacted the prospective commissioners. (The labor organization was heavily political and had worked closely with the CIA since the late 1940s to construct "free" European trade unions sympathetic to US foreign-policy goals.[42] More recently, the AFL-CIO had cooperated with agency operatives in Chile to support the Chilean truckers' strike against the government of Salvador Allende.)[43]

Even Erwin Griswold, the commissioner thought to be most sympathetic to civil-liberty concerns, had contact with the defense and intelligence establishments. As solicitor general, Griswold had defended the US Army's domestic surveillance of civilians in the late 1960s.[44] John Connor had retired from public service and was serving as chairman and CEO of the large multinational corporation, Allied Chemical. Though best known as a Tennyson scholar and former president of the University of Virginia, Edgar Shannon had served with distinction in the US Navy during World War II and was on the Board of Consultants of the National War College.[45]

The commission's staff was also carefully chosen. Although it was less visible than the commissioners themselves, the importance of this group should not be underestimated. The attorneys who served as counsel to the panel worked closely with the commissioners, conducted the research itself, and, as one commissioner admitted frankly, "ended up writing ninety-seven percent of the final report."[46]

Heading this group was the commission's executive director, David Belin. A Des Moines attorney who had served as chairman of Lawyers for Nixon-Agnew, Belin was best known for his work as counsel to the Warren Commission. Ford's "good impression" of Belin's service on that panel led him to personally select him for that important post.[47] By the mid-1970s, criticism of the Warren Commission report was growing, and Belin—a staunch defender of the report—had remained in the public eye because of his strong defense of the lone-assassin theory in the death of President Kennedy.[48] Despite the fact that the panel's chairman would have to rely heavily on the integrity and judgment of the executive director, Ford did not solicit Rockefeller's advice in making the appointment.[49] Belin would play an important role in the course of the investigation, a role that often went beyond supervisory and administrative responsibilities.

Working with Belin were eight attorneys who served the commission in the capacity of senior counsel, assistant counsel, or special counsel. Each was either an established member of the legal community or a rising star just out of the nation's most prestigious law schools. They were, in most cases, selected to serve on the commission through their association with Belin or one of the commissioners. In the White House, Phil Areeda,

Buchen's assistant in the counsel's office, also played a significant role in the selection process. Areeda had taught law at Harvard and was thus well positioned to recommend promising young attorneys for service.

Those selected to serve shared many of the ideological predispositions of the commissioners. One staffer acknowledged the similarities within the group.

> Most [of the staff members] shared the same general political orientation. There were not any SDS [Students for a Democratic Society] members, but on the other hand there were no John Birchers either.... Because of the type of individual on the commission and on the staff, little credence was given to the wilder accusations regarding the CIA.[50]

The conservative nature of the panel raised some immediate protests. Predictably, the reaction was fiercest from the political left. Representative Ron Dellums (Democrat-California) wrote to Ford expressing his concern: "Its [the panel's] makeup negates its integrity and its potential usefulness ... you have fumbled an opportunity to restore morale and balance to public opinion by your selection of the CIA investigating team."[51]

Even some Republicans questioned the commission's composition. Senator Richard Schweiker (Republican-Pennsylvania) told *Time* magazine that he, too, doubted the objectivity of a body so dominated by "those oriented to Government and the military intelligence establishment."[52] *Newsweek* presciently gauged the political consequences of the selections, noting that the panel's makeup "guaranteed that it would not have the field to itself."[53] Perhaps most important, the American public also took a dim view of the personnel appointments. A Harris poll conducted in early February revealed that 43 percent of those surveyed felt the commission's investigation would likely result in a coverup.[54]

Certain Other Matters

Even as the investigation into the CIA's domestic activities got under way, a corollary inquiry was developing on the issue of the agency's plots to assassinate foreign leaders. Ford's first clue that such activities had occurred came during his vacation in Vail. In Colby's initial response to Ford about the allegations, he indicated there were "certain other matters in the history of the Agency which are subject to question."[55] Kissinger was even more direct in his letter to Ford on December 25.

> There are other activities in the history of the agency which, though unconnected to the NYT article, are also open to question. I have discussed these activities with [Colby], and must tell you that some few of them clearly were illegal, while others—though technically not illegal—raise profound moral questions.[56]

Ford discovered exactly what these "profound" questions were during his 3 January briefing by Colby in the Oval Office. The DCI detailed agency plans, and in some cases attempts, to kill leaders such as Cuba's Fidel Castro, Patrice Lumumba in the Congo, and Rafael Trujillo in the Dominican Republic.

It is thus clear that Ford was fully aware of the foreign assassination plots and the legal/ethical questions they raised before he created the Rockefeller Commission. Yet even with this knowledge, he chose to limit the commission's investigative powers to the one issue, domestic spying, that had already been made public. Even though he directed the panel away from the issue, Ford was shocked to learn of the plots and remained preoccupied by the entire issue. He also proved incapable of keeping the matter secret.[57]

At a White House luncheon with top executives from the *New York Times* on 16 January 1975, Ford attempted to defend the conservative nature of the panel's membership by emphasizing the need for discretion. When *New York Times* editor A. M. Rosenthal pressed for elaboration, Ford hinted at the existence of "things that could blacken the name of every president since Truman," and then proceeded to relay the essence of Colby's "horror stories" on the assassination of foreign leaders. According to Press Secretary Nessen, the president sat calmly, smoking his pipe as the conversation developed. "If you knew what they were doing," he told the captivated journalists, "it would curl your hair." Nessen recalls that Ford sounded "genuinely appalled."[58] It is difficult to imagine what possible political benefit he might have sought from leaking the story. That the president could commit such a huge blunder, particularly in front of such an unforgiving audience, is nothing short of remarkable.

Although the editors present agreed, at Nessen's urging, not to report the luncheon incident, details of Ford's slip began to spread. CBS newsman Daniel Schorr aired the assassination story on 28 February 1975.[59] With the issue now in the open, the CIA commission came under pressure to investigate. After consulting with Rockefeller on the subject, Ford concurred that the panel should look into the allegations more closely.[60] In sanctioning this part of the probe, Ford chose to ignore the fact that he was asking the commission to operate outside its official mandate by investigating an issue that had little to do with domestic spying. Buchen assured Ford privately, however, that he had asked Executive Director Belin to keep the president informed of the progress of the assassination investigation. Buchen also assured the president that he would have the opportunity to decide "whether the issue should eventually be included as an integral part of the commission's final report."[61]

But even before Schorr's story aired, some commission insiders had begun to look into the assassination question. Belin had been aware of the plots since the beginning of the investigation and had pursued his own line of inquiry "without telling any member of the commission."[62] His rationale for extending the investigation was based on the premise that because the foreign assassination plots stemmed from discussions held inside the United States, they qualified as "domestic activity" under the scope of the commission's executive order. One top CIA official noted wryly that this questionable reasoning "opened the door to anything the commission might be curious about."[63]

Even as the commission expanded its investigation, however, some critics began to wonder aloud about the politics behind this turn of events. Specifically, some Kennedy-era officials speculated that the move was designed to take the heat off the CIA by focusing instead on presidential directives related to plots against Fidel Castro in the early 1960s. A former aide to Senator Robert Kennedy charged that Ford and Rockefeller were conspiring to absolve the agency of responsibility for its "scummy activities" by pointing the finger at "public officials who are, from the CIA's point of view, conveniently dead."[64] Senator Edward Kennedy also defended his brothers, suggesting that the issue was raised "to pass the buck" from the intelligence agencies.[65]

Whatever its source, the introduction of the new issue crowded the commission's already overburdened investigative schedule. The assassination inquiry would place new demands on the research staff that would make it impossible to meet the three-month deadline Ford had set. At Belin's request, the president agreed to grant the commission an extension. Executive Order 11848, issued on 29 March, amended Ford's initial order and extended the panel's life by an additional two months.

Though he empowered the CIA panel to investigate the assassination question, Ford was personally averse to playing "Monday morning quarterback" with the issue.[66] Throughout the year of intelligence inquiries, Ford cautioned against judging the decisions of previous presidents outside their historical context. In a memorable PBS interview on 7 August 1975, he emphatically made the case for not "passing judgment" or "finger pointing" at least seven times. His last comment on the topic was the most impassioned of all.

> Now, the United States has to compete in this real world. It's a tough world, and our national security on many occasions involves doing things in a covert way....
>
> I am not going to pass judgment on what other Presidents did. They were good men, whether they were Democrats or Republicans. They thought they were doing right. I can only pass judgment on what I want us to do.[67]

Even though some suggested that Ford deliberately leaked the assassination story to direct attention away from the CIA, it is difficult to reconcile that judgment with his other statements and actions during the period.[68] If anything, Ford seemed ill at ease with the issue and even acted late in the investigation to rid himself and the Rockefeller panel of the entire question.

Another investigation developed over the issue of alleged CIA involvement in the assassination of President Kennedy. Although certainly falling under the heading of possible "domestic activity," the decision of the panel to re-enter the Kennedy case appears to have been driven by personal motives. In the years after the Warren Commission inquest, both Ford and Belin had remained active in the debate over the lone-assassin theory. During the course of the Rockefeller probe, the CIA inspector general met with Belin and noted that his service on the earlier panel "had left an understandable interest" in John Kennedy's death.[69] One of Belin's associates was less kind. He suggested that the director's obsession with the assassination had led him to drag the commission back into the Kennedy case to "exorcise his own ghosts."[70]

Reopening the case certainly provided a means of responding to the conspiracy theorists. Not surprisingly, however, this part of the probe was soon swept up in the ongoing debate over the Warren Commission's findings. Dr. Cyril Wecht, an expert medical witness, went public with the charge that the Rockefeller Commission had deliberately misrepresented his testimony to support the lone-assassin theory. The questions directed to him, he claimed, "were much more in the form of cross examination than simple elicitation of direct testimony."[71] Even among the commissioners, the issue was the subject of considerable discussion. In its final report, though, the panel concluded that there was "no credible evidence of CIA involvement" in the assassination.[72]

Operating Procedure

The commission held its first meeting within a week of its establishment. Thereafter the commissioners assembled at least once each week, normally on Monday to accommodate those who commuted to Washington. Many of the sessions were held in the vice president's office in the Old Executive Office Building. The staff, however, needed a more permanent location from which to conduct the investigation. To accommodate this need, a base of operations was established in a well-guarded townhouse at 712 Jackson Place off Lafayette Square.

As is the case with most presidential commissions, the commissioners themselves exhibited varying degrees of interest and participation. Members of the staff recall that Griswold, Rockefeller, and Lemnitzer were particularly energetic. With one exception, the other commissioners also joined the debate and contributed to the investigation. The exception was Commissioner Reagan, whose role was limited due to his poor attendance record. He offered to resign after missing four of the first five meetings and would eventually attend only ten of the commission's twenty-six sessions. Griswold noted that even when Reagan was present, "his participation—other than the anecdotes he told—was minimal."[73]

As the investigation progressed, differences of opinion began to emerge. Individual points of view coalesced into informal blocs, the members of which tended to agree on the key issues involved. One camp included Rockefeller, Lemnitzer, and Dillon, and was inclined to stress the importance of a vigilant intelligence capability and the need for secrecy on national security issues. The other camp was more attuned to civil-liberty concerns and the deleterious effects of excessive secrecy in a democratic society. Erwin Griswold was most closely identified with this position, although Shannon and Connor often sided with him during discussions. Reagan became more involved as the commission drew to a close. According to one commission insider, he played an important role as conciliator between the two camps during the drafting process.[74]

The commission's staff conducted the research. Due to the serious time constraints under which the panel operated, the investigators were heavily dependent on the CIA to produce the needed documentation. E. Henry Knoche, assistant deputy to the DCI, was appointed the agency's liaison with the commission.[75] Those associated with the commission were impressed by Knoche's competence and willingness to cooperate. There was no suggestion of delay or tampering with the needed information. Belin suggests that the CIA's cooperation rested on the realization that undue damage would result if the commission was forced "to extract the facts a tooth at a time."[76] One senior staffer also raised the point that, by 1975, most of the agency's files were computerized and were thus less vulnerable to alteration.[77]

Still, this reliance on the organization that was itself at the center of the controversy inevitably gives rise to questions of objectivity and thoroughness. The starting point for the entire investigation was, in fact, the family jewels—the collection that had been assembled by the agency itself two years earlier. One staffer admitted it would have been difficult to uncover information that the CIA wanted to keep hidden.[78] This highlights a unique challenge for blue-ribbon panels of this type. It is very difficult for an ad hoc team of investigators to penetrate the secretive world of the national security apparatus. This dilemma was not unique to the CIA panel, though Rockefeller's group was certainly one of the first to confront the problem so directly.

The only alternative to relying on the CIA for documentation would have been for the commission itself to undertake the arduous task of identifying and compiling the necessary information. That, according to one commission insider, was impractical and would have required "an army of staffers" and time that the commission simply did not have.[79] As noted earlier, Ford had already extended the commission's mandate by two months, and to prolong the life of the panel any more would have led critics to charge the administration with stalling. It also would have denied Ford the benefit of having the commission's report in hand as the congressional committees intensified their own investigations.

But the commission did not wholly depend on the CIA for its information. During the five-month investigation, the commissioners and staff interviewed fifty-one witnesses and compiled almost 3,000 pages of testimony. Among the more prominent figures called upon to testify were Colby and Helms. Colby's account of his interview with the panel, however, raises more questions than it answers. The DCI recounted that only Griswold was "anything that could be called aggressive" during the questioning. His later encounter with the commission's chairman was particularly memorable.

> Rockefeller drew me aside into his office at the Executive Office Building and said in his most charming manner, "Bill, do you really have to present all this material to us? We realize that there are secrets that you fellows need to keep and so nobody here is going to take it amiss if you feel that there are some questions you can't answer quite as fully as you seem to feel you have to." I got the message quite unmistakably, and I didn't like it.[80]

Rockefeller's reputation as a political moderate did not extend to the issues involved in the intelligence inquiry. As chairman he emerged as one of the more conservative members of the panel. Some staffers reported that his advocacy for particular positions often bordered on inflexibility. "Rockefeller," said one insider, "really hadn't learned anything from our investigation of the CIA .... he was a completely unreconstructed cold warrior."[81]

Despite Rockefeller's strong political beliefs, he is generally given high marks for his administrative ability. Those present at the panel's meetings note that, even given a broad spectrum of views, the vice president did an admirable job of "steering the committee toward something acceptable to all."[82] Even Griswold, the member most frequently at odds with Rockefeller on substantive points of debate, stated that he was "very pleased" with the chairman's leadership.[83] The fact that Rockefeller also happened to be vice president worked to the panel's advantage. It reduced the need for official liaison between the panel and the Ford administration. When the commission needed clarification or additional information from the White House, Rockefeller would handle the communication and report back quickly. Conversely, this also meant that Ford had easy access to the commission. The danger inherent in this arrangement was that Ford could use such access to exert political pressure or interfere with the progress of the investigation. With the important exception of one issue, however, most of the contact between the White House and the committee concerned procedural, not substantive, questions.[84]

Pressure from the White House

The issue that did attract significant White House attention was that of the foreign assassination plots. As late as 12 May 1975, commission Vice Chairman Dillon reported that the subject was still under investigation and that the final report would cover that issue. When the report was released, however, the preface acknowledged that some research into the topic had been undertaken, but "time did not permit a full investigation before this report was due."[85] Buchen defended the commission's decision, noting that "if they [the commissioners] were to go into the whole thing, it would have taken more time and resources than they had."[86]

It is clear, however, that time constraints were not the primary factor at work in the decision to omit the assassination report. The investigation into that topic had progressed much further than the preface suggested and was in fact nearing completion. Commissioner Griswold recalls that a draft report on the issue was circulated as the inquiry drew to a close—a draft that would have become a chapter in the commission's final report. But due to Buchen's promise to keep Ford informed of the progress of the investigation, the president was aware that the report dealt with extremely sensitive matters. In late May of 1975 the White House began to exert pressure to remove the draft from consideration. Belin recalled one such instance: "The request came to Rockefeller directly through the president. 'The State Department'—that meant Kissinger—felt it would be 'inappropriate for a presidentially appointed commission' to report that the CIA had been involved in plans to assassinate leaders of foreign countries in peacetime."[87]

Griswold recalls that the commissioners themselves later voted not to include the section.[88] Given Ford's well-chronicled aversion to dealing with the assassination question, coupled with Kissinger's reservations, it is apparent that White House pressure was the crucial factor in killing that part of the report. Among the commission members, there was a sense of relief at having avoided the topic. When queried on the topic years later, Rockefeller candidly expressed his own feeling that the decision "got the president off the hook ... and got it [the assassination issue] right where it belonged in the Congress."[89] When the commission was terminated, Ford quickly turned the files on the subject over to the congressional investigators.

A Senate select committee, better known as the [Frank] Church Committee, would eventually delve the deepest into the assassination question.[90] In the House, the Pike Committee examined the quality of the CIA's intelligence estimates. Although the Pike report was ultimately censored by the House, and then later leaked to the press, there is a curious respect for that investigation from those associated with the Rockefeller Commission. One staffer argued that the House committee was "the one asking all the right questions."[91] In his memoirs, Ford blasts the Church Committee as "sensational and irresponsible," yet remains mute on the House probe.[92]

The Final Report

The Rockefeller Commission delivered its final report to President Ford in an Oval Office ceremony on 6 June 1975. Controversy erupted at the ensuing press conference when Press Secretary Nessen announced that the president was "undecided" on whether or not to release the document to the public. The revelation that Ford might withhold the report stunned White House correspondents. They had assumed that, like other blue-ribbon commission reports, the panel's work would be marked for general distribution. Although Nessen tried to change the subject several times, the reporters continued to focus on the issue. When asked if former President Nixon "had been consulted on this coverup," Nessen abruptly terminated the press conference and stormed from the room.[93]

The indecision surrounding the final report led to a new round of charges that the entire investigation had been conducted in suspect fashion. In an 8 June editorial *New York Times* columnist Tom Wicker argued the case against the commission.

> It seems clear that if a report on this matter that will satisfy a suspicious public can be made, it is going to have to be made by one or both of the Congressional committees now at work.
> An establishment commission whose chairman is loyal to the Administration, several of whose members served in past Administrations, and which was set up at least partially to limit the damage investigation could do to the CIA, just does not have, and cannot attain, the required credibility.[94]

In the end, the public outcry was so sharp that Ford was forced to relent. On 10 June the White House released the document. Since the congressional investigations were just getting under way at that time, the report quickly became the focal point of public debate on the intelligence issue.

The 299-page report was divided into nineteen chapters, almost half of which were devoted to the CIA's history and statutory status. The remaining chapters covered the individual charges that had been leveled against the agency, the findings of the commission regarding each allegation, and recommendations for reform in those areas where abuses were uncovered. The panel determined that although "the great majority" of the CIA's activities were legal, some were more "doubtful," and still others were "plainly unlawful."[95] Among the findings considered most damning were those concerning the infiltration of dissident groups inside the United States, mail-opening operations, the testing of behavior-influencing drugs on unsuspecting citizens, and the physical abuse and prolonged confinement of defectors. To the credit of the commission, the congressional investigations that followed in 1975–1976 uncovered no instance of domestic abuse that was not covered in the Rockefeller Commission Report. Seven appendixes were also attached to the end of the report, ranging from the essential (National Security Act of 1947), to the normal (biographical information on the members and staff), to the curious (highlights of civil disturbances in the United States, 1966–1973).

The report carried the unanimous endorsement of all eight commissioners. There was, however, spirited discussion regarding the wording of the final draft. Griswold even threatened at one point to issue a formal dissent over the agency's ability to operate inside the country. He disagreed with the wording of a recommendation that urged that the National Security Act of 1947 be amended to make it clear that the CIA's activities must be "related to" foreign intelligence.[96] Griswold complained that, as worded, the recommendation did not prohibit domestic activity by the CIA, but only served to specify the necessary preconditions for it to occur. He felt the commission should instead call for a complete ban on all domestic activity by the agency. Other moderates on the panel, however, refused to join Griswold. Noting that he had "no desire to become a minority of one," he chose to drop the dissent and agreed to a compromise in which his reservations were placed in a footnote to the text.[97]

With the issuance of its final report, the Rockefeller Commission quietly disbanded. The commissioners and staffers returned to their occupations, and the investigation was quickly overshadowed by the ongoing congressional probes that would dominate the media's attention throughout the autumn of 1975. Aside from dealing with congressional requests for documents, the Ford administration seemed content to rest on the commission's report and let the congressional committees grapple with the unwieldy issue.

The Commission and the Policy Process

Ford waited until February 1976 to retake the initiative on the intelligence issue. At that time he released Executive Order 11905, which contained his own package of reforms. Buchen was the principal architect of that document, though he shared responsibility for the task with (future Supreme Court Justice) Antonin Scalia, a young attorney working in the Justice Department. The timing of the move was strategically designed to play on growing public sentiment that the intelligence disclosures had gone far enough. The various investigations had been under way for more than a year, and the murder of the CIA station chief in Greece two months earlier had been used by the administration to "prove" the dangers in opening up the agency to external scrutiny.[98]

It is also curious to note that almost nine months had passed between the close of the Rockefeller panel investigation and the issuing of Ford's executive order. Loch Johnson, a Church Committee staffer, suggests that Ford deliberately waited until Congress was concluding its own investigation to issue the order. He argues that the timing was designed to "pull the rug out from under the Church Committee."[99] In his state of the union address in January, Ford had certainly set the stage for the administration's countermove by attacking the "sensational" legislative probes that, he suggested, were responsible for the "crippling of our foreign intelligence services."[100]

Though moderate in nature, many of the correctives in Ford's executive order owed a considerable debt to the findings and recommendations of the CIA panel.[101] To strengthen the external controls on the agency, for instance, Ford created three new oversight bodies within the executive branch. These included (1) a committee on foreign intelligence to supervise all such activities under the direct supervision of the National Security Council; (2) a new operations advisory group of top administration officials to meet and vote on all future clandestine operations; and (3) a permanent independent oversight board that would have responsibility for alerting the president to any illegal undertakings on the part of the intelligence community. The order also broadened the supervisory powers of the DCI in an effort to ensure greater accountability for future CIA operations.

Ford also acted on the Rockefeller Commission's recommendation that the DCI should be selected from outside the ranks of intelligence professionals. He had asked for Colby's resignation in the fall, as part of a more general personnel shake-up known as the "Halloween Massacre."[102] Ford's first choice to replace Colby was none other than Ed Williams, the attorney whose advice had helped convince the president of the need for a special investigation. Williams declined, however, citing his inability to keep his "mouth shut" and his unwillingness to give up business opportunities in real estate.[103]

Williams's refusal to accept the nomination sent Ford back to the drawing board. In January 1976 he submitted the name of George Herbert Walker Bush as his second pick for the job.[104] Though Bush was certainly an outsider to the agency, his nomination was not universally welcomed.

Congressional Democrats questioned his independence and willingness to make tough calls on the legality and propriety of presidential intelligence directives. Much of this skepticism stemmed from Bush's strong partisan credentials; he had recently served as chair of the Republican National Committee. During the confirmation hearing that followed, Senator Church charged that the selection of such a political figure was "astonishing," given the legacy of CIA involvement in the Watergate scandal.[105] Despite these objections, Bush was confirmed by the Senate and went on to serve as the CIA's eleventh director.

Critics noted that most of the reform measures proposed by Ford actually served to increase presidential involvement in agency activities. Frank Church was again the point man for the attack, arguing that the executive order "gave the CIA a bigger shield and a longer sword with which to stab about."[106] Ford worked hard to portray the intelligence abuses as isolated incidents that had occurred without presidential authorization. In large part, the report of the Rockefeller Commission adopted this same point of view, thus giving Ford's argument something of an official basis. The other side of this contention was, of course, that there was no need for an expanded congressional role in the process of intelligence oversight. Along these lines, the president actually sought to reduce the number of legislators involved in this activity by proposing that a joint intelligence oversight committee be created by Congress to limit access to classified data on the CIA and other agencies.

It was true that some of the abuses were the work of intelligence free-lancers, but it was equally true that others had resulted from orders on high. Former DCI Helms lamented that the press "failed to stress that a number of these questionable activities were initiated or ordered by the various incumbent presidents."[107] Nowhere was this more apparent than in the case of the foreign assassination plots. In this light, it becomes even more apparent why Ford was determined to avoid the inclusion of that issue in the commission's final report. The assassination chapter-that-never-was would have weakened the "rogue agency" argument and thus pointed to the need for greater congressional supervision of executive-branch intelligence activities. In short, by influencing the report's contents, Ford was able to assure that the president's authority over the intelligence apparatus would not be challenged by the commission's findings.

Evaluation

The case of the CIA panel serves as a useful reminder that presidential commissions are products of the political environment in which they operate. Gerald Ford dusted off an investigative mechanism as old as the republic itself, then used it as a tool of presidential power to fend off those who challenged his control of the national security apparatus. On a number of key points, commission politics significantly affected the course of the investigation and the content of the final report.

First, it is abundantly clear that the decision to appoint the Rockefeller panel was a preemptive maneuver designed to outflank Congress on the intelligence issue. This raises important questions regarding the tendency of commission scholars to de-emphasize the political motivations that often underlie the creation of blue-ribbon advisory groups. Even after it was clear that the appointment of the commission would not deter Congress from investigating the issue, Ford continued to use the panel as a preemptive tool. Months after the commission concluded its work, he was able to control the reform agenda by basing his recommendations on the panel's findings. His ability to exert such influence, particularly given the weakened state of the presidency at the time, would have been considerably less had the Church and Pike committee reports been the only body of evidence introduced into the public debate.   ·

Second, it is interesting to note the importance of structural and personnel decisions in determining the course of the commission's investigation. The narrow mandate given to the commission, for instance, was designed to limit the field of inquiry before the commission ever began its work. Even with a sixty-day extension, the commission was forced to grapple with a cumbersome issue and produce a detailed final report in a remarkably short time. This, too, served to limit the scope of the commission's investigation. Finally, the selection of the commissioners and staff attest to Ford's determination to preside over a manageable investigation. The appointment of Rockefeller to head the inquiry and the selection of Belin as staff director must be deemed crucial. A more independent-minded investigative team might have balked at White House interference, but Rockefeller and Belin appeared as eager as Ford to make sure the administration was not confronted with any unnecessary controversy.

Even with a tightly controlled commission, however, pressures can build to expand the investigation. This point has been better documented in the literature, and is certainly supported by this case study.[108] For example, the fact that a commission originally appointed to investigate "domestic" intelligence activity could end up looking into plots against Fidel Castro and Patrice Lumumba is striking. In requesting additional time with which to expand its investigation, the commission was also following what in recent years has become standard operating procedure for presidential advisory panels.

Finally, it is clear that political pressure played a key role in shaping the commission's activity. There was a high level of contact between the White House and the commission as the investigation progressed. On at least one issue—the assassination plots against foreign heads of state—

Ford and Kissinger acted decisively to determine the course of the investigation and the content of the final report. In short, there is considerable evidence here with which to challenge the benign view of commissions as objective fact-finding bodies operating with only loose White House supervision.

Notes

An earlier version of this chapter appeared under the title of "Commission Politics and National Security: Gerald Ford's Response to the CIA Controversy of 1975," *Presidential Studies Quarterly* 26:4 (Fall 1996), 1,081–1,098.

1. Tom Wicker wrote a critique of the agency entitled "Destroy the Monster," in the *New York Times*, 12 September 1975, p. 33.

2. David Wise and Thomas B. Ross, *The Invisible Government* (New York: Vintage Books, 1974).

3. Seymour M. Hersh, "Huge CIA Operation Reported in U.S. Against Antiwar Dissidents in Nixon Years," *New York Times*, 22 December 1974, p. 1.

4. Frank J. Smist, *Congress Oversees the United States Intelligence Community* (Knoxville: University of Tennessee Press, 1990), p. 56.

5. Hersh, "Huge CIA Operation Reported in U.S."

6. Ibid.

7. "Washington Wire," *Wall Street Journal*, 3 January 1975, p. 1.

8. Seymour M. Hersh, "Three More Aides Quit in CIA Shake-Up," *New York Times*, 30 December 1974, p. 1.

9. "Playing Games with the CIA," *The Nation* 220 (11 January 1975), p. 2.

10. Kissinger's influence over the administration's foreign and security policy was thought by many to be excessive. For an example of such criticism, see Richard Reeves, *A Ford Not a Lincoln* (New York: Harcourt, Brace, Jovanovich, 1975), pp. 120–133.

11. Memo, Marsh to Ford, 24 December 1974, Folder Intelligence—Rockefeller Commission General, Box 7, Richard Cheney Files, Gerald R. Ford Library (hereafter cited as GRFL).

12. Memo, Kissinger to Ford, 25 December 1974, Folder Intelligence—Colby Report, Box 5, Richard Cheney Files, GRFL.

13. Notes, Cheney Meeting with Ford, 27 December 1974, Folder Intelligence—Colby Report, Box 5, Richard Cheney Files, GRFL.

14. Evan Thomas, *The Man to See: Edward Bennett Williams—Ultimate Insider; Legendary Trial Lawyer* (New York: Simon and Schuster, 1991), p. 334.

15. Notes, Cheney Meeting with Ford, 30 December 1974, Folder Intelligence—Rockefeller Commission General, Box 7, Richard Cheney Files, GRFL.

16. Gerald Ford, *A Time to Heal* (New York: Harper and Row, 1979), p. 230.

17. Memorandum of Conversation, Ford with Helms, Marsh, Buchen, and Scowcroft, 4 January 1975, Folder "Ford, Former CIA Director Richard Helms," Box 8, National Security Advisor Memorandum of Conversation, 1973–1977, GRFL. Cited in Brett Garson, "Clandestine Operations in the CIA: When Secrecy Becomes Overextended," *Michigan Journal of History* (Winter 2004) <http://www.umich.edu/~historyj/papers/ winter2004/garsonart.htm>.

18. Memo, Marsh to Ford, 24 December 1974, Folder Intelligence—Rockefeller Commission General, Richard Cheney Files, GRFL.

19. William Colby and Peter Forbath, *Honorable Men: My Life in the CIA* (New York: Simon and Schuster, 1978), p. 398.

20. The 1967 probe was not a presidential commission in the formal sense. It contained no "citizen" members from outside the executive branch, and thus functioned much like a high-level interagency task force.

21. Letter, Pawley to Ford, 6 January 1975, Folder Commission on CIA Activities Within the US, Box 9, Presidential Handwriting File, GRFL.

22. Seymour M. Hersh, "Ford Names Rockefeller to Head Inquiry into CIA," *New York Times*, 6 January 1975, p. 18.

23. Walter Rugaber, "Ford Sets Up Commission on CIA's Domestic Role," *New York Times*, 5 January 1975, p. 42.

24. Hersh, "Three More Aides Quit in CIA Shake-Up."

25. Ron Nessen, *It Sure Looks Different from the Inside* (Chicago: Playboy Press, 1979), p. 61.

26. Memo, Kissinger to Rumsfeld, 23 December 1974, Folder Intelligence— General, Box 6, Richard Cheney Files, GRFL.

27. Talking Points to Prospective Commissioners, 3 January 1975, Folder Commission on CIA Activities Within the U.S., Box 9, Presidential Handwriting File, GRFL.

28. Executive Order No. 11828, *Public Papers of the Presidents* (Washington, DC: Government Printing Office), Gerald R. Ford, 1975, p. 19.

29. John M. Oseth, *Regulating U.S. Intelligence Operations* (Lexington: University of Kentucky Press, 1985), p. 73.

30. Terrence R. Tutchings, *Rhetoric and Reality: Presidential Commissions and the Making of Public Policy* (Boulder, CO: Westview, 1979), p. 24.

31. Nessen, *It Sure Looks Different from the Inside*, p. 57.

32. Notes, Cheney's Meeting with Ford, Folder Intelligence—Rockefeller Commission General, Box 7, Richard Cheney Files, GRFL.

33. Letter, Friendly to Ford, 6 January 1975, Folder FG-393: Commission on CIA Activities Within the United States, White House Central Files, GRFL. Chief Justice Earl Warren's service on the commission probing the death of J. F. Kennedy stands out as a noteworthy example of judicial service on a presidential commission. Such interbranch service has, however, been criticized on the grounds that it violates Madisonian principles. For a discussion of this dispute, see Wendy E. Ackerman, "Separation of Powers and Judicial Service on Presidential Commissions," *University of Chicago Law Review* 53 (1986), 993–1,025.

34. Ford, *A Time to Heal*, p. 230. It also bears mentioning that the American people were suspicious of Rockefeller's appointment as chairman. According to a Harris poll, fully 49 percent of the public disagreed with the vice president's selection to head the CIA panel. See *New York Times*, 14 February 1975, p. 10.

35. Nessen, *It Sure Looks Different from the Inside*, p. 56.

36. Memorandum, Areeda to White House, 4 January 1975, Folder CIA Commission, Box 10, Edward C. Schmults Papers, GRFL.

37. Telephone interview with Erwin Griswold, 27 September 1993.

38. Memo, Leppert to Friedersdorf, 21 January 1975, Folder CIA Investigation, Box 10, Max Friedersdorf Files, GRFL.

39. Executive Director Belin suggests that subpoena power might have been useful in the case of Robert Maheu, a CIA employee who functioned as an intermediary between the agency and several organized-crime figures. See David W. Belin, *Final Disclosure: The Full Truth About the Assassination of President Kennedy* (New York: Charles Scribner's Sons, 1988), p. 100.

40. Joseph E. Persico, *The Imperial Rockefeller* (New York: Simon and Schuster, 1982), p. 86.

41. Hersh, "Ford Names Rockefeller."

42. John Ranelagh, *The Agency: The Rise and Decline of the CIA* (New York: Simon and Schuster, 1987), pp. 248–249.

43. A discussion of the labor organization's ties to the CIA may be found in Sidney Lens, "Partners: Labor and the CIA," *The Progressive* 39 (February 1975), 339.

44. Hersh, "Ford Names Rockefeller."

45. There was some ideological diversity among the members. Both Connor and Shannon had spoken out against US policy during the Vietnam War.

46. Telephone interview with Griswold.

47. Memo, Buchen to Rustand, 30 May 1975, Folder FG 393—4/1/75–1/20/77, White House Central Files, GRFL.

48. Both Ford and Belin wrote books defending the Warren Commission's conclusions. See Belin, *You Are the Jury* (New York: Quadrangle Books, 1973) and Gerald Ford, *Portrait of the Assassin* (New York: Simon and Schuster, 1965). Griswold recalls that the members of the Rockefeller Commission agreed at the outset not to publish insider accounts of the panel's operation or findings. The agreement was apparently taken seriously. Aside from the occasional mention in various memoirs, little has been written about the panel by the commissioners themselves.

49. Michael Turner, *The Vice-President as Policy Maker* (Westport, CT: Greenwood Press, 1982), p. 224n.

50. Telephone interview with Marvin Gray, 31 August 1993.

51. Letter, Dellums to Ford, 7 January 1975, Folder FG 393—Commission on CIA Activities Within the United States, White House Central Files, GRFL.

52. "Examining the Examiners," *Time*, 20 January 1975, p. 31.

53. "A True Blue Ribbon Panel," *Newsweek*, 20 January 1975, p. 5.

54. "Majority in Poll Oppose Rockefeller CIA Inquiry," *New York Times*, 14 February 1975, p. 10.

55. Letter, Colby to Ford, 24 December 1974, Folder Intelligence—Colby Report, Box 5, Richard Cheney Files, GRFL.

56. Memo, Kissinger to Ford, 25 December 1974, Folder Intelligence—Colby Report, Box 5, Richard Cheney Files, GRFL.

57. This was not the first time Ford had leaked classified information. His *Portrait of the Assassin* included excerpts from secret transcripts of Warren Commission testimony. The issue was serious enough to be raised during the confirmation hearings for Ford's appointment to the vice presidency.

58. Nessen, *It Sure Looks Different from the Inside*, p. 58. Though there remains some dispute regarding whether or not Ford's remarks were off the record, the other first-hand accounts of the luncheon agree on the basics of the president's remarks. See, for instance, Tom Wicker, *On Press* (New York: Viking Press, 1978), pp. 190–195.

59. Schorr continued to follow the progress of the intelligence investigations, even though many at the CIA did not appreciate his zeal for disclosing classified information. The dislike surfaced in a remarkable incident on 28 April 1975. Schorr confronted Helms outside Rockefeller's office, where the former DCI had just appeared before the CIA commission. Helms, unable to control his resentment, turned on Schorr and began cursing the newsman loudly. A full account of the episode may be found in Thomas Powers, *The Man Who Kept the Secrets* (New York: Alfred A. Knopf, 1979), pp. 291–294.

60. Letter, Buchen to Belin, 31 March 1975, Folder FG 393—Commission on CIA Activities Within the United States, White House Central Files, GRFL.

61. Memo, Buchen to Belin, 31 March 1975, Folder Intelligence—8/9/74–8/23/75, ND-6, White House Central Files, GRFL.

62. Belin argues that two factors led him to keep the issue away from the commissioners. First, the commission's investigation was originally set to end in early April, and Belin felt that there simply was not time to introduce this new concern. Second, he was unsure whether Ford's directions to the commission covered an area that was only loosely related to "domestic activity." Belin, *Final Disclosure*, pp. 92–93.

63. Scott C. Breckinridge, *The CIA and the Cold War* (Westport, CT: Praeger Publishers, 1993), p. 213.

64. Clifton Daniel, "The Assassination Plot Rumors," *New York Times*, 6 June 1975, p. 66.

65. Ibid.

66. The phrase "Monday morning quarterback" was used by Ford on a number of occasions in responding to questions regarding the assassination investigation. An outstanding football player at the University of Michigan, Ford used football analogies throughout his political career to explain his policies. For one aide's recollections of this interesting habit, see Nessen's *It Sure Looks Different from the Inside*, p. 346.

67. "Interview With Paul Duke and Martin Agronsky of the Public Broadcasting Service," 7 August 1975, *Public Papers of the Presidents*, Gerald Ford, 1975, p. 1,131.

68. Tom Wicker, among those present at the luncheon, later wrote of his suspicions that "Ford had deliberately let a very dark cat out of the bag." *On Press*, p. 195.

69. Breckinridge, *The CIA and the Cold War*, p. 214.

70. Confidential telephone interview.

71. See Cyril H. Wecht, "Why Is the Rockefeller Commission So Single-Minded about a Lone Assassin in the Kennedy Case?" *Journal of Legal Medicine* 3 (1975), 22–25. Wecht, a noted forensic pathologist, testified before the commission on 7 May 1975. He writes that his "questioning by a commission staff member was detailed and tenacious."

72. Chapter 19 of the final report is devoted entirely to the Kennedy assassination. *Report to the President by the Commission on CIA Activities Within the United States* (Washington, DC: Government Printing Office, 1975).

73. Erwin Griswold, *Ould Fields, New Corn* (St. Paul: West Publishing, 1992), p. 358.

74. Telephone interview with Marvin Gray, 31 August 1993.

75. Knoche would go on to become deputy director of the CIA the following year. He retired from the agency in 1977.

76. Belin, *Final Disclosure*, p. 85.

77. Telephone interview with Ernest Gellhorn, 7 September 1993.

78. Telephone interview with Gray. Belin also noted that the compartmentalization of the agency made it difficult to guarantee that all relevant information was uncovered. *Final Disclosure*, p. 89.

79. Telephone interview with Gray.

80. Colby and Forbath, *Honorable Men*, p. 400.

81. Confidential telephone interview.

82. Telephone interview with Ronald Greene, 17 September 1993.

83. Telephone interview with Griswold.

84. Aside from Belin, none of the participants interviewed (Commissioner Griswold, staffers Gellhorn, Greene, and Gray) were aware of any political pressure from the White House.

85. *Report to the President*, p. xi.

86. "Leaving Murky Murders to the Senate," *Time*, 16 June 1975, p. 9.

87. Belin, *Final Disclosure*, p. 163.

88. Telephone interview with Griswold.

89. Turner, *The Vice President as Policy Maker*, p. 224n.

90. U.S., Congress, Senate, Select Committee to Study Government Operations with Respect to Intelligence Activities, *Final Report*, 95th Congress, 1st session, 1976.

91. Telephone interview with Gray.

92. Ford, *A Time to Heal*, p. 265.

93. Nicholas M. Horrock, "Rockefeller Gives Ford Report on CIA," *New York Times*, 7 June 1975, p. 8.

94. Tom Wicker, "CIA–Confusion," *New York Times*, 8 June 1975, p. 17.

95. *Report to the President*, p. 10.

96. Ibid., 12.

97. Ibid., 81.

98. The link of the Welch murder in Athens to the congressional intelligence investigations was much more suspect than the administration was willing to admit. There Welch had long been identified as a CIA employee (also, an East German publication had identified him as an intelligence officer as early as 1967). See Ranelagh, *The Agency*, p. 473.

99. Johnson, *A Season of Inquiry*, p. 213.

100. "Transcript of President's State of the Union Message," *New York Times*, 20 January 1976, p. 18.

101. A discussion of the specifics of Ford's reform package may be found in Oseth's *Regulating U.S. Intelligence Operations*, Chapter 4.

102. The shake-up also resulted in the elevation of Brent Scowcroft to the post of national security advisor. Kissinger, who previously had held that position while also serving as secretary of state, suffered a demotion of sorts, and would serve only in the latter capacity through the remainder of the Ford administration.

103. Thomas, *The Man to See*, p. 334.

104. Ibid.

105. Bernard J. Firestone and Alexej Ugrinsky, eds. *Gerald R. Ford and the Politics of Post-Watergate America* (Westport, CT: Greenwood Press, 1993), p. 496.

106. "CIA Shake-Up," *Newsweek*, 1 March 1976, p. 18.

107. Richard Helms with William Hood, *A Look over My Shoulder: A Life in the Central Intelligence Agency* (New York: Random House, 2003), p. 429.

108. Morton Halperin detailed this same phenomenon in the case of the Gaither Commission. See "The Gaither Committee and the Policy Process," in *The Presidential Advisory System*, eds. Thomas E. Cronin and Sanford D. Greenberg (New York: Harper and Row, 1969), pp. 185–209.

4

The Politics of Armageddon: The Scowcroft Commission and the MX Missile

The nation must keep expanding the stockpiles, then, partly because of the convolutions of the deterrence argument: we need these additional warheads to deter those other ones they are now building. But there is an additional psychological factor: namely, if we don't keep building the weapons, we risk the possibility of viewing both them as evil and ourselves as having been long associated with that evil.
—Robert Jay Lifton and Eric Markusen,
The Genocidal Mentality: Nazi Holocaust and Nuclear Threat

I'm telling you, it's coming. Go read your Scripture.
—Ronald Reagan on superpower nuclear conflict,
quoted in Robert McFarlane, *Special Trust*

By the dawn of 1981 US relations with the Soviet Union had sunk to their lowest point in a decade. Stung by the Kremlin's invasion of Afghanistan two years earlier, many US citizens felt that the detente-based policies of the previous decade had only encouraged a more aggressive Soviet posture around the globe. Conservative policymakers called for a greater emphasis on military preparedness. And no one preached the gospel of peace—through strength—more consistently or with more fervor than Ronald Reagan. Elected to the presidency by a narrow margin in 1980, Reagan promised to restore US prestige around the globe, demonstrate that the country could project its power when necessary, and provide the leadership necessary to reinvigorate the West in its ideological battle with Soviet communism.

In Reagan's view of the world, however, this revival depended on a concentrated effort to restore US military capabilities across the spectrum. This was especially true in the field of strategic nuclear weapons. There, Reagan argued, recent administrations had permitted a "window of vulnerability" to develop, which placed the United States in the shadow of Soviet missiles. But plans for a strategic buildup sparked opposition from those frightened by the specter of more missiles, more warheads, and more nuclear megatons. Because the resulting controversy came early in Reagan's first term, the issue assumed additional importance as one of the first tests of the president's ideological commitment and political skill. In this context, Reagan turned to a blue-ribbon panel of defense experts to help rescue the administration's strategic-weapons program. The work of the President's Commission on Strategic Forces is the subject of this chapter.

Political Context

The centerpiece of the Reagan administration's strategic modernization effort was the MX missile, so named for its original designation as "missile experimental." The MX's development dated to the Nixon administration, when it had been conceived as a successor to the Minuteman II and III intercontinental ballistic missiles (ICBMs), which constituted the bulk of the US land-based deterrent. An impressive weapon, the MX stood 71 feet tall, weighed 97 tons, and carried 10 multiple independently targetable re-entry vehicle (MIRV) W78 warheads capable of delivering 3.5 megatons of explosive power. It was also extremely accurate. With a mean-miss distance of only 300 feet, the MX could threaten even the most hardened Soviet missile silos.[1] Of course, that same destructive potential could just as easily threaten the very fabric of life in the Soviet Union. In an effort to draw attention away from such unpleasantness, Reagan euphemized the weapon as the "Peacekeeper" shortly after taking office.[2]

To MX supporters, deployment of the missile represented the best opportunity for the United States to offset the Soviet advantage in heavy-missile development. In the 1970s, the Kremlin had developed a new generation of ICBMs that had begun to close the technological gap between the superpower arsenals. The most formidable of these were the ten-warhead SS-18 and the six-warhead SS-19. Over 600 of these weapons had been deployed by the time Reagan assumed office, leaving the United States with a significant deficit in land-based warheads. With their own strategic modernization program complete, the Soviets were eager to negotiate to keep the MX program from moving ahead. Soviet Foreign Minister Andrei Gromyko had lobbied hard since the late 1970s for a ban on new ICBM development.

But while Reagan's security advisers agreed on the need for the MX, there had been much heated debate over which deployment scheme would best accommodate the new missile. This was an important concern. Reagan himself had criticized the fixed silo method, used for the Minuteman force, as too vulnerable to any surprise Soviet attack. The search for a more survivable basing mode had led to over thirty proposals in the preceding decade. These ran the gamut from the plausible to the fantastic. Among those seriously considered: a wheel-shaped system that would permit the missile to be moved secretly among different silos located in the outer reaches of the system's spokes; placing the missiles on a fleet of C-5A cargo planes (the "Big Bird" proposal), a portion of which would be airborne at any given time; placing the MX on long-platform trucks that would be moved frequently to sites on remote military bases; and dumping the missiles in canisters at sea during times of crisis, where they could be triggered electronically should the need arise. One by one, however, each scheme proposed had been dismissed as too expensive, too cumbersome, or too environmentally unsound.

The Carter administration's answer to the dilemma was a deployment configuration known as multiple protective shelters (MPS). Officially proposed in September 1979, the plan called for the construction of 4,600 protective missile shelters along giant rail "racetracks" in the western states.[3] Using the logic of the shell game, the Soviets would be kept guessing which shelters contained the 200 MX missiles the administration wished to deploy in this manner. In the event of a nuclear exchange, they would thus be forced to target each shelter individually to ensure the destruction of the ICBM force. Strategists reasoned that such a demand would overextend the Soviet's offensive delivery capabilities. The racetrack scheme held out the prospect of enhanced missile survivability, but it also promised to be extremely expensive to build. A price tag approaching $50 billion alarmed even those members of Congress who were normally desensitized to huge defense outlays.[4] As a result, the MPS proposal was rejected and the unwieldy issue was passed along to the next administration.

Political considerations kept President Reagan from reviving the idea. Even though many in the administration believed the theory behind MPS to be sound, there was considerable opposition from Republicans. Senator Paul Laxalt of Nevada, one of the president's closest friends, led a group of western-states' lawmakers in an effort to bury the racetrack proposal once and for all. Laxalt realized that if the MPS system were to work, the individual missile shelters would have to be built far enough apart to permit a reasonable degree of survivability in the event of a Soviet strike. He feared that the attendant geographical requirements would cause considerable land-use disruption in rural areas in the western states.[5] This was not an unjustified concern; a 1981 congressional study had warned that "severe social and economic impacts" would occur wherever the system was constructed.[6]

At the same time, a special Pentagon study group headed by the Nobel physicist Charles Townes had concluded that the Soviets could meet the MPS challenge by simply deploying more MIRV missiles. The SS-18s and SS-19s alone contained enough warheads to threaten the system's effectiveness. Combined with the environmental concerns, the Townes report convinced Reagan to abandon the racetrack proposal in October 1981. Although frustrated by the prospect of another delay in MX production, administration officials reopened the search for a permanent basing mode.

As an interim measure, Reagan asked Congress to consider deploying the MX in existing Minuteman silos, a plan that had received some support from the Townes panel.

Lawmakers greeted the idea with skepticism. John Tower, chairman of the Senate Armed Services Committee, charged that the proposal would create "just so many more sitting ducks for the Russians to shoot at." Senator Pete Domenici of New Mexico agreed that "the existing silos would make a nice target for Soviet planners."[7] In November 1981, the Senate adopted an amendment to the Defense Appropriations Act sponsored by William Cohen and Sam Nunn, which effectively killed the proposal and blocked MX production until a more acceptable deployment scheme could be agreed upon.

Early the following year, the Pentagon created a second study group, again headed by Townes, to revisit the issue. Although the panel's work was inconclusive, a majority of the members recommended additional study of a new deployment scheme known as closely spaced basing (CSB).[8] The CSB proposal, commonly referred to as "densepack," was based on the strategic concept of fratricide, that is, a belief that incoming Soviet missiles would destroy one another in an attack on a highly concentrated "missile plot," some 20 square miles in size, to be located at Warren Air Force Base near Cheyenne, Wyoming. There was little consensus within the defense community regarding the proposal. Three members of the Joint Chiefs of Staff had serious reservations about the viability of densepack.[9] But Secretary of Defense Caspar Weinberger was more enthusiastic about the plan. He urged the White House to accept the Townes report and develop CSB as a legislative initiative.

The idea of concentrating the ICBM force in such a confined space was as controversial as it was revolutionary. Nevertheless, a number of factors led Reagan to embrace the idea. First, the plan was acceptable to Republicans from the western states because its land-use requirement was low. Second, the system would be a bargain to build, especially when compared to the MPS proposal. Initial cost estimates put the price tag of CSB at $26 billion, just over half the cost of a racetrack system.[10] Third, by invoking the concept of fratricide, Reagan could argue to Congress that the new basing system promised, in theory, greater survivability than the single silo method. Finally, densepack appealed to hawks in the administration because it opened the door to future consideration of a ballistic missile defense (BMD) system. With one entire leg of the US nuclear triad crammed into a small corner of Wyoming, it would be only a matter of time before proposals were put forth to ring the area with antiballistic missiles (ABMs). One source within the administration admitted as much, noting that "an ABM [system] was in the wings."[11]

On 22 November 1982 Reagan forwarded a proposal to Congress to build and deploy 100 MX missiles in the densepack mode. The debate that followed was unusually sharp. Questions went beyond the strategic modernization program to include Reagan's conduct of foreign policy, the state of superpower relations, and the administration's commitment to arms control. A Republican member of Congress told the *New York Times* that the MX had become "a symbol for the whole nuclear issue."[12] Attention soon settled on the House of Representatives, the first chamber to consider the administration's request as part of a continuing budget resolution for 1983.

The climactic vote was scheduled for 7 December, Pearl Harbor day, a coincidence not lost on those involved in the decision. Representative Joseph Addabbo, Democrat of New York, led opposition forces in the House. Addabbo took to the floor to urge his colleagues "not to create another Pearl Harbor by putting all our missiles in one basket in one location." Representative William Ratchford (Democrat-Connecticut) echoed the sentiment, labeling densepack "one of the all-time turkeys in the history of this country." Even some Republicans spoke against the measure. Congressman Bill Green of Manhattan wondered if the administration's plan was constructed primarily to "placate the Pentagon bureaucracies involved."[13]

But most House Republicans argued forcefully that voting against the measure would leave the country dangerously unprepared in the face of the Soviet challenge. Minority leader Robert Michel of Illinois compared those opposed to the MX to the isolationist forces of the 1930s.[14] "Well-meaning, patriotic people were tragically wrong," he charged, yet "the hard facts of the defense of freedom and peace remain the same ... it's always a sacrifice."[15] But Michel was fighting an uphill battle. Reagan's staffers had done an uncharacteristically poor job of packaging the proposal for legislative consideration. More important, densepack was simply too radical a plan to win the quick approval the administration sought.

In the end, and in a stunning defeat for the administration, 195 Democrats and 50 Republicans in the House joined forces to reject the CSB system. The *New York Times* noted that it was the first time since World War II that Congress had defeated a major weapons program backed by the president.[16] Reagan reacted strongly to the vote, issuing a statement later the same day castigating those responsible for the outcome:

> I had hoped that most of the members in the House had awakened to the threat facing the United States. That hope was apparently unfounded. A majority chose to go sleepwalking into the future....
>
> The Soviets will not negotiate with us when we disarm ourselves. Why should they negotiate seriously when we give up weapons systems voluntarily, asking nothing of them in return?
>
> It would be tragically ironic if this of all days—December 7—once again marked a time when America was unprepared to keep the peace.[17]

The president also vowed to continue the fight by taking his case directly to the American people.

But Reagan's effort to save the MX would soon face new obstacles. As a result of the November midterm elections, the Democrats were poised to gain twenty-six additional House seats in the ninety-eighth Congress.[18] Moreover, Gen. John Vessey, chairman of the Joint Chiefs of Staff, revealed on 8 December that the joint chiefs were themselves of different minds on the densepack scheme. That announcement did little to bolster confidence in the administration. After all, how could the American people be expected to endorse a strategic-weapons plan that did not enjoy the support of the top brass?[19]

Creating the Commission

Significantly, the House vote in December, though decisive, left the door open for another review of the strategic modernization program. The appropriations bill set aside $2.5 billion for additional research and development of the MX, though it specifically prohibited flight-testing the missile.[20] More important, an amendment to the bill directed the administration to provide a fresh assessment of alternative basing modes, to be delivered to Congress not earlier than 1 March 1983.[21] The language of the proviso held out the possibility of another congressional vote on the MX at that time. Although the amendment did not specify the mechanism for this new assessment, some members of Congress pressed for the issue to be removed from Pentagon control. Among these members, there existed a feeling that Secretary of Defense Caspar Weinberger had contributed to the administration's defeat through his poor management of the densepack proposal. The *New York Times* noted that his appearances before Congress and the press had been "uninspired." Senator Paul Tsongas (Democrat-Massachusetts) accused Weinberger of squandering the mandate for higher defense spending, which had accompanied Reagan's election in 1980.[22] Senator Sam Nunn of Georgia, widely regarded as the Democrat's leading expert on defense matters, was also troubled by the secretary's performance. Privately he warned White House aides that the next MX proposal would "surely fail" if Weinberger were too involved.[23]

Members of the National Security Council (NSC) planning group agreed that the MX needed a fresh political start. With Weinberger pushed to the sidelines, Deputy National Security Advisor Robert McFarlane became the administration's new point man in the strategic modernization effort. McFarlane, too, was deeply concerned by Weinberger's "inability to develop and promote our defense policy successfully."[24] He also believed that the new study ordered by Congress represented the last opportunity to save the MX. He felt strongly that the administration "just has to win this one."[25]

In devising a political strategy, McFarlane had considerable autonomy to act since his immediate supervisor, National Security Advisor William P. Clark, had little background in defense-related issues. Moreover, Clark had left Washington in mid-December to accompany the president on an extended Christmas vacation at the California estate of Ambassador Walter Annenberg. Consequently he was absent from the key strategy sessions that were held in the wake of the densepack vote.

Pushed by Congress, distrustful of Weinberger, and committed to saving the MX, McFarlane began to toy with the idea of creating a presidential commission to respond to Congress's demand for a new study of basing alternatives. While working at the State Department in 1981, he had been greatly impressed with the work of the Greenspan Commission on Social Security reform and felt that a blue-ribbon study represented the best chance of resuscitating the MX program.[26] Senator William Cohen (Republican-Maine) encouraged McFarlane to pursue the idea. He argued that a bipartisan panel might help bridge the deep divisions that existed on the issue.[27]

McFarlane's initial efforts focused on developing a list of names for commission service. Ideologically, he was careful to seek out only those individuals who shared his "ideas about the nuclear balance."[28] But it was apparent that political skill, not ideological commitment, would determine the fate of the MX. McFarlane knew that the individuals selected to serve would have to couple defense expertise with a keen awareness of congressional sensitivities. In this sense, the commission would be markedly different from the two Townes panels that had already examined the issue. As in-house Defense Department (DOD) studies those groups had focused heavily on the technical, not political, aspects of missile deployment.

The list of names compiled by McFarlane was heavy with establishment figures. To head the commission, he recommended Henry Kissinger, the ubiquitous security guru whose influence had shaped US foreign and security policy for the preceding decade. Others selected to serve included Thomas Reed, special assistant for national security policy; Alexander Haig, former secretary of state and supreme allied commander in Europe; William Clements, former governor of Texas and deputy secretary of defense; John M. Deutch, dean of sciences at M.I.T. and former undersecretary of research at the Department of Energy; Richard Helms, former DCI; James Woolsey, former undersecretary of the navy; Nicholas Brady, an investment banker and former senator from New Jersey; John H. Lyons, vice president of the AFL-CIO's defense subcommittee; and Levering Smith, a retired vice admiral with experience in weapons systems development. To give Democrats a voice in the deliberations, McFarlane also included two Carter-era officials: former secretary of defense Harold Brown and former undersecretary of defense William Perry.[29]

McFarlane forwarded the list to Palm Springs, California, for Reagan's approval. With one notable exception, the president agreed with each of the personnel recommendations. The exception was Henry Kissinger, whose appointment Reagan vetoed because of his close association with the policy of detente. An aide close to the decision recalled that the president "just didn't feel like Kissinger would be simpatico to his views."[30] Seeking to preempt criticism of the decision, presidential aides constructed a cover story that Kissinger had declined to serve due to scheduling conflicts associated with his consulting business.[31] The truth behind the matter was never disclosed.

McFarlane's search for a suitable replacement to head the commission led to his close friend Brent Scowcroft. A longtime security aide, Scowcroft was best known for his service as national security advisor in the Ford White House. He was also closely aligned with Kissinger on matters of military strategy. That association became an issue when Scowcroft was nominated for an NSC post at the beginning of the Reagan administration. As McFarlane explains: "Because of my respect for him, I had been disappointed when he wasn't brought into the Reagan administration in 1981, since he was viewed as a moderate and a friend of Kissinger's who didn't pass the conservative litmus test Reagan's aides applied to most appointments in the early years."[32]

But the prospect of appointing Scowcroft to head a fixed-term commission was apparently less threatening to administration stalwarts. Reagan approved his appointment as chair, and the panel's membership appeared to be set.[33]

There was, however, some last-minute lobbying on the part of former defense officials to join the panel. Not wanting to exclude any key constituencies, McFarlane agreed to add these individuals to the commission under the title of "senior counselors." Kissinger joined in this fashion, as did presidential assistant Lloyd Cutler and former CIA chief John McCone. The list was completed with the addition of three former secretaries of defense: Melvin Laird, Donald Rumsfeld, and James Schlesinger. The counselors shared equally in the commission's work. They attended all meetings, contributed to the deliberations, and even helped draft the final report. In fact, when queried on the topic, none of the key participants could recall a single instance in which the member-counselor distinction became an issue.[34] As a practical matter, the addition of the group expanded the size of the commission from twelve to eighteen.

The President's Commission on Strategic Forces was officially brought to life on 3 January 1983 by Executive Order 12400. Reagan authorized the panel to "review the strategic modernization program for United States forces, with particular reference to the intercontinental ballistic missile system."[35] The order provided for a study lasting only six weeks, an extraordinarily short period, given the complexity of the issue. Senator Ernest Hollings (Democrat-South Carolina) complained that he did not "see the need or rationale for this rush to judgment."[36] However, Vice Chairman Reed explained that the deadline had been set with another goal in mind.

> The purpose of setting the early time deadline was to make it clear that this was not to be a lifelong project, and it sent the signal that we intended to impact the budget process that fiscal year.... A beautiful piece of literature in December [1983] would have been pointless. I set that date, but we all knew it couldn't possibly be met.[37]

The order went on to note that the panel's members had been selected for their "particular knowledge and expertise" in foreign and military policy. This was an unusual admission, since blue-ribbon panels traditionally include nonspecialists appointed to give the commission a broader political base.[38]

The White House released a list of the panel's members and counselors along with the executive order. Critics charged that such a "handpicked" group could hardly be expected to conduct an objective assessment of defense needs.[39] Former National Security Advisor McGeorge Bundy dismissed the members as "strategic notables—all preselected friends of the MX."[40] These were not idle objections. None of the individuals selected to serve had expressed serious concerns about the direction or scope of the Reagan defense buildup. This was particularly true of General Scowcroft, whose concern for military preparedness once led him to advocate the expansion of the Triad (the dispersion of nuclear weapons to land, sea, and air platforms) "to a Quadrad or even a Pentad."[41] Along with Woolsey, he had already tried to find a home for the MX as a member of the first Townes Commission in 1981. On the day he was named to head the new panel, he told a reporter that the missile continued to represent a "very important part of our future defense posture."[42]

Others on the commission were similarly predisposed. James Schlesinger was considered the father of the MX since work on the new missile had begun on his watch at the Pentagon in the early 1970s. To match the Soviet effort in counterforce weapons, he felt it might be necessary to deploy over 200 new ICBMs. During the Carter administration, Harold Brown had argued forcefully for the MX as the cornerstone of the MPS ("racetrack") system. He told reporters in early January that producing the missile would solve the "equality problem" of Soviet superiority in land-based weapons. Donald Rumsfeld also felt it imperative to develop "deterrents across the spectrum." Warning that "nuclear age perceptions of the military balance are important," he judged the MX to be necessary *regardless* of whether or not a survivable basing mode could be found.[43]

The Commission in Operation

Unlike most presidential advisory panels, the Scowcroft Commission had no need for an extensive staff network. Previous DOD studies had explored the various basing options thoroughly, and there was little new information to be uncovered through a labor-intensive inquiry. For this reason, it is misleading to describe the commission's work as an investigation or even a study. Commissioner Woolsey characterized it more appropriately as "an intellectual exercise," an effort to resolve the MX dispute in a manner that would be politically acceptable to both the administration and a majority of the nation's lawmakers.[44]

The panel assembled for the first time on 7 January 1983. Thereafter the group met once or twice weekly in Room 3E333 of the Pentagon. Commissioner Reed, a member of the NSC staff, served as informal liaison between the panel and the Reagan White House. But Scowcroft also worked to keep the lines of communication open. He met with the president on two occasions and spoke frequently with both Weinberger and McFarlane. According to the chairman, administration officials went to great lengths to cooperate when approached for information or technical assistance.[45] They could scarcely have done otherwise. "They needed us," one commissioner observed, "more than we needed them."[46]

Over 200 individuals came before the board to offer their views on the state and prospects of US strategic nuclear policy. While most of the testimony came from past or current government experts who supported the MX, the panel did solicit the views of critics concerned with the direction of the administration's defense effort. On 31 January Dr. Jeremy Stone, director of the Federation of American Scientists, told the panel members that the country "would not get its money's worth" from the MX. Even more troubling, he noted, was the possibility that deploying the missile could threaten the very security that the administration sought to achieve.[47]

A host of critics shared Stone's concerns. To them the MX represented an illogical addition to a nuclear force designed to deter Soviet aggression. Because no one had been able to solve the problem of silo vulnerability, it was accepted that the MX would be unable to survive a Soviet strike. Thus, if the missile were to have significant military value, it would have to be launched *before* Soviet missiles struck the US heartland. This launch-on-warning philosophy obviously carried a great many risks, including the possibility that crises would escalate as decisionmakers confronted the choice of "using or losing" one entire leg of the strategic triad. "The MX invites attack," charged one defense scholar. "The Soviets can get ten warheads by using only one or two of theirs."[48]

Comments made by administration strategists did little to ease the critics' fears. Colin Gray, a consultant to the Arms Control and Disarmament Agency, called for a greater "freedom of offensive nuclear action."[49] Deputy Secretary of Defense Thomas White suggested that fears of a nuclear Armageddon were overblown: "If there are enough shovels around, everyone's going to make it."[50] Federal Emergency Management Authority (FEMA) Director Louis Guiffrida argued that "nuclear war would be a terrible mess, but it wouldn't be unmanageable."[51] Stunned by this brashness, a prominent administration critic noted wryly that "crazier analysts have risen to higher positions than is normally the case."[52]

But the combined weight of the critics' objections and the administration's belligerency had little effect on the panel. McFarlane had done his homework well. The conservative disposition of the members precluded the option of discontinuing the MX program. "We started out with a wide variety of views on stability, MIRVing, and arms control," recalled one commissioner, "but no one on the commission was opposed to modernizing the ICBM force.... It was a very collegial operation."[53] Still, the critics had called attention to a fundamental question that could not be easily dismissed: Minus a survivable basing mode, did it make strategic sense to build and deploy the MX?

The Compromise

By late January, less than one month into the commission's inquiry, the members had reached agreement on a proposal to save the MX program. The plan was structured to appeal to different parts of the policymaking community. To accommodate the administration, the commission would recommend that 100 MXs be built and deployed in existing Minuteman silos. The members hoped that the production goal of "only" 100 missiles would help allay the fears of administration critics. After all, they could point out, the Carter administration had sought twice that number as part of its MPS proposal in 1979.

The real trick, however, would be to sell the country on the use of existing silos to house the new missile. Critics were certain to point out that the administration had based much of its argument for the MX on the vulnerability of the Minuteman force. To get around this problem, the commission would treat the recommendation as an "interim measure" designed to bridge the gap between the older ICBMs and the next generation of strategic weapons. But this would be a difficult point to argue since the administration had consistently championed the MX as the weapon of the future.

To bolster its case, the commission decided that vague references to the "next generation of weapons" would have to be replaced by a more concrete proposal. Attention soon focused on the prospect of a weapon known variously as the small intercontinental ballistic missile (SICBM) or "Midgetman." Standing only 38 feet tall and with a weight only a fraction of the MX's, Midgetman promised to be both mobile and concealable. More important, plans called for each missile to carry only a single 500-kiloton warhead. The modest yield of the weapon would, in theory, create stability in superpower relations. Because the weapon would not be counterforce-capable, the Soviets would have less incentive to strike preemptively in a crisis situation. (The MX, containing ten warheads and situated in fixed silos, was more threatening to the Soviets—and represented a more tempting target of opportunity.) Conversely, US decisionmakers would face less pressure to launch on warning since the SICBM offered greater survivability than the silo-based behemoths.

Deployment plans for the SICBM were as yet undecided. Some strategists were enthusiastic about the prospects of a specially designed transport vehicle known as the "armadillo." Plans called for the armadillo to be built low to the ground with thick armor on all sides. It also would feature a self-contained anchoring system that would permit the vehicle to survive all but the closest nuclear blasts (strategists had less to say about the effects of a nuclear near-miss on the crew's morale).

It is clear that political considerations led the panel to embrace the SICBM proposal. As a commission member explained: "For most of the members of the commission the small missile was a way of buying in political support on the basis that the total package would go through [Congress] and the MX would survive. Very few shared the belief on the Hill that somehow or other the small missile was a panacea."[54]

As the deliberations continued, however, some members became convinced that Midgetman represented a viable alternative to continued reliance on MIRVs. Commissioner Woolsey was reported to be a particularly strong advocate of the proposal.[55] Even so, none of the members were willing to suggest that resources be directed from the MX to speed up Midgetman's development.

The final recommendation agreed upon involved the issue of arms control. Since the signing of SALT I in 1972, negotiators had focused on missiles, not warheads, as the accepted unit of limitation in disarmament talks. As a result, the number of MIRVs held by both superpowers had increased exponentially. This, the commission felt, could be addressed if attention was focused instead on limiting the number of warheads each side could possess. The recommendation was partly self-serving; the Soviets would be expected to make more drastic cuts since their own strategic modernization program, undertaken in the 1970s, had swelled their warhead inventories to unprecedented levels.

This was the essence of the plan that began to emerge in late January 1983. The commissioners dubbed it a "compromise" proposal to enhance its appeal on Capitol Hill. Scowcroft charged Woolsey with responsibility for drafting the recommendations into a publishable report. Woolsey had an initial draft of the document ready as the first month of the inquiry drew to a close. He explains how the panel proceeded thereafter:

> We used the meetings to rework the draft ... Brent ran it in such a way that people got to express themselves but we didn't try to sit around the table with all those bright and high-powered people and discuss the thing in detail. He got them to agree on general direction, and then I would write it up, and he would rewrite it, and then we would get out another draft—often overnight—for them to look at the next day.[56]

Woolsey was concerned that details of the plan would be leaked prematurely, giving opposition forces the opportunity to mount a campaign that could kill the proposal in its infancy. As a precaution, he labeled the draft "Option One," reasoning that this would protect the report's integrity even if a leak occurred.[57]

Star Wars

Unbeknown to the commissioners, the MX was not the only strategic program receiving significant White House attention. In an 11 February meeting between the president and the Joint Chiefs of Staff, Adm. James Watkins discussed the emergence of new technologies that could possibly be used to construct a defensive shield against ballistic missile attack. Reagan was instantly taken with the idea and encouraged the group to pursue the matter further.[58] Three weeks later, the chiefs submitted a formal proposal to the president calling for a concerted effort to build high-energy lasers and particle beams as the centerpiece of a major new program known officially as the Strategic Defense Initiative (SDI). Soon the rest of the world would know it as "star wars."

The implications of the proposal were staggering. Building such a system would require an unprecedented commitment of human and material resources. It also would entail a major philosophical shift away from the deterrence-based strategies that had guided the nation's search for nuclear security since the signing of the ABM Treaty in 1972. For this reason, SDI represented a challenge to the Scowcroft Commission's work, geared as it was toward strengthening the forces of deterrence. Critics would inevitably question the wisdom of committing resources to the MX if a viable defense system was just around the corner.

The nuances of this dilemma were not lost on McFarlane, who feared that the commission would feel "blindsided by SDI ... some members might even quit."[59] This was not an unjustified concern. Among the commission members there was "some spread of views" on the desirability of a ballistic missile defense system.[60] McFarlane pleaded with Reagan to postpone announcing the initiative until the MX issue had been decided.[61] But the president was committed to going public with the idea as soon as possible. To appease McFarlane, however, he directed his assistants to inform the commission of the coming announcement. One panel member recalled what followed: "One of Reagan's aides approached Brent. He said that the president was going to announce the initiative, and that needless to say the White House would welcome, if not an endorsement, at least an open mind on the part of the commission. Brent understood."[62]

Reagan revealed his vision to the nation in a televised address on 23 March. He opened the speech by hinting of "a decision which offers a new hope for our children in the twenty-first century." Later, he sprang the surprise: "What if free people could live secure in the knowledge that their security did not rest upon the threat of instant U.S. retaliation to deter a Soviet attack, that we could intercept and destroy strategic ballistic missiles before they reached our own soil and that of our allies?"

Reagan acknowledged that building such a defensive shield would be a "formidable, technical task." He used the point to emphasize the need for continuation of the strategic modernization program. Because SDI was still some years away, he warned the nation, "we must remain constant in preserving the nuclear deterrent and maintaining a solid capability for flexible response."[63] In short, Reagan's answer to the defense or deterrence question was "both." But the commission members realized that the president's announcement would make it harder to sell the MX. It would be difficult to argue forcefully for deterrence without foreclosing the possibility of a nuclear defense. The commission's job had just become much more difficult.

Courting Congress

With the compromise proposal in hand, the commission turned its attention to Congress. The members were aware that any proposal that called for MX development would encounter resistance. Some lawmakers were concerned that deployment of the weapon would destabilize relations with the Soviet Union. Others questioned the need to spend enormous sums of money on a system that was undeniably vulnerable. In Congress, even some hawks argued that defense funds could be better spent on further improvements to the ballistic missile submarine force.

The commission received an unwelcome surprise on 10 February when the Congressional Budget Office (CBO) released its assessment of the MX program. The CBO's annual report on deficit reduction listed fourteen possible reductions that could be made in Reagan's proposed $273 billion military budget. Canceling the MX program, the report noted, would provide the largest saving of any of the cost-cutting measures, eliminating over $28 billion in spending over a five-year period.[64]

But the CBO report only strengthened the commission's resolve. The members realized that, since the administration had already lost one key MX vote, a second defeat would likely kill the program forever. Accordingly, the commission devised a strategy to bring key figures on Capitol Hill into the deliberative process. Max Friedersdorf, a legislative specialist from the Ford administration, was brought in to assist in the effort. House members credited him with helping swing congressional sentiment in favor of the compromise.[65] Scowcroft even tried to gain the cooperation of Representative Addabbo, the New York Democrat who had led the successful fight against densepack. But Addabbo was firm. He urged Scowcroft to "forget the MX."[66]

In the House, the commission concentrated its efforts on recruiting the services of Representative Les Aspin, the influential Wisconsin Democrat who served on the Armed Services Committee. Aspin had established a reputation as a knowledgeable critic of defense procurement procedures. He had also voted against the densepack proposal in December. It thus came as a shock to all concerned when Aspin volunteered to help the commission broker a deal on the MX. One journalist monitoring the commission's activity reported that personal motives drove Aspin's decision.

> The less charitable of his colleagues suggest that a strong motivation for Aspin is that he wants to be Secretary of Defense someday. To reach such a goal, one cannot have been simply a critic of the Pentagon. It is a fact that a sizable portion of the Washington population ... consists of people "positioning" themselves for a high job in some future Administration.[67]

In a series of Sunday afternoon meetings with Scowcroft and Woolsey, Aspin reported on congressional reaction to various aspects of the commission's proposed compromise. Through these efforts, he eventually emerged as the head of a bloc of moderate House Democrats that included Thomas Foley, Albert Gore, Vic Fazio, Dan Glickman, and Norman Dicks. Collectively, the group controlled enough votes to determine the MX's future.[68]

Aspin was aware that the MX was only one of three key defense issues scheduled to come before Congress in March. The others included a vote on a nuclear freeze resolution, and the confirmation decision on Reagan's nomination of Kenneth Adelman to head the Arms Control and Disarmament Agency. Aspin feared that "if the Scowcroft report was up first it would sink. We wanted it to come up a little bit after the freeze vote. The usual pattern of this place is that people begin to get a little uncomfortable if they've gone too far one way and start looking for a way to pop back the other way."[69] Because of this concern, Aspin concluded that the MX decision should be pushed back to May. He convinced Scowcroft to request an extension for the commission in order to delay the report. The White House agreed. Executive Order 12406, issued on 18 February, granted the panel an additional two months to complete its inquiry.[70]

The strategy worked exactly as Aspin had hoped. On 4 May, the House adopted the freeze resolution urging the president to negotiate with the Soviets to halt the testing and development of new nuclear weapons systems. In the wake of that vote congressional moderates began to view the MX more favorably. "They went with the freeze," a legislative aide noted, "and then they wanted to get back to the center."[71] That search for a political center, of course, coincided nicely with the release of the commission's report.

The Final Report

Differences of opinion came to the surface as the commission struggled to complete its final report. Some members objected to the strident language of proposed recommendations. Passages that compared opposition to US defense policies with disloyalty were excised, as were phrases that "conveyed more hostility about the Soviet system than was wise."[72] But these were minor disruptions. On the whole, the members were like-minded enough to keep the deliberations moving. No formal dissents were issued.

The commission presented its final report to President Reagan on 11 April 1983.[73] Just over twenty-five pages long, it was short by the standards of blue-ribbon commissions. Woolsey had done his job well. The document had to be concise to produce the immediate political impact the administration sought. The *New York Times* devoted four full pages to the commission and its report in its 12 April edition.

The report contained few surprises. The content closely reflected the details of the compromise that had been negotiated between the commission, the administration, and Congress. On the sensitive issue of ballistic-missile defense, the commission took pains not to undermine SDI. Although the report noted that current technology offered "no real promise of being able to defend the United States against massive nuclear attack in this century," it nonetheless advocated "vigorous research and development" of nonnuclear defensive systems.[74] As expected, the commission also recommended spending $5 billion on development of the Midgetman, with the goal of bringing the missile into operation in the early 1990s.

Buried beneath these provisions was the more controversial issue of MX deployment. The report listed four reasons for moving ahead with the

MX program: (1) to drive the Soviets to the negotiating table; (2) to demonstrate national will and cohesion; (3) to offset Soviet numerical superiority in land-based missiles; and (4) to replace the aging Titan II and Minuteman missiles that were the backbone of the ICBM force.[75] The commission also took pains to link the missile's deployment to other, less threatening goals. The report argued that the MX was necessary to aid in the transition to Midgetman. This, the members argued, would eventually contribute to a more stable environment "in which individual targets are of lower value."[76]

But this line of reasoning was rife with contradictions. To pave the way for a single-warhead missile, a ten-warhead missile was needed. To emphasize the advantages of low-value weapons, a weapon with extremely high value would have to be built. The commissioners realized that the report would lose its appeal if the specific recommendations were viewed in isolation. Consequently, Scowcroft constantly stressed that the recommendations regarding the MX, Midgetman, and arms control constituted an "integral package—not intended as separate and distinct paths of action."[77]

The commission had less to say about the use of existing silos to base the MX. In a subsection titled "Strategic Forces as a Whole," the report noted that the issue of silo vulnerability "would be far more serious if we did not have a force of ballistic missile submarines at sea and a bomber force."[78] In its recommendations, the panel returned to the issue.

> In the judgment of the Commission, the vulnerability of such silos in the near term, viewed in isolation, is not a sufficiently dominant part of the overall problem of ICBM modernization to warrant other immediate steps being taken such as closely-spaced new silos.... In any circumstances other than that of a particular kind of massive surprise attack on the U.S. by the Soviet Union, Soviet planners would have to account for the possibility that MX missiles in Minuteman silos would be available for use, and they thus would help deter such attacks.[79]

Critics seized on these passages as evidence that the administration's claims of a "window of vulnerability" had been overstated from the beginning.[80] Using the logic of the report, they noted, one could make a convincing case that the existing Minuteman III force provided an effective deterrent even without the addition of the MX.[81]

A *New York Times* editorial found the report "not persuasive" in its defense of the MX, but went on to praise the "clear and comprehensive analysis" that urged development of the small, single-warhead ICBM.[82] Former national security advisor McGeorge Bundy was less kind. In a commentary titled, "The MX Paper: Appealing, But Mostly Appalling," he scored the panel for ignoring the impact of more MIRV weapons on superpower relations.

What is wrong? Only the centerpiece of the report. It goes in the [wrong] direction by placing the first-strike multiple-warhead MX in Minuteman silos, right where Soviet MIRVs could knock it out if ever the Kremlin thought we were about to use it.... If there was ever a "use it or lose it" system, ill-designed for stability in crisis, it is this one.[83]

Tom Wicker argued that the deployment of 100 MXs was "a high price to pay" to buy the administration's support for Midgetman.[84] Herbert Scoville, a former deputy director for research at CIA, reiterated his belief that the MX was "the most dangerous weapon designed to date ... they make nuclear holocaust much more likely."[85] However, even those opposed to the MX conceded that, by treating the MX as an "interim" weapon designed to bridge the technological gap to Midgetman, the commission had framed the issue in a manner that would appeal to many of those still undecided.

The Congressional Vote

With the report released, the commission intensified its lobbying effort in anticipation of the upcoming congressional vote on the MX. In a series of breakfast meetings held at Blair House, the panel members discussed their recommendations with key lawmakers. Aspin was a regular fixture at the meetings, representing those House moderates who had announced their support for the commission's report. Also present was William Cohen, who performed a similar function in attempting to sell the report in the Senate. Commissioner Reed later recalled the challenge of "stitching together a majority one vote at a time."

Aspin was careful not to appear overly enthusiastic about the recommendations regarding the MX. He told his House colleagues: "This is as good a decision as you're going to get to a problem that has no good answer."[86] His reluctance to embrace the report fully was part of a grand political act designed to buttress the appeal of the commission's work as a "middle ground." For the scheme to work, Aspin realized that conservatives would also have to react cautiously. "Don't crow when this comes out," he warned Weinberger, "we need you to grouse. Say this isn't very good, but, etc., etc."[87] Unfortunately for Aspin, however, key figures on the right failed to strike the appropriate posture. In fact, administration officials reacted so favorably to the report that many observers were left wondering exactly how much ground hawks had really given up to arrive at the compromise. Aspin was shocked by the lack of protest. "Paul Weyrich and Richard Viguerie," he wondered, "where are you when we really need you?"[88]

Reagan endorsed the panel's recommendations on 19 April. Thanking the members for a "tough job extraordinarily well done," he noted that the

National Security Council and the Joint Chiefs of Staff had also approved the report. Predictably, he chose to emphasize that portion of the report that advocated improvements in strategic capabilities.

> Time and again, America has exercised unilateral restraint, good will, and a sincere commitment to effective arms control. Unfortunately, these actions alone have not yet made us truly safer, and they haven't reduced the danger of nuclear war.... History teaches us that when the United States has shown the resolve to remain strong, stabilizing arms control can be achieved.[89]

Reagan forwarded the commission's proposal to the House and Senate leadership for formal consideration under the terms of the congressional resolution passed the previous December. The stage was now set for the final showdown over the administration's strategic modernization proposal.

As a prelude to the upcoming vote on the MX, the commissioners journeyed to Capitol Hill throughout late April and early May to defend their recommendations before various standing committees. The liveliest exchanges took place in hearings before the Senate Armed Services Committee. Chaired by Texas Senator John Tower, the committee heard testimony from commission members Scowcroft, Deutch, and Perry, as well as from senior counselors Brown and Schlesinger.[90] Senators James Exon (Democrat-Nevada) and Carl Levin (Democrat-Michigan) led the attack on the commission's report. On the first day of hearings, Levin challenged Scowcroft to defend the panel's credibility.

> Levin: My question is, did anyone on the Commission advocate the position that we should not build MX unless there were a way to put it into a survivable basing mode?
> Deutch: Senator, may I?
> Levin: No, I would like the General first to answer.... It is a straightforward question. Did anybody advocate the position at any time during the deliberations [of] the Commission: Let us not build it unless we have a survivable way to base it?
> Scowcroft: I could not state that categorically.[91]

Both lawmakers also pressed hard on the issue of silo vulnerability. Exon noted that many of the panel members "were the ones that sowed the seeds of MX in the first instance." He wondered if this personal investment in the weapon's future had blinded the commission to the problem of survivability. By advocating the use of existing silos, he charged, the panel "has taken us back to square one."[92]

Key members of the Senate Appropriations Committee also took issue with the report. Democrats Ernest Hollings and Daniel Inouye pointed out that, during the densepack debate of 1981–1982, many defense officials had argued forcefully *against* the use of existing silos to house the MX. Paradoxically, a number of those same officials now embraced the Scowcroft Report. Two commission members were cited for experiencing such a change of heart. In November 1981, then Undersecretary of Defense William Perry had argued that placing a heavily MIRVed missile in unprotected silos would create a "hair trigger" effect in the event of a crisis. That same month, Harold Brown told Congress that advances in Soviet guidance systems would soon place even the most hardened silos at risk.[93]

Despite these objections, the administration's proposal was brought before both chambers with favorable committee recommendations. As with the densepack decision in December, attention focused on the House where opposition to the MX was strongest. The administration again turned to the commission for help. On 23 May, the evening before the House vote, the White House hosted a dinner for twenty-five members of Congress who remained undecided on the issue.

The event was planned for maximum political effect. Distributed strategically among the tables, commission members and counselors used the opportunity to make one last push for the MX. They pointed out to the lawmakers that the MX vote was tied, by their report, to more general arms-control goals. Scowcroft spoke at one point, assuring the invitees that the president shared the commission's commitment to an eventual build-down of MIRV weapons. But Reagan's following remarks were less than convincing. When Representative Elliott Levitas (Democrat-Georgia) asked the president how he envisioned the build-down would proceed, Reagan appeared confused and referred the question to Scowcroft. Although Levitas went on to support the administration's plan, other Democrats were appalled by the president's inability to defend the report. Representative Robert Matsui of California confided that the episode weighed heavily in his decision to vote against the proposal.[94]

The last-minute lobbying effort worked. By a vote of 239 to 186, the House voted to release $625 million to permit flight-testing of the MX. The Senate followed suit the following day, approving the measure by a vote of 59 to 39. Even though major expenditure decisions remained—$6 billion would be necessary for the missile's procurement—opposition forces realized the battle had been lost. With initial funding having been granted, the MX would soon acquire a political and industrial constituency all its own. Local politics would be a major factor in all future spending decisions. The issue would never again be framed so clearly.

Many Democrats were bitter that moderates in their own party had played such a crucial role in selling the commission's report. Representative Les Au Coin (Democrat-Oregon) was particularly blunt in his assessment.

> I was thinking these clowns would give away the Midwest for a shoeshine and a smile.... And what [we're] bitter about is the presumption on the part of members that they could give Ronald Reagan religion on arms control. It's preposterous. And, even more, the idea that an Administration has to be bargained into sincerity about arms control—what kind of Administration is that?[95]

Senator Alan Cranston agreed with Au Coin, calling the compromise a "cruel hoax."[96]

But it was impossible to deny that the administration had scored an impressive political victory. Reagan himself made no bones about the influence of the commission on the legislative process. He hosted a reception for the commission and its staff on a Friday in late May. Reed remembers it as "one of the greatest TGIF parties of all time.... There were very appreciative words from Reagan and photos all around."[97]

Most knowledgeable observers agreed that the Scowcroft Commission had saved the day for the administration. No less an insider than McFarlane concluded that the MX would have been "completely lost" without the intervention of the panel.[98] The *New York Times* judged the commission's report to have been the "critical factor" in the vote.[99] A legislative aide was equally direct.

> Without the Scowcroft Commission, we'd never have the MX. If Weinberger had said he wanted to put the MX in Minuteman silos, he'd have been laughed off the Hill. But you had Brent Scowcroft and Harold Brown—who advise Democrats—saying it, and you had a bipartisan commission of genuine experts. It was a beautiful move.[100]

By joining Democratic and Republican policymakers together under one roof, the panel effectively preempted much of the opposition to the MX. As Hugh Sidey noted in a *Time* editorial, "would-be doubters were instantly humbled since virtually every top expert in strategic affairs had signed on."[101]

Aftermath

Following the MX vote, Reagan took the unusual step of once again extending the commission's official life. In Executive Order 12424, issued on 10 June, he asked the panel to serve through the remainder of 1983 to review the administration's progress in implementing the recommendations contained in the report.[102] Of the panel's eleven official members, ten agreed to continue to serve.[103] However, the activity of the commission during that period was minimal. Meetings were held only infrequently, and Scowcroft handled reports to the president informally.[104]

The administration acted decisively on two of the commission's three major recommendations. The House and Senate approved procurement funds for the MX in July, and the Pentagon began to deploy the missile the following year. But the end of the Cold War accomplished what Reagan's critics could not—an interruption in MX production. Only fifty missiles, half the number recommended by the commission, were ultimately brought into service.

The administration also showed some movement in arms control negotiations. On 8 June, Reagan ordered a shift in the US negotiating position at the Strategic Arms Reduction Talks (START) under way in Geneva. He instructed Gen. Edwin Rowny, head of the US delegation, to focus attention on strategic warheads as the unit of limitation, instead of launchers as had previously been the case.[105] This, Reagan argued, would encourage both superpowers to de-emphasize large, multiwarhead weapons in favor of smaller, less threatening weapons such as the SICBM.

But Reagan's efforts to achieve an agreement on strategic warheads proved fruitless. Two factors account for this failure. First, the Soviets took a dim view of any agreement that focused primarily on MIRV ICBMs. Those weapons constituted the backbone of the Soviet strategic arsenal, a situation that contrasted sharply with the US emphasis on submarine-launched missiles. To the Kremlin, Reagan's talk of reducing the number of MIRVs was simply an attempt to deny the Soviet advantage in that leg of the triad. Second, the Soviets were reluctant to conclude any agreement that did not also address SDI. Behind in key defensive technologies, they had much to fear from the abandonment of deterrent-based strategies. But Reagan was unwilling to forgo the initiative to secure an arms-control agreement. Even so, the commission's emphasis on counting warheads permanently altered the terms of debate and paved the way for the START treaties concluded under the administration of George H. W. Bush.

Evaluation

Unlike the Rockefeller Commission, the Scowcroft Commission was not designed to preempt congressional action. Indeed, it was apparent that lawmakers would have to act for the MX program to be saved. Instead, what Reagan sought was a mechanism for mobilizing public and congressional support for an established goal. The evidence does not support claims that the commission achieved a policy compromise in which the administration sacrificed some of its own priorities. The fact that defense hawks, both within and outside the government, embraced the report so quickly was particularly telling. The only real dissent came from critics outside the administration.

Of more general significance, this analysis gives rise to three observations regarding the role of presidential commissions in the policy process. First, the study illustrates that commission politics can, at times, be quite overt. The Scowcroft Commission was heavily political even by the standards of the ad hoc advisory system. The members made little effort to conceal their feelings that the MX program needed to move forward. When asked about the charge that the panel's sole purpose was to save the missile, one commissioner responded with unusual frankness: "Yes, the critics were right, but that's not an indictment, that's what the American system is all about."[106] At no point did the commission assert its authority in dealing with the administration. If anything, the members demonstrated a willingness to subordinate their own preferences to those of the White House—a fact that was underscored by the panel's accommodation of the president on SDI.

Second, the study indicates how remarkably responsive presidential commissions are as political mechanisms. Should the need arise, they can be modified to help meet new challenges or to advance personal and institutional goals. McFarlane dealt with pressures to increase the size of the panel's membership by creating the category of senior counselor in order to avoid alienating key individuals. Later, when sympathetic legislators advised that the report should be delayed to maximize its impact, Reagan extended the panel's life with the stroke of a pen.

Finally, this case demonstrates the political weight carried by blue-ribbon commissions. The recommendations of the Scowcroft Commission regarding the MX were virtually identical to those of the first Pentagon study headed by Charles Townes. Both panels recommended placing the missile in existing Minuteman silos. Yet the Townes Commission's recommendations resulted in legislative defeat, while the Scowcroft report paved the way for the resuscitation of the MX program. A number of factors led to these different outcomes, but it is clear that the Scowcroft Commission simply brought more influence to bear than the earlier panel. This highlights the unique and powerful position of presidential commissions in the universe of government advisory bodies.

Notes

1. In comparison, the mean-miss distance for the Minuteman III ICBM is 730 feet. Peter R. Beckman et al., *The Nuclear Predicament: Nuclear Weapons in the Cold War and Beyond*, 2d ed. (Englewood Cliffs, NJ: Prentice Hall, 1992), p. 100.

2. Reagan originally chose the name "peacemaker" for the weapon, but some administration insiders worried that critics would dub the weapon a "pacemaker" instead. Gregg Herken, *Counsels of War* (New York: Alfred A. Knopf, 1985), p. 332.

3. In its original conception, the MPS system was to be constructed along an oval-track design. Due to rising cost estimates, however, this was changed to a linear-track configuration in late 1979.

4. US Congress, Senate, *Resolution to Approve the Obligation and Expenditure of Funds for Full-Scale Engineering Development of a Basing Mode for the MX Missile*, Senate Report 98–95 to accompany S. Con. Res. 26, 98th Congress, 1st session, 1983, p. 21.

5. McGeorge Bundy, *Danger and Survival* (New York: Random House, 1988), p. 563.

6. US Congress, House of Representatives, Committee on Interior and Insular Affairs, *Basing the MX Missile*, 97th Congress, 1st session, August 1981, p. 14.

7. US Congress, Senate, *Resolution to Approve the Obligation and Expenditure of Funds for the MX*, pp. 61, 64.

8. Herken, *Counsels of War*, p. 332.

9. Richard Halloran, "Basic Military Issues Loom," *New York Times,* 31 December 1982, p. 1.

10. Ibid., 19.

11. Anonymous administration source, quoted in Herken, *Counsels of War*, p. 303.

12. Steven V. Roberts, "Reagan Loss on MX," *New York Times*, 8 December 1982, p. D23.

13. Ibid.

14. There was rich irony in Michel's reference to the congressional isolationists of the pre–World War II era. With a handful of exceptions, those most opposed to Roosevelt's military build-up—LaFollette, Nye, Vandenberg, and Taft in the Senate; Fish, Case, and Burdick in the House—were Republicans.

15. "Excerpts from MX Debate in House," *New York Times*, 8 December 1982, p. D23.

16. Roberts, "Reagan Loss on MX."

17. "Statement on Action by the House of Representatives on Production of the MX Missile," 7 December 1982, *Public Papers of the Presidents* (Washington, DC: Government Printing Office), Ronald W. Reagan, 1982, p. 1,573.

18. The partisan balance in the Senate remained the same.

19. Paul Lettow, *Ronald Reagan and His Quest to Abolish Nuclear Weapons* (New York: Random House, 2005), p. 85.

20. Public Law 377, 97th Congress, 2d session (8 December 1982), Department of Defense Appropriations Act.

21. The amendment to the Defense Appropriations Act was originally offered in the Senate by Henry Jackson. It was approved by both chambers in late 1982.

22. Richard Halloran, "Weinberger Faces First Real Attacks," *New York Times*, 27 December 1982, p. B8.

23. Robert McFarlane, *Special Trust* (New York: Cadell and Davies, 1994), p. 224.

24. Ibid., 281.

25. Elizabeth Drew, "A Political Journal," *The New Yorker* 20 June 1983, p. 46.

26. Telephone interview with Robert McFarlane, 30 March 1995.

27. Ibid. See also Charles A. Sorrels, "The Scowcroft Commission," in *Triumphs and Tragedies of the Modern Presidency*, ed. David Abshire (Washington, DC: Center for the Study of the Presidency, 2001), pp. 160–163.

28. Telephone interview with Robert McFarlane, 30 March 1995.

29. Early in the commission's inquiry, Harold Brown came under some criticism for his consulting work with TRW, a company involved in the MX program. As a result, he resigned from the panel as an official member and served thereafter

as a senior counselor. See Charles Mohr, "Ex-Defense Chief, Citing Conflict, Quits MX Panel," *New York Times*, 22 January 1983, p. 30.

30. Confidential telephone interview.

31. Steven R. Weisman, "Tax Increase Options Unlikely, Reagan Aides Say," *New York Times*, 1 January 1983, p. 6.

32. McFarlane, *Special Trust*, p. 339.

33. Scowcroft later served as a member of the Tower Commission on the Iran-Contra issue. In 2001, another "Scowcroft Commission" came to life when President George W. Bush appointed the retired general to head an eight-member panel tasked with conducting a review of US intelligence capabilities. See Vernon Loeb, "CIA Panel May Lack Voice for Change," *Washington Post*, 7 August 2001, p. A13.

34. Telephone interviews with commission members and counselors.

35. "Executive Order 12400—President's Commission on Strategic Forces," 3 January 1983, *Public Papers of the Presidents*, Ronald Reagan, 1983, p. 3.

36. Francis X. Clines, "Reagan Appoints a Panel to Study MX Missile," *New York Times*, 4 January 1983, p. 15.

37. Telephone interview with Thomas Reed, 9 March 1995.

38. *Public Papers of the Presidents*, Ronald W. Reagan, 1983, p. 3.

39. Clines, "Reagan Appoints a Panel to Study MX Missile."

40. McGeorge Bundy, *Danger and Survival* (New York: Random House, 1988), p. 563.

41. Brent Scowcroft, "Understanding the U.S. Strategic Arsenal," in *Nuclear Arms: Ethics, Strategy, Politics*, ed. James Woolsey (San Francisco: Institute for Contemporary Studies, 1984), p. 82.

42. *New York Times*, 4 January 1983, p. 15.

43. The comments of Schlesinger, Brown, and Rumsfeld appeared in "How Superpowers Stand Now," *U.S. News and World Report* (10 January 1983), p. 19.

44. Telephone interview with James Woolsey, 7 April 1995.

45. Telephone interview with Brent Scowcroft, 24 April 1995.

46. Confidential telephone interview.

47. Stone's remarks before the commission appear in US Congress, Senate, Committee on Armed Services, *Hearings on the MX Missile Basing System*, p. 243.

48. Stephen J. Cimbala, "Midgetman: Major Problems," *Bulletin of the Atomic Scientists* 40 (February 1984), 7.

49. Quoted in Robert Jay Lifton and Eric Markusen, *The Genocidal Mentality: Nazi Holocaust and Nuclear Threat* (New York: Basic Books, 1990), p. 209.

50. Quoted in Ronald E. Powaski, *March to Armageddon* (New York: Oxford University Press, 1987), p. 188.

51. Quoted in Michael Parenti, *The Sword and the Dollar: Imperialism, Revolution, and the Arms Race* (New York: St. Martin's, 1989), p. 168.

52. Herbert York, quoted in Lifton and Markusen, *The Genocidal Mentality*, p. 34.

53. Confidential telephone interview.

54. Anonymous commission source, quoted in Herken, *Counsels of War,* p. 334.

55. Confidential telephone interview.

56. Telephone interview with Woolsey.

57. The effort to keep the commission's plans from the press was not entirely successful. See Hedrick Smith, "Basing MX in Minuteman Silos Expected as Panel's Interim Plan," *New York Times*, 23 March 1983, p. 23.

58. McFarlane, *Special Trust,* p. 229.

59. Telephone interview with Robert McFarlane, 30 March 1995.

60. Confidential telephone interview.

61. Lettow, *Ronald Reagan and His Quest to Abolish Nuclear Weapons*, p. 101.

62. Confidential telephone interview.

63. "Address to the Nation on Defense and National Security," 23 March 1983, *Public Papers of the Presidents*, Ronald Reagan, 1983, p. 437.

64. *New York Times*, 11 February 1983, p. 18. A summary of the CBO report appears in US Congress, Senate, *A Resolution to Approve the Obligation and Expenditure of Funds for Full-Scale Engineering Development of a Basing Mode for the MX Missile*, 98th Congress, 1st session, 1983.

65. Smith, "Basing MX in Minuteman Silos Expected as Panel's Interim Plan."

66. Ibid.

67. Drew, "A Political Journal," p. 49.

68. For additional detail on negotiations between the administration and Congress on the MX issue, see William W. Newmann, "The Structures of National Security Decision Making: Leadership, Institutions, and Politics in the Carter, Reagan, and G. H. W. Bush Years," *Presidential Studies Quarterly* 34:2 (June 2004), 272–306.

69. Drew, "A Political Journal," p. 55.

70. Executive Order 12406, *Public Papers of the Presidents,* Ronald Reagan, 1983, p. 249.

71. Drew, "A Political Journal," p. 56.

72. Anonymous commission source, quoted in Herken, *Counsels of War*, p. 334.

73. President's Commission on Strategic Forces, *Report of the President's Commission on Strategic Forces* (Washington, DC: Government Printing Office, 1983).

74. Ibid., 12.

75. Ibid., 16–17.

76. Ibid., 14.

77. US Congress, Senate, Committee on Armed Services, *Hearings on the MX Missile Basing System*, p .90.

78. *Report of the President's Commission on Strategic Forces*, p. 7.

79. Ibid., 17.

80. During congressional hearings in late April, Senator Joseph Biden thanked the commission for "putting to bed" the window of vulnerability argument. Such interpretations of the report irritated the commission members, who felt that their conclusions on the subject had been taken out of context. For more details on this exchange, see US Congress, Senate, Committee on Foreign Relations, *Hearings on the Arms Control and Foreign Policy Implications of the Scowcroft Commission Report*, 98th Congress, 1st session, 1983, p. 28.

81. Steven E. Miller, "The Politics of Saving the MX," *New Leader* 66 (2 May 1983), 7.

82. "Beyond the MX at Last," *New York Times*, 13 April 1983, p. 30.

83. McGeorge Bundy, "The MX Report: Appealing, But Mostly Appalling," *New York Times,* 17 April 1983, p. E19.

84. Tom Wicker, "And Still the MX," *New York Times*, 15 April 1983, p. A31.

85. Steven V. Roberts, "MX Opponents Call Basing Plan Too Costly and Short of Objective," *New York Times,* 13 April 1983, p. 21.

86. Steven V. Roberts, "Congressmen Say MX Still Faces a Tough Battle," *New York Times,* 12 April 1983, p. 20.

87. Drew, "A Political Journal," p. 55.

88. Les Aspin, "The MX Bargain," *Bulletin of the Atomic Scientists* 39 (November 1983), 53.

89. "Remarks Endorsing the Recommendations in the Report of the President's Commission on Strategic Forces," 19 April 1983, *Public Papers of the Presidents,* Ronald Reagan, 1983, p. 555.

90. The committee also heard testimony from four outspoken critics of the commission's report: Dr. Jeremy Stone, director of the Federation of American Scientists; Dr. Herbert Scoville, head of the Arms Control Association; Dr. Henry Kendall, chairman of the Union of Concerned Scientists; and former National Security Advisor McGeorge Bundy.

91. US Congress, Senate, Committee on Armed Services, *Hearings on the MX Missile Basing System and Related Issues,* 98th Congress, 1st session, 1983, p. 25.

92. Ibid., 17.

93. US Congress, Senate, Committee on Appropriations, *Resolution to Approve the Obligation and Expenditure of Funds for Full-Scale Engineering Development of a Basing Mode for the MX Missile,* 98th Congress, 1st session, 1983, pp. 57–63.

94. The perceptions and comments of the House members invited to the White House dinner were reported by Drew in "A Political Journal," pp. 64–66.

95. Ibid., 73.

96. Steven V. Roberts, "Senate, by 59 to 39, Votes $625 Million for Testing of MX," *New York Times,* 26 May 1983, p. 18.

97. Thomas C. Reed, *At the Abyss: An Insider's History of the Cold War* (New York: Presidio Press, 2004), p. 254.

98. Telephone interview with McFarlane.

99. Roberts, "Senate, by 59 to 39, Votes $625 Million."

100. Drew, "A Political Journal," p. 55.

101. Hugh Sidey, "The Buck Stops Here," *Time,* 30 May 1983, p. 14.

102. Executive Order 12424, *Public Papers of the Presidents,* Ronald Reagan, 1983, p. 849.

103. The exception was Thomas Reed, who resigned from the NSC staff in the summer of 1983.

104. The participants interviewed were unable to recall any events of significance that occurred in the period following the congressional vote. Most agreed that, as a practical matter, the commission concluded its work in May 1983.

105. "Remarks Announcing Changes in the United States Position at the Strategic Arms Reduction Talks," 8 June 1983, *Public Papers of the Presidents,* Ronald Reagan, 1983, p. 831.

106. Confidential telephone interview.

5

The Politics of Scandal: The Tower Commission and Iran-Contra

A bad cause seldom fails to betray itself.
—James Madison, *Federalist No. 41*

We dug up a snake and followed it where it went.
—John Tower, Chair of the President's Special Review Board

As the sixth year of his presidency drew to a close, Ronald Reagan was in an enviable position. It had been twenty-five years since a US president had completed two full terms in office, and Reagan had every reason to believe he would preside over an end to the string of failed presidencies that dated back to the tumultuous days of Vietnam and Watergate. His popularity showed no signs of waning as he reached the midpoint of his lame-duck term. Polls taken at the end of October 1986 indicated that 81 percent of the American people held a favorable image of him as an individual; 67 percent approved of his job performance.[1] These ratings were among the best of his time in office, and even compared favorably with poll results from his honeymoon period in early 1981.[2]

Then came the Iran-Contra affair. Almost overnight, the Reagan presidency was brought to a political standstill amid charges that the administration had negotiated secretly with terrorists, waged an illegal war in Central America, and conspired to shut Congress out of the foreign-policy process. The growing scandal took a heavy personal toll on the president. His behavior was punctuated by long periods of inactivity and acrimonious exchanges with top White House personnel.[3] Desperately seeking to regain control of events, Reagan created a three-member advisory panel, headed by former Senator John Tower, to examine the issue. The work of the President's Special Review Board is the focus of this chapter.

Political Context

The chain of events leading to the appointment of the commission began on 3 November 1986. On that date, the Lebanese newspaper *Al-Shiraa* published an account of former National Security Advisor Robert McFarlane's trip to Tehran the previous May.[4] According to the story, McFarlane and US Marine Lt. Col. Oliver North had made the journey in an effort to swap Hawk missile components for Iranian assistance in securing the release of US hostages being held in Lebanon. The American press picked up the story quickly, and it soon became apparent that the contact with the Iranians had not been an isolated incident. Even as the details began to unfold in the news media, the arms deals continued in the Middle East. On 7 November 1986, the CIA delivered 500 TOW (tube-launched, optically tracked, wire-guided) missiles to Israel to replace weapons the Israelis had sent to Iran earlier in the year. In all, it was later revealed, the arms shipments to Iran—whether handled directly by administration representatives or indirectly through Israeli intermediaries—had been under way for fifteen months.

But the 7 November delivery of TOWs was to be the last in the arms-for-hostages effort. The issue of secret administration dealings with Iran, a country long identified with support for international terrorism, was simply too interesting for the press to ignore. McFarlane realized the impact of the revelations, later stating that he "knew without a shadow of a doubt that the spotlight was about to be turned full force on the White House."[5] Others in the administration shared McFarlane's assessment. During the first week of November, there was a flurry of activity between top decisionmakers regarding the *Al-Shiraa* story. National Security Advisor John Poindexter wrote to Secretary of State George Schultz that "we must remain absolutely close-mouthed" to avoid complicating last-minute negotiations for the hostages' release.[6] Schultz agreed that "only the key facts" of the issue should be disclosed to the public.[7] White House Chief of Staff Donald Regan dissented, however, arguing that White House reticence would only arouse further speculation.[8] But President Reagan was inclined to follow Poindexter's lead on the issue. He made it clear that there would be no public discussion of the allegations.

By the following week it was apparent that the strategy of silence was not working. In a 10 November White House strategy session, Reagan complained that he was being "held out to dry" by the press.[9] At the urging of his advisers, the president agreed to make his first public comment on the matter in a nationally televised address on 13 November. In that speech, written in part by Oliver North, Reagan admitted selling arms to Iran, but forcefully defended the policy as a means of pursuing a strategic opening with moderate contacts in Tehran. He tried to assure the nation that the most damning charges, "attributed to Danish sailors and unnamed observers at Italian ports and Spanish harbors," were unfounded.

The charge has been made that the United States has shipped weapons to Iran as ransom payment for the release of American hostages in Lebanon,

that the United States undercut its allies and secretly violated American policy against trafficking with terrorists. Those charges are utterly false....
    We did not—repeat—did not trade weapons or anything else for hostages nor will we.[10]

But this was not entirely true. Whatever Reagan's own recollection of the intent behind the policy, McFarlane found his denial of an arms-for-hostages deal to be "just this side of an outright lie."[11] President Reagan went on to tell the nation that all his top foreign-policy advisers had been included in the decision to pursue the opening with Iran. This, too, was false. Both Schultz and Secretary of Defense Caspar Weinberger had been left out of many key strategy sessions and were unaware of the magnitude of the effort.[12] The president's denials also failed to erase the doubts of the American people. A *Los Angeles Times* poll taken after the speech revealed that only 14 percent of the public believed that the arms sales had not been used as ransom payments.[13] It was clear that the televised address had completely failed to quiet the furor, as the White House had hoped.

A presidential press conference held on 19 November proved equally futile. By this time the Washington press corps was beginning to learn more details of the policy, including the extensive use of Israeli intermediaries to facilitate the arms transfers. The questioning was relentless, and Chief of Staff Regan was alarmed to find the president "stumbling all over the place and looking very inept and weak."[14] Reagan admitted that the arms sales had generated "considerable debate within administration circles," but refused to concede that laws had been broken or even that errors in judgment had been made. He realized that the policy involved a certain amount of risk, but denied that it had been a "fiasco or a great failure of any kind." When asked if Congress should have been notified of the contact with Iran, under the provisions of the Arms Export Control Act, Reagan responded that he had been justified in withholding such information on the grounds of national security.[15]

Angered by the president's recalcitrance, key members of Congress began to press the issue with more vigor. Senator Sam Nunn, the Georgia Democrat slated to chair the Armed Services Committee in the new Congress, appeared before the press on 20 November and proceeded to list by category the contradictions in the administration's official line. Senate Minority Leader Robert Byrd (Democrat-West Virginia) was more blunt, telling the press that the dealings clearly amounted to an arms-for-hostages swap. Even Robert Dole, the Senate Republican leader, urged the president "to admit that a mistake was made."[16]

A similar sense of disillusionment settled over the American people. The last two weeks of November would bring the sharpest drop in Reagan's approval rating of his eight years in the White House. By the end of the month, only 46 percent of the American people viewed his performance favorably.[17] That drop of twenty-one points was the sharpest one-month decline ever recorded in presidential approval polls. For the president, however, the situation was about to become even more distressing.

At Reagan's request, Attorney General Edwin Meese had already launched an investigation of the arms sales. In a meeting at the White House on the morning of 24 November, he informed the president that an undetermined—though significant—portion of the profits from the sales had been diverted to the contra forces fighting to overthrow the Sandinista government of Nicaragua. That revelation raised serious questions of legality in light of a series of congressional enactments known as the Boland amendments which, to varying degrees, either limited or proscribed support for the Nicaraguan opposition. Regan recalled that the president "blanched when he heard Meese's words."[18] Reagan's own diary entry from the meeting deemed the diversion a "smoking gun" and concluded with an ominous prediction: "This may call for resignations."[19]

Meese, Regan, and the president agreed to hold a press conference the following day to get the story out and avoid charges of a coverup. But Regan was determined not to stage a repeat of Reagan's disastrous performance of 19 November. He convinced Meese to preside over the conference, citing his concern that the president would not "be able to handle press inquiries."[20]

Meese tried his best to downplay the issue. He told reporters that Israeli representatives had been primarily responsible for the diversion and that "no one in the chain of command had been informed."[21] But knowledgeable observers were quick to realize the impact of the announcement. Senator Dave Durenberger, a Minnesota Republican, confided that the revelation "exceeded even our most creative imaginations."[22] A *New York Times* headline on 26 November proclaimed "A Presidency Damaged." The story that followed suggested that discovery of the contra angle had appreciably dimmed Reagan's chances for a political recovery.[23]

Thus, what had begun as a story in an otherwise obscure Lebanese newspaper had become a full-fledged scandal for the administration. It was now apparent that the story would not die on its own, nor would a skeptical public be mollified by official explanations couched in terms of national security imperatives or the demands of diplomatic *realpolitik*. The Democrats had recaptured control of the Senate in the midterm elections and, as the new majority party in Congress, promised to convene extensive committee hearings in January. For Reagan the outlook had never appeared so bleak. He knew, as did his advisers, that the very fate of his presidency would hinge on his ability to stop the free-fall and restore some measure of control over the course of events.

Creating the Commission

The idea of creating a blue-ribbon panel to deal with the growing scandal began to take shape in the days following the president's 19 November news conference. Within the White House, one of the first to push for an ad hoc review was Deputy Chief of Staff Dennis Thomas. Significantly, Thomas had been instrumental in setting up a presidential commission to investigate the space shuttle *Challenger* disaster in February 1986. He realized the usefulness of such panels in "pulling the pin on political pressure," and felt that a commission-based review could be used effectively to quiet the furor over Iran-Contra: "The pressures were coming for a hill inquiry. The best way to address those, probably the only way to address those, was to say an independent review was being conducted ... and being conducted by someone with congressional standing."[24]

Regan agreed—the chief of staff was at the center of all the key decisions made regarding the commission—and plans for an advisory "review board" began to take shape.

Others in the administration greeted the idea enthusiastically. Members of the NSC Planning Group pressured Regan to act quickly in setting up the commission.[25] These key decisionmakers understood that revelation of the diversion of funds to the contras would worsen an already dire situation, and thus realized that extraordinary measures were called for. They also were aware of the skepticism that would greet any attempt to leave the issue to the attorney general's office.[26] Representative Stephen Solarz (Democrat-New York) had already stated publicly that such an inquiry would be unacceptable to congressional Democrats.

Secretary of State Schultz was a particularly strong backer of the commission proposal.[27] He had every reason to push for a special inquiry. Reports filtering out of Washington indicated that the NSC staff had seriously encroached on State Department authority in developing foreign-policy initiatives. The secretary knew his bureaucratic turf was threatened and must have dreaded the inevitable comparison with Kissinger's end run around the State Department during the Nixon years. Moreover, Schultz had less to fear from public scrutiny than many other officials; he had been left out of the more questionable decisions taken in the Iran-Contra drama.

On the afternoon of 24 November, Regan brought the commission proposal to the president in an Oval Office meeting that also included Attorney General Meese. His notes from the meeting, drawn up in a "plan of action" memo, indicate that he argued for a panel containing "at least one member with congressional connections and a Democrat." In selling the idea, Regan also made it clear that the commission would function as part of a more general damage-control effort.

> Tough as it seems, blame must be put at NSC's door—rogue operation, going on without President's knowledge or sanction. When suspicions arose he took charge, ordered investigation, had meeting of top advisors to get at facts, and find out who knew what. Try to make the best of a sensational story. Anticipate charges of "out of control," "President doesn't know what's going on," "Who's in charge"[28]

The president agreed that decisive action was needed and gave permission for the staff to move ahead with preparations for the commission.[29]

With the president's endorsement in hand, Regan began to work on the board's size and composition. On the afternoon of 25 November he assembled a group of White House aides to assist in the task. There was some initial sentiment to select former secretary of state William P. Rogers to head the board.[30] His name had been under active discussion since a 20 November meeting between Schultz and Regan. However, Rogers had chaired the commission on the space shuttle tragedy earlier in the year, and Regan argued successfully that it would be unfair to press him into service again so soon.

Instead Regan recommended that former senator John G. Tower, a Texas Republican, be offered the chairmanship. While in the Senate, Tower had built a reputation as an articulate, if somewhat acerbic, conservative well versed in national security issues. Regan had already discussed this possibility with Thomas, and both men were convinced that Tower had the right mix of experience, toughness, and political savvy for the job.[31]

The second member selected was Edmund Muskie, the former senator from Maine who had also served briefly as secretary of state in the final year of the Carter administration. The onetime Democratic presidential candidate was held in high regard on Capitol Hill and was considered something of an elder statesman. As with Tower, Regan's influence was instrumental in bringing Muskie's name to the fore.[32] The chief of staff realized that Muskie's inclusion would give the commission bipartisan appeal and help preempt charges of a coverup inquiry.

Brent Scowcroft, the final member appointed to the board, was no stranger to blue-ribbon inquiries. In addition to chairing the Commission on Strategic Forces, he had served as a member of the 1985 Packard Commission on Pentagon management procedures. That experience had helped build his reputation as a thoughtful and knowledgeable observer of the political process. More important, Scowcroft was also intimately familiar with the inner workings of the NSC system—an important consideration in the context of the Iran-Contra issue.

With only three members, the Tower Commission was very small by the standards of the ad hoc advisory system.[33] When queried on the significance of the commission's size, one aide involved in the decision argued that it was simply difficult to find individuals who were available to serve, had credibility with Congress, and were sufficiently knowledgeable of NSC operating procedures.[34] Equally important, though, was the fact that Regan had decided to lobby for a small commission. He was aware that a split among the commission members would seriously weaken the impact of the board's work and felt that a lean panel would be better able to "work quickly and report decisively."[35]

The president approved the selections without objection. Regan personally contacted the prospective commissioners on the evening of 25 November. All three agreed to serve, though Regan noted that "none leapt at the chance to undertake this difficult assignment."[36] Interestingly, both Tower and Muskie expressed reservations about working together under such demanding circumstances. The two men knew each other from their days in the Senate, where they had crossed swords on a number of issues. Muskie knew that Tower could be tenacious when challenged, and worried about the thoroughness of an investigation led by such a partisan figure.[37] Tower had similar reservations. When Regan informed him that Muskie had been selected to serve, he pointed to the former secretary's "famous short fuse" as a cause for concern.[38]

In retrospect, Regan and his assistants handled the job of membership selection expertly. The three members selected certainly delivered the blue-ribbon prestige necessary to guarantee the panel media attention and a significant voice in the general debate over Iran-Contra, an important concern given the fact that congressional committees were set to begin new hearings on the scandal in the spring.

The President's Special Review Board was officially established on 1 December by Executive Order 12575. The language of the order was vague. The president directed the board to "conduct a comprehensive study of the future role and procedures of the National Security Council staff." There was no mention of Iran-Contra, though the mandate did authorize the board to review the NSC staff's role in "extremely sensitive diplomatic, military, and intelligence missions." The order directed all executive departments and agencies to provide, on request, "such information as it may require for purposes of carrying out its functions."[39] To facilitate communication, the president recalled David Abshire from his post as ambassador to NATO and placed him on temporary duty as White House liaison with the investigation.[40] Abshire was an experienced hand with this sort of task, having served as State Department liaison with Congress during the Watergate scandal.

Reagan ordered the board to report within sixty days. On average, ad hoc security commissions have a lifespan of eight months, more than three times longer than the period specified for the Tower Commission. In light of this, it is remarkable to note that the White House had originally sought an even shorter investigation lasting only thirty days. Muskie was responsible for derailing that plan. He complained to the press on 27 November that he "did not want to be rushed into a hasty report."[41] The White House could ill afford to ignore his objections. As the lone Democrat on the panel, Muskie's support was essential if the inquiry was to have credibility.

Public reaction to the announcement of the board's creation was generally favorable. The *Washington Post* opined that the composition of the commission would ensure a "penetrating inquiry."[42] From Tower's home state, the *Dallas Morning News* editorialized that "the public will best be served by the non-political deliberations that the Tower panel promises."[43] There were, however, some scattered objections to the board's membership. Commentator Pat Buchanan complained that asking Muskie to serve was the political equivalent of "calling in an air strike" on the White House.[44] On Capitol Hill, Senator Patrick Moynihan (Democrat-New York) noted that McFarlane had served as a staff aide to Senator Tower in the late 1970s. He expressed his hope that this personal relationship would not alter the commission's view of events.[45] Aware of these reservations, Tower sought to preempt further criticism by vowing that he would be "coldly objective."[46]

The commissioners wasted little time in pulling together a staff to assist in the inquiry. Tower called on Rhett Dawson, one of his former legislative aides, to serve as executive director of the board. Dawson was an experienced hand at conducting this type of review, having served the previous year as director of the Packard Commission on defense procurement procedures.[47] Muskie selected W. Clark McFadden, a Washington attorney and onetime Senate staffer, as the commission's general counsel. With these two key selections in hand, the commissioners went on to assemble a staff that included twenty-six administrative and investigative personnel. Whenever possible, the members sought out individuals who already had the required security clearances in hand. This avoided unnecessary delays and, according to Tower, permitted the panel to "jump start the investigation."[48]

By the end of the first week in December the commission was ready to proceed. One of the first decisions taken involved the scope of the investigation. As noted earlier, Reagan's executive order establishing the commission did not mention the Iran-Contra issue specifically, but rather provided for a review of the NSC as part of the larger policymaking process. But in the president's meeting with the commission on 1 December, he indicated that he desired a more tightly focused investigation.

> I want to assure you and the American people that I want all the facts to come out about learning of a possible transfer of funds from the sale of arms to Iran to those fighting the Sandinista government....
> If we're to maintain confidence in our government's foreign policy apparatus, there must be a full and complete airing of all the facts. And I

am determined to get all the facts out and take whatever action is necessary.... Just as soon as your findings and recommendations are complete,
they will be shared with the American people and the Congress. So, with
that, I say, go to it![49]

Reagan's directive to focus on Iran-Contra reinforced the commissioners'
feelings that the inquiry needed to be more than an academic exercise.[50] As
a result, the board plunged directly into the labyrinth of secret administration dealings that literally spanned the globe.[51]

The Investigation Begins

From the outset the commission was hindered by a lack of documentary
evidence about the NSC's role in the scandal. Cooperation from executive
agencies was not always forthcoming. For example, Tower knew that the
FBI had already launched a criminal investigation into the matter. He
phoned FBI Director William Webster on 5 December to request access to
relevant files in order to "avoid having the board duplicating the investigative effort of the FBI."[52] But because the files pertained to an ongoing
investigation, Webster declined to cooperate.

Deprived of this material, the commission was forced to place unusually heavy emphasis on personal interviews. Fifty-three individuals appeared
before the board to offer their recollection of related events or to shed light
on the dynamics of the NSC as an advisory mechanism. The list included a
who's who of key decisionmakers from recent administrations, including
four presidents, three vice presidents, and every living individual who had
served as secretary of state or defense or as national security advisor.
Former directors of the CIA and members of the Joint Chiefs of Staff also
participated. Most of the interviews were conducted in Washington, though
the commission did travel to Paris in late January to meet with Adnan
Khashoggi, a Saudi Arabian businessman, and Manucher Ghorbanifar, an
Iranian arms dealer with close ties to Israeli intelligence.

Despite the impressive list of interviews compiled by the commission,
the panel had no legal authority to summon witnesses or take sworn testimony. The administration could have asked Congress to grant the board
this power, but no such action was taken. Several commission insiders
argued this was an appropriate limitation given their mandate to conduct a
policy review. In their view, such a move would have diverted the board's
attention from its primary task of conducting a policy review. "With subpoena power," said one staffer, "everyone shows up with their attorneys in
tow, and that would have made the proceedings unnecessarily adversarial."[53]

Still, the inability to issue subpoenas meant that persons called upon to
testify could refuse without penalty. Six individuals did just that, a list that

included Poindexter, North, and retired Air Force Maj. Gen. Richard Secord.[54] Because Poindexter and North were still on active duty in the armed forces at the time of the inquiry, Tower wrote to President Reagan asking that he use his authority as commander in chief to order the two men to cooperate.

The request caught the White House by surprise. Several of Reagan's top aides were reported to be angry that the commission had involved the president in the controversy.[55] Political sensitivities aside, the president's legal advisers were also concerned by the constitutionality of the request. White House counsel Peter Wallison sought a legal opinion from the DOD. Pentagon counsel H. Lawrence Garrett wrote to Wallison on 5 February 1987 that such an order would violate North and Poindexter's Fifth Amendment rights unless accompanied by a grant of testimonial immunity. He argued that even with such a provision, the president's order would set "an extremely poor precedent" by placing the question of immunity in the hands of military commanders.[56] As a result Reagan refused the commission's request. Wallison wrote to Tower on 6 February to explain that the right of North and Poindexter to remain silent "must be respected even when its assertion unduly hinders the disclosure process the President himself has set in motion."[57]

Even though Wallison's letter settled the issue as a legal matter, Tower felt that the White House had misinterpreted the commission's intent. He revisited the issue the following summer as he watched the congressional select committees grapple with the same constitutional questions.

> If those committees want to get maximum benefit from [North and Poindexter's] testimony, they are going to have to grant them some immunity. In fact, that is what we sought when we requested that the president, as commander-in-chief, order them to appear. In our legal view, that would have been tantamount to granting them use immunity for anything they said to us. The White House legal advisers, however, came up with the wrong conclusion.[58]

The absence of North and Poindexter deprived the commission of vital information. Consequently, the commission was forced to rely more heavily on those NSC participants who were willing to cooperate.

Tower hit a similar roadblock with Lawrence E. Walsh. A former federal district court judge with a distinguished resume, Walsh had been operating as independent counsel in the Iran-Contra investigation since 19 December of the previous year. His initial meeting with Tower got off to a bad start when the chairman kept Walsh waiting in a cold lobby for a half-hour. Once under way, Tower wasted no time in asking Walsh to issue proxy subpoenas to aid in the board's investigation. "He wanted us to use our power ... to get information for him so that he could publish the information in his report," Walsh recalled. But Walsh was not inclined to function as a glorified research assistant. He deemed the request "contrary to the law" and rejected it out of hand.[59]

The McFarlane Interviews

The most forthcoming witness to appear before the board was Robert McFarlane.[60] As national security advisor from October 1983 to December 1985, McFarlane had been at the center of the Iran initiative from the beginning. His testimony helped the commission make sense of a complex policy that had undergone a number of transformations in its fifteen-month history. In his first interview with the board on 11 December 1986, McFarlane told the commissioners of the crucial role played by Israeli intermediaries in establishing contact between the administration and Iran. Tower later deemed this information "invaluable ... he pointed the board in the right direction."[61]

Significantly, McFarlane also indicated that President Reagan had played an important role in shaping the initiative, a role that included granting prior approval for the initial arms shipments that took place in the fall of 1985. The legal ramifications of this were enormous, for the president did not sign an intelligence directive authorizing the arms transfers until January 1986. McFarlane's willingness to speak freely was driven in part by anger; he believed that he was being set up to take the fall for a president who "lacked the moral conviction and intellectual courage to stand up in our defense and in defense of his policy."[62] He also suspected that the White House staff had orchestrated a plan to portray the scandal as the product of rogue NSC elements:

> I was willing to take the responsibility for having initiated the talks with Iran, but not against the backdrop of utter and official White House silence and disapproval.... Everyone in the White House national security circle ... had known about and supported, or acquiesced to, the Iran opening, but now chose to sit sphinx-like in the face of the media onslaught.[63]

Scowcroft also sensed that an effort was under way to shift blame away from the president. He contacted McFarlane in the middle of November—before the commission was appointed—to issue a blunt warning: "Regan is hanging you out to dry."[64] On 21 February, McFarlane again voiced his feelings regarding the president's role in shaping the decisionmaking environment that led to the Iran-Contra situation.

> It has been, I think, misleading, at least, and wrong, at worst, for me to overly gild the President's motives for his decision in this, to portray them as mostly directed toward political outcomes. The President acknowledged those and recognized that those were clearly important. However ... it is very clear that his concerns here were for the return of the hostages.[65]

McFarlane's openness irritated Regan, who was determined to keep the controversy as far away from the White House as possible. But in reality, the Tower Board's inquiry only exacerbated the deep personal feud that already existed between the two men. The dispute had a long history, dating back to Regan's appointment as chief of staff in January 1985. McFarlane later cited his "fractious" relationship with Regan as a key reason behind his decision to resign as national security advisor later that year.[66]

Regan appeared before the commission on 7 January to refute McFarlane's charge that the president had been "four-square behind" the Iranian initiative. Far from authorizing the policy, he recalled, the president had been "upset" to discover that US arms had been shipped to Iran.[67] Regan also felt that McFarlane should bear more of the responsibility for the Iran-Contra mess. "When you give lousy advice," he noted, "you get lousy results."[68]

Regan's testimony aside, however, McFarlane already bore a deep sense of guilt for his role in the scandal. His sense of failure almost led to tragedy: on 9 February, the day before he was scheduled to appear before the board for his second interview, he attempted to commit suicide by taking an overdose of Valium at his home outside Washington. Although he survived, McFarlane spent the next ten days at Bethesda Naval Hospital. The attempt deeply affected the commission's members and staff, many of whom were close personal acquaintances of McFarlane. Tower and Muskie knew him from their days in the Senate, where he had served with (commission director) Rhett Dawson on the staff of the Armed Services Committee. Several members of the board's legal staff had also worked with McFarlane at the NSC under Nixon and Ford. But none was as close to McFarlane as Brent Scowcroft.

> Brent was one of my oldest friends, a colleague with whom I had shared my professional life in public service for almost 20 years, and he was close to my family and children. In many senses, he had been almost like a father to me since I first went to work for him and Kissinger during the Nixon administration.... And I know Brent had come to trust me absolutely.[69]

The bond between the two men survived the Tower Commission's probe. McFarlane even called Scowcroft on one occasion—presumably as a friend and not as a material witness—to find out what Reagan had told the commission about the arms sales.[70]

The Reagan Interviews

In a strange turn of events, McFarlane's charge that the White House had been deeply involved in the Iran initiative received support from an unlikely source—President Reagan. The commission interviewed the president twice, first on 26 January 1987 and again on 11 February 1987. This was something of a coup for the board, since it marked the first time that Reagan had agreed to offer his own recollection of events before an investigating body. Tower led the questioning on both occasions, given his "experience with the president's tendency to ramble on and tell stories."[71]

During the first interview, Reagan stunned the board members by stating unequivocally that he had personally approved the initial shipment of US arms to Iran in August 1985. A staff member recalled the scene that followed: "I was there when they returned to the office. Their faces were ashen. They were absolutely flattened ... the president had said he had authorized it and would do it again. They sat around talking and worrying about the Twenty-Fifth Amendment to the U.S. Constitution."[72]

The president's frank admission also alarmed those in the White House who were seeking to distance him from the controversy. Peter Wallison had expected the president to deny responsibility for the 1985 shipments. Four days after the commission's visit, he joined Regan in an attempt to convince the president that he had been mistaken in his testimony before the board. Reagan seemed genuinely confused regarding the entire chain of events and eventually arrived at the position that he had not, in fact, authorized the arms transfer in advance.

Wallison set up another meeting with the commission to give the president an opportunity to clarify his remarks. During the second interview on 11 February Reagan stunned the board once again. This time he stated emphatically that he had *not* granted prior authorization for the arms transfers—a complete reversal of his previous testimony. Tower recalled that the president became uncomfortable when pressed for details. "While starting to repeat his previous answer, he stood up and went over to his desk. He picked up a sheet of paper and, as I remember his words, said to the board, 'This is what I am supposed to say,' and proceeded to read us an answer prepared by Peter Wallison, the White House counsel."[73]

Sitting in on the interview, Wallison was embarrassed to hear Reagan reading the memo in the second person. He felt such a "weak performance" might lead the commission to conclude that White House aides were seeking to protect themselves by altering the president's testimony.[74]

As it turned out, that was exactly what the commission believed.[75] Tower felt the second interview

> bore all the earmarks of a deliberate effort to conceal White House Chief of Staff Donald Regan's involvement in the Iran-Contra affair. By convincing the president that he, the president, had not authorized the arms shipment, Regan was buttressing his own contention that he had been completely unaware of the transaction despite a reputation for tightly controlling the chain of command within the White House staff.[76]

Other commission insiders shared these concerns. One staffer came away wondering if "Wallison was more loyal to Regan than to Reagan."[77] The president's reversal on the question was serious enough to catch the attention of other investigators. Even after the close of the board's inquiry, Walsh considered pursuing the issue as a legal matter. He noted that, despite the fact the board had no subpoena power, there *were* grounds for penalizing those who made false statements before the commission.[78]

Political Pressure

Inside the White House, Reagan's lieutenants were aware that the second interview was the source of considerable skepticism among the commissioners. Wallison met with Tower Board staffers on 14 February to discuss the president's testimony. Five days later, David Abshire phoned Tower to see if the commission would like to pursue a third interview with Reagan to clear the air. But the chairman feared what surprises a third interview might yield. Instead he requested that the president write to the commission if he wished to offer additional information or clarification.[79]

In a letter sent to the commission soon after, Reagan explained contritely that he had "let himself be influenced by others' recollections" in preparing his testimony. The "simple truth," he wrote, was that he could not recall whether or not he had authorized the Israeli transfer of arms in advance.[80]

By this time the board members were beginning to question the president's competence. Tower later wrote that Reagan was "probably the most naive man who ever served as president of the United States."[81] Muskie was even more direct in his assessment: "We were appalled by the absence of the kind of alertness and vigilance to his job and to these policies that one expects of a president.... We do not regard him as a mental case. But we do regard him as a president who didn't do his job."[82]

Of more immediate concern, Reagan's letter meant that the board now had three conflicting pieces of testimony regarding the president's involvement at the beginning of the Iran initiative: (1) that he had approved the initial arms deal in advance; (2) that he had not approved the deal in advance; and (3) that he could not recall what action he had taken.

The interviews with the president also generated behind-the-scenes pressure on the commission. Some White House officials took the risky step of contacting Tower directly to ask that the board ignore Reagan's initial declaration that he had approved of the first arms shipment. As time wore on, the lobbying effort intensified. A commission insider recalled:

There were clearly a number of contacts made to Senator Tower that pointed out to him the various implications of what he was doing and how important it was … politically and personally. I can remember being in his office a couple of times when he got these calls … it was clear what they were saying. Then he'd hang up the phone and say "they're at it again" and joke that he would hate to have to take more than three or four of these things a day.[83]

To his credit, Tower fended off these attempts to interfere with the investigation. He apparently bore the burden in silence; Commissioner Muskie was completely unaware of the White House effort.[84] In its final report, the board recounted Reagan's change of testimony in some detail.[85]

Tower's leadership on other issues was similarly impressive. Every individual who served on the panel—Democrat or Republican, commissioner or staff officer—credited the Texan with ensuring the investigation would not become politicized. General Counsel Clark McFadden admitted that he went into the investigation concerned by Tower's reputation as one "highly attuned to political sensitivities." But his fears were allayed. McFadden found Tower a highly capable leader who insisted on an "absolutely straight down the line, on the merits" investigation.[86]

Executive Director Dawson recalled a telling incident that occurred immediately after the board's first interview with the president. As the group left the White House, Muskie, the board's lone Democrat, turned to Tower and congratulated him for being "very forceful and persistent" in his questioning of Reagan.[87] This was high praise coming from one who had been initially concerned that the chairman's partisan loyalties would preclude a thorough investigation.

A Last-Minute Discovery

Tower later recalled that a "bleakness" settled over the board in the wake of its interviews with Reagan. The president's changing testimony created obvious difficulties for a board that owed its very existence to the man who was the source of so much suspicion and confusion. Unbeknown to the board members, however, the key turning point of the investigation was just around the corner.

On 11 February, Kenneth Krieg, a Pentagon analyst assigned to work on the commission's staff, informed Tower that he had discovered a wealth of computer files on NSC activity during the period of the arms shipments to Iran and the contra resupply effort.[88] The files were part of an internal communications network known as Professional Office System (PROFS) software. An early form of e-mail, the PROFS network was used as a means of sending private communications between top NSC officials. The individuals using the system assumed that messages saved to memory were well protected from outside scrutiny and could be deleted on command.

They were wrong. White House technicians routinely copied saved materials onto the main White House computer to safeguard important files. The FBI was aware of this and had already tried, unsuccessfully, to access the saved messages.[89] Krieg was highly skilled at manipulating the system, however, and was able to deliver where the bureau had failed.

The recovered PROFS notes, assembled into a stack almost 4 feet high, painted a damning picture of NSC involvement in the events of Iran-Contra. Oliver North had made particularly heavy use of the computer system. The resulting paper trail erased any lingering doubts regarding his central role in shaping the Iran initiative. To a lesser degree the notes also incriminated McFarlane and Poindexter. This was the proof the commission so desperately needed. It corroborated much of McFarlane's testimony and made North and Poindexter's refusal to testify less consequential. Tower later compared the impact of the discovery to "switching on a bright overhead light" in a darkened room.[90] As testimony to the importance of the breakthrough, both the congressional investigators and the independent counsel made heavy use of the PROFS evidence in their own reports.

The ordeal of processing the new material also placed new demands on the commission's small staff. Unable to meet its original sixty-day deadline, the board had already requested and received a three-week extension to complete its probe. But Krieg's discovery meant that more time was needed. At Tower's urging, the White House added an additional week to the commission's life, with the stipulation that no further extensions would be granted. Congress was increasing the pace of its own investigation, and the White House risked losing the political initiative unless it soon produced its own set of findings on the scandal.

The Final Report

The commission's already hectic pace increased as the 26 February deadline neared. Eighteen-hour days became the norm as staffers worked to assemble the evidence in preparation for the final report. But unlike many blue-ribbon panels, the commissioners themselves also played an active role in overseeing the process. The basic analysis was accomplished through a three-way division of labor: a legal analysis, headed by Muskie, to determine what laws might have been broken; an organizational analysis, headed by Scowcroft, of the NSC's role and performance; and a political analysis, headed by Tower, that focused on the "ideas that motivated the participants."[91]

Two members of the commission's legal staff, Stephen Hadley and Nicholas Rostow, were selected to draft the report. Hadley (a future national security advisor under President George W. Bush) had first worked on the NSC with Scowcroft during the Ford administration. He was given responsibility for the first portion of the report that included a general overview of the issue and the board's recommendations. Rostow, on loan from the State Department, wrote the narrative of Iran-Contra that took up two-thirds of the final report. Tower recalled that both men "spent weeks chained to word processors."[92] But the commissioners themselves remained active even as the drafting process got under way. "It was their report," Hadley recalled, "they had put a lot of time in on it, they had mastered the details, they had signed off on every word." Rostow agreed that the commissioners treated the task "exceedingly seriously ... they knew their briefs."[93]

The finished report, classified as top secret, was almost 500 pages long. As a condition of its release, it was forwarded to an interagency declassification board assembled for the express purpose of reviewing the text for sensitive materials. The commission members, however, were not passive players in this process. They threatened at one point to delay release of the final report if too much material was deleted.[94] In the end only minor changes were made. Some administration insiders were dismayed by the amount of material made public. Michael Ledeen charged that the commission's report was the "major hemorrhage" of secret documents in the entire Iran-Contra drama.[95] Richard Secord also found the board's disclosures "irresponsible."[96]

On the morning of 26 February the board members met privately with the president to discuss their findings. This was the only advance notice given to Reagan regarding the contents of the commission's report. Chief of Staff Regan felt such an arrangement was "unfair and demeaning to the President." He had argued earlier that Reagan should be given time to read the report before it was made public.[97] But David Abshire, the presidential aide serving as liaison with the commission, feared that any delay would lead to charges of a coverup. He refused to raise the issue with Tower.

Immediately after leaving the White House, the board assembled for a news conference to discuss its report. The electronic media gave the report full coverage. All the major networks interrupted their regularly scheduled programming to televise the conference.[98] Reagan opened the session by promising to read the report carefully and do "whatever is necessary" to put the Iran-Contra affair behind him. The commissioners were then given the opportunity to make general comments before the questioning began, and all three stressed the collaborative nature of the inquiry and noted that the report was unanimously endorsed. Scowcroft made the case that the panel had operated "not in a bipartisan but a nonpartisan fashion ... we had a great many arguments about semantics, but I recall not a single one about substance."[99]

The report was direct in its criticism of the administration. Part IV of the document, "What Was Wrong," noted that problems existed in both the decisionmaking process as well as in the process of policy implementation. On the key question of administration dealings with Iran, the board noted that such activity could not be reconciled with the administration's publicly stated position of not dealing with terrorists. It rejected the argument that the initiative was primarily designed to create a strategic opening to Iranian moderates. "The whole arrangement," the commission concluded, "was premised on Iran's ability to secure [the hostages'] release."[100]

The report had considerably less to say about the diversion of profits from the arms sales to the contras. This was, in part, a reflection of the fact that full details concerning that portion of the scandal were only beginning to emerge during the period of the board's inquiry. The commissioners knew that North had told Attorney General Meese that millions in "residual funds" had been used to purchase supplies for the contras, but could find no evidence to indicate that the president knew of the diversion. In addition, much of the money was routed through Swiss bank accounts that could not be accessed by the panel's investigative staff. For these reasons, the board simply noted that there was "considerable evidence" that such a diversion had occurred.[101]

Much of the board's criticism fell at the feet of the NSC staff. The report took a dim view of the legal argument—consistently forwarded by key administration figures—that the staff's unique status rendered it exempt from congressional restrictions, such as the Boland amendments, which applied to other executive agencies. Such reasoning "could only touch off a firestorm in the Congress and threaten the Administration's whole policy."[102] The board was especially critical of Lt. Col. North. It found that in his zeal to maintain operational control of the Iranian initiative, he had misrepresented his access to the president and ignored the jurisdiction of the State and Defense departments. As a result, the initiative was pursued without the benefit of serious review. Consequences and alternatives were not discussed, and procedures for policy assessment were overlooked. The proper environment for a "presidential judgment" was not created.[103]

Other administration figures were also singled out for criticism. Secretaries Weinberger and Schultz were reproached for distancing themselves from a policy they questioned. Chief of Staff Regan was cited for his role in managing the White House response to the disclosures of November 1986. Noting that Regan exercised great control over the president's staff, the commission concluded that he "must bear primary responsibility for the chaos that descended upon the White House" in the days following publication of the *Al Shiraa* story.[104]

But the commission also concluded that, as an advisory mechanism, the National Security Council system was not irreparably flawed. It detailed the advantages of having such an advisory group divorced from bureaucratic responsibility for implementation. It recommended that no changes be made to the "structure and operation" of the NSC system. The board also argued against Senate confirmation for the national security advisor, noting that "confirmation would tend to institutionalize" differences between the NSA and the president's other foreign policy advisers.[105] A move in that direction, the commission warned, might tempt the president to turn to an even more informal arrangement for the development of national security policy.

Perhaps most important, the board also found reason to fault President Reagan's performance. In language that has since become famous, the report argued that "the NSC system will not work unless the President makes it work."[106] It went on to suggest that Reagan had not taken the proper measures to ensure that review procedures were implemented. Moreover, by emphasizing the hostages' fate to the exclusion of other policy goals, he had given the NSC staff a green light to proceed with its secret dealings.

Public reaction to the report was generally favorable. A *Wall Street Journal* editorial praised the "good, common sense expressed by the members of the Tower Commission."[107] The *New York Times* judged the commission's conclusions to be "blunt, fair, and humiliating."[108] Senate minority leader Dole conceded that the report demonstrated beyond doubt that "blunders were made of colossal proportions."[109] Conservative Congressman Newt Gingrich feared that the scandal had left an indelible imprint on the president. "He will never again," predicted Gingrich, "be the Reagan that he was before he blew it."[110]

Publicly, Reagan stood behind the Tower Report. White House spokesman Marlin Fitzwater described the president as "rightfully angry at the mismanagement" described by the commission. Behind the scenes, however, the president was irritated by the board's condemnation of his detached management style. Press coverage only heightened his sensitivity. A page one headline in the 27 February *New York Times* offered a blunt characterization: "Tower Panel Portrays the President as Remote and Confused Man."[111]

The morning after the release of the report, Reagan announced to several advisers that he planned to tell the nation once again that there had been no effort on the part of the administration to swap arms for hostages. Regan, Tower, and Vice President Bush rushed to prevent this from happening. They gently dissuaded Reagan from creating further embarrassment by pointing out that such a claim could not be sustained in the wake of the commission's report. There is also reason to believe that the president did not read the report closely. During the trial of John Poindexter in February

1990—three years after the issuance of the commission's report—Reagan claimed to be unaware that the board had found evidence of a diversion of funds to the contras.[112]

Others in the administration were also unhappy with the board's portrayal of their actions. Regan, the man most responsible for the commission's creation, was more rankled than most. He charged that the board had failed to interview enough White House personnel to understand his conduct as chief of staff. Schultz and Weinberger used their testimony before the congressional select committees to respond to the charge that they had distanced themselves from an unwise policy. Both men told investigators that they had spoken out repeatedly and forcefully against the Iranian initiative. Oliver North simply referred reporters to chapter five of the Gospel of Matthew: "Blessed are they which are persecuted for righteousness' sake."[113]

But the sharpest, and most enduring, criticism of the Tower Commission's work came from those who agreed with Richard Secord that the commission's "real agenda seemed to be fending off criticism of President Reagan."[114] Michael Ledeen expanded on the point:

> The major error in the Tower Commission analysis lies in the president's role. Far from being a detached observer, or a laid-back overseer of the foreign policy process, the president played a very active role at the beginning of Iran-Contra, and intervened as late as the winter of 1985-86 to insist, over the objections of his secretaries of State and Defense, that the Iran initiative continue. The president wanted the hostages out, and wanted the Contras on the battlefield, and was prepared to run substantial risks in order to achieve those ends.... The basic policies were those the president strongly desired, and they were put into effect because of his formal approval.[115]

An editorial in *The Nation* echoed the sentiment, blasting the "Reaganite" members of the board for ignoring evidence that pointed to a more direct and persistent presidential role in the affair.[116] Senator Sam Nunn agreed, stating that he was "not sure we can construct any group of people down there that can make up and compensate totally for that lack of presidential involvement in major matters."[117]

Aftermath

In the short term, the Tower report did little to bolster Reagan's image with the American people. A poll taken the day after the report's release showed that his approval rating had fallen another five percentage points to stand at 42 percent, his poorest rating since the economic downturn of 1982–1983. Almost half the respondents believed the president had lied about his own involvement in the scandal.[118]

Reagan decided to take his case directly to the American people in an effort to bring a close to the episode. In a televised address on 4 March 1987 he admitted that it was "pretty hard to find any good news in the board's report." The commission's findings, he said, had convinced him that the opening to Iran had indeed become little more than an arms-for-hostages swap. Reagan expressed his anger at the "freelancing" that had taken place by certain members of the NSC staff but acknowledged that he bore responsibility for the acts since they "happened on my watch."

The president stated explicitly that he endorsed each of the commission's recommendations and pledged that, in the future, a more concerted effort would be made to consult with Congress on sensitive national security issues. He also announced two changes designed to guard against similar policy failures. First, he issued a directive prohibiting the NSC staff from undertaking covert operations. Second, he created the post of NSC legal adviser to "assure a greater sensitivity to matters of law." In closing, he promised to learn from his mistakes and construct a more open decision-making environment.[119]

Reagan's speech, however, came up short in the judgment of at least one inside observer. Lieutenant General Colin Powell, an aide at the NSC, had worked on an earlier draft of the address. He was dismayed to hear key lines omitted that would have exonerated Schultz and Weinberger and made it clear that the president pursued the arms-for-hostages scheme over their objections.[120]

The report led to a significant shake-up in administration personnel. Former senator Howard Baker was brought in to replace Regan as White House chief of staff. Momentum had been building for Regan's removal for some time, due in no small part to his bitter feud with first lady Nancy Reagan. Mrs. Reagan was alarmed by the political fallout from the scandal and was convinced that her husband had been poorly served by his closest advisers.[121] The president's national security team was also significantly revamped. North and Poindexter were already gone, having been removed from their NSC posts soon after the scandal broke. Frank Carlucci, a former deputy director of intelligence, moved in as the new national security advisor. FBI director William Webster was transferred to head the CIA, a post that had been vacant since the resignation of William Casey on 2 February.[122]

Of the three members of the Iran-Contra panel, Tower remained the most visible in the wake of the commission's inquiry. In April 1987 he testified before the House Armed Services Committee regarding the review board's recommendations. He urged the lawmakers not to make substantial changes in the 1947 National Security Act and spoke against Senate confirmation for the national security advisor. He was successful on both counts.

On 11 August, one week after the close of congressional hearings on the subject, Tower went public with criticism of the select committee's conduct. He argued that by choosing to televise the proceedings, Congress had unwittingly provided Oliver North a stage on which to showcase the misty-eyed patriotism that endeared him to millions of citizens. But the congressional investigators were quick to respond that Tower's own investigation had been far from complete. Representative Jack Brooks, a Texas Democrat, suggested that Tower's partisan connections had colored his view of the hearings. "As a lifetime Republican, you can understand where John Tower is coming from.... The congressional committees fleshed out what the Tower Commission could only outline. The hearings focused the American people's attention on how fragile our constitutional system can be and how it can be abused."[123]

Tower's subsequent political activity took part on behalf of Vice President Bush, who had emerged unscathed from the board's investigation. In January 1988, less than a year after the close of the commission's investigation, Bush asked Tower to join his presidential campaign as Southern regional cochairman. Tower denied any connection between this appointment and his service on the Iran-Contra board.[124] Once elected, Bush nominated Tower to serve as secretary of defense. When that effort failed, Bush appointed Tower to chair the President's Foreign Intelligence Advisory Board, a six-member group designed to help the president oversee sensitive intelligence activities.[125] He served in that capacity until his death in a plane crash in April 1991.

Evaluation

The appointment of the Special Review Board stands as a textbook example of the use of an ad hoc commission to try to defuse an explosive political issue. Created amid chaos in the White House, the commission bought invaluable time for administration officials to gather their collective wits before responding to the charges at hand. Dennis Thomas, the presidential assistant who conceived the commission, elaborated on this function:

> It was a blunt instrument that was necessary at the time ... it was an activity that was essential to seeing President Reagan through a very difficult time and allowed there to be some passage of time to put a little more perspective on what happened. Those were critical months, and in that sense the commission will be found to have served a very good purpose.[126]

Beyond this, however, any objective assessment of the Tower Commission must deal with a pivotal question. Did the board protect President Reagan from the heat of the Iran-Contra scandal? The debate surrounding this question centers on two key points: (1) the commission's portrayal of Reagan as a detached leader only vaguely familiar with the details of the arms sales to Iran; and (2) the commission's decision to focus heavily on the Iran initiative at the expense of the contra resupply effort.

The board's report offered a sympathetic evaluation of Reagan's activity in the Iran initiative, especially when compared with the findings of the congressional select committees and the independent counsel. Broadly put, the commission faulted Reagan for sins of omission, the failure to oversee the activities of his subordinates, while the later investigators found sins of commission, which included the more damning charge that Reagan had actively presided over an illegal and politically unsound policy.

But those who worked on the commission refused to concede that they had accorded the president special treatment. "If we had had evidence that Ronald Reagan had orchestrated the whole thing, it would have come out," a staffer argued, "but we did not."[127] Muskie agreed, pointing out that the board's ability to gain a full appreciation of the decisionmaking process was hampered by its small investigative staff, the constant and severe time pressures, and the lack of subpoena power.[128]

Yet no individual's testimony figured so prominently in the report as that of Robert McFarlane. And it was McFarlane who, more than any other witness, made it clear that the president had played an active role in the decision to pursue the opening with Iran. Consequently, the board's failure to address his claims more fully raises important questions about the overall tenor of the report.

Additional questions stem from the board's treatment of the diversion of funds to the contras. That portion of the scandal was potentially the most damaging for the president. The resupply effort simply could not be reconciled with existing congressional enactments that prohibited such assistance, yet only thirty pages of the board's report were devoted to the subject. The Iran initiative, though legally questionable in its own right, was less troubling since Reagan could argue that his own intelligence "findings" of 1985–1986 permitted administration officials to act with some discretion under the terms of the 1974 Hughes-Ryan Amendment.[129] But the language of the Boland amendments offered no comparable loophole. And that raised serious questions—even raising the issue of impeachment—regarding the president's attention to the rule of law.

But details concerning the contra angle were only beginning to emerge during the period of the board's inquiry. The NSC officials most directly involved in the resupply effort, North and Poindexter, refused to testify before the commission. The PROFS notes that provided the necessary evidence of their dealings were discovered only at the close of the investigation as the members struggled to complete the final report. In addition, many of the diverted funds were routed through Swiss bank accounts that could not be examined by the panel's investigative staff. For these reasons, the board's tentative conclusion that there was "considerable evidence" of a diversion of funds should not be judged too harshly.

In the final analysis, the case of the Tower Commission provides a different perspective on the concept of damage control. Reagan administration officials knew that external inquiries into the Iran-Contra affair were unavoidable. What they sought with the blue-ribbon panel, then, was not preemption of other actors but a more sympathetic inquiry. They needed an alternative story line that would put the president's conduct in a more favorable light. When completed, the board's findings were not flattering to Reagan. They were, however, less politically damning than the judgment rendered by Congress and the independent counsel.

Notes

1. Richard J. Meislin, "President Invites Inquiry Counsel; Poll Rating Dives," *New York Times*, 2 December 1986, p 1.

2. In February 1981, Reagan's job approval rating stood at 55 percent. It would crest at 68 percent the following May. George C. Edwards and Alec M. Gallup, *Presidential Approval: A Sourcebook* (Baltimore: Johns Hopkins Press, 1990), p. 132.

3. For an account of Reagan's activity during November-December 1986, see chapters 23 ("Panic") and 24 ("The Bitter End") of Theodore Draper, *A Very Thin Line: The Iran-Contra Affairs* (New York: Hill and Wang, 1991).

4. The *Al-Shiraa* story was not entirely accurate. It reported that McFarlane's trip had taken place in September, not May as was actually the case. Moreover, it now appears that the story was deliberately leaked by the Iranian opposition in an effort to embarrass both the Khomeini government and the Reagan administration. Draper, *A Very Thin Line*, pp. 452–457.

5. Robert C. McFarlane, *Special Trust* (New York: Cadell and Davies, 1994), p. 89.

6. John Poindexter, Cable to George Schultz, "U.S. Policy on Iran," 5 November 1986, cited in Peter Kornbluh and Malcolm Byrne, eds., *The Iran-Contra Scandal: The Declassified History* (New York: The New Press, 1993), p. 312.

7. Ibid., 404.

8. CIA Director William Casey also realized the futility of trying to contain the story. He told North that the press revelations represented "the end" of the Iranian initiative. Draper, *A Very Thin Line*, p. 458.

9. Donald Regan recorded the president's comments at the 10 November meeting. His notes were made public during his testimony before the congressional select committees the following summer. See US, Congress, *Joint Hearings Before the House Select Committee to Investigate Covert Arms Transactions with Iran and the Senate Select Committee on Secret Military Assistance to Iran and the Nicaraguan Opposition*, 100th Congress, 1st session, Volume 100-10, p. 764.

10. "Address to the Nation on the Iran Arms and Contra Aid Controversy," 13 November 1986, *Public Papers of the Presidents,* Ronald Reagan, 1986 (Washington, DC: Government Printing Office, 1987), pp. 1,546–1,548.

11. McFarlane, *Special Trust*, p. 95.

12. Draper, *A Very Thin Line*, p. 476.

13. Ibid., 474.

14. Regan testimony to grand jury, 26 February 1988, in Lawrence E. Walsh, *Iran-Contra: The Final Report*, Times Books Edition (New York: Times Books, 1994), p. 508.

15. Text of Reagan's November 19 Press Conference, cited in Patricia Ann O'Connor, ed., *The Iran-Contra Puzzle* (Washington, DC: Congressional Quarterly, Inc., 1987), p. D-3. The Arms Export Control Act was amended in August 1986 to prohibit the transfer of weapons to countries identified with support for international terrorism. Iran had been so designated by the State Department in January 1984.

16. Ibid., 19.

17. Meislin, "President Invites Inquiry Counsel."

18. Donald T. Regan, *For the Record: From Wall Street to Washington* (New York: Harcourt Brace Jovanovich, 1988), p. 38.

19. Ronald Reagan, *An American Life* (New York: Simon and Schuster, 1990), p. 530.

20. Draper, *A Very Thin Line*, p. 529.

21. "Comments by Meese," *New York Times*, 26 November 1986, pp. A10-A11.

22. Ibid.

23. R. W. Apple Jr., "A Presidency Damaged," *New York Times*, 26 November 1986, p. 1.

24. Telephone interview with Dennis Thomas, 14 December 1994.

25. Regan, *For the Record,* p. 44. The National Security Planning Group included the statutory members of the NSC but few of the other officials that routinely sat in on NSC meetings. In its final report, the Tower Commission noted that President Reagan made increasingly heavy use of the NSPG because of its smaller size. See *Report of the President's Special Review Board* (Washington, DC: U.S. Government Printing Office, 1987), p. II-5.

26. Regan recalls that Meese advocated an independent counsel that, unlike a special counsel, would operate outside the Justice Department. Congressional investigators were unable to verify this information, however, and concluded that most discussion centered on appointment of a special counsel. See US Congress, *Report of the Congressional Committees Investigating the Iran-Contra Affair with Supplemental, Minority, and Additional Views, November 1987* (Washington, DC: Government Printing Office, 1987), p. 319.

27. *The Fairfax Journal*, 28 November 1986, in Folder 6–Press Clippings, Accn. 92-08-20, Box 25, Papers of John G. Tower, Southwestern University, Georgetown, Texas (hereafter cited as JTP-Southwestern).

28. Memorandum from Regan, 24 November 1986, in US Congress, *Joint Hearings Before the House Select Committee to Investigate Covert Arms Transactions with Iran and the Senate Select Committee on Secret Military Assistance to Iran and the Nicaraguan Opposition,* 100th Congress, 1st session, Volume 100-10, p. 428.

29. Regan, *For the Record*, p. 39.

30. Files of M. Charles Hill, in Walsh, *Iran-Contra: The Final Report*, pp. 508–509.

31. Regan, *For the Record*, p. 44.

32. Regan felt that Democrats in Congress would "say we had selected a good person to represent that side." Regan Testimony, *Joint Hearings Before the Select Committees on Iran-Contra*, Volume 100-10, p. 80.

33. Only one other national security commission, the 1954 Doolittle Commission on covert operations, had fewer than five members.

34. Telephone interview with Thomas.

35. Regan, *For the Record*, p. 44.

36. Ibid., 45.

37. Telephone interview with Edmund Muskie, 14 February 1995.

38. The reference to Muskie appeared in an early draft of Tower's memoirs, which were published in 1991 as *Consequences: A Personal and Political Memoir* (Boston: Little, Brown and Company, 1991). The unedited remarks are taken from Folder Confirmation, Accn. 92-08-31, Box 34, JTP-Southwestern.

39. Executive Order 12575, 1 December 1986, *Public Papers of the Presidents*, Ronald Reagan, 1986, p. 1,592.

40. David Abshire, ed., *Triumphs and Tragedies of the Modern Presidency* (Westport, CT: Praeger Publishers, 2001), p. xiii.

41. Bernard Weinraub, "Muskie Opposes Haste," *New York Times*, 28 November 1986, p. 10.

42. The *Post* editorial appears in its entirety in Tower, *Consequences,* p. 272.

43. *Dallas Morning News*, 2 December 1986, in Folder 6–Press Clippings, Accn. 92-08-20, Box 25, JTP-Southwestern.

44. Jane Mayer and Doyle McManus, *Landslide: The Unmaking of the President, 1984–1988* (Boston: Houghton Mifflin Company, 1988), p. 360.

45. Bernard Weinraub, "Reagan Names Three to Examine National Security Council," *New York Times*, 27 November 1986, p. 1.

46. "Excerpts from Session with President's Panel," *New York Times*, 2 December 1986, p. A15.

47. Asked to compare the two commissions, Dawson responded that they were "totally different animals." He noted that the political pressure on the Tower Commission was more intense "by several orders of magnitude." Telephone interview, 13 October 1994.

48. Tower, *Consequences*, p. 275.

49. "Remarks at a Meeting with the President's Special Review Board," 1 December 1986, *Public Papers of the Presidents*, Ronald Reagan, 1986, p. 1,591.

50. Tower, *Consequences*, p. 274.

51. Each Tower Commission participant who agreed to be interviewed for this study defended the board's decision to focus heavily on Iran-Contra. To have done otherwise, they suggested, would have destroyed the board's credibility.

52. Talking Points for Telephone Call to FBI Director William Webster, Folder Memorandums to Commission/White House, Box 43, Accn. 92-08-31, JTP-Southwestern.

53. Confidential telephone interview.

54. The other individuals who refused to appear before the commission included two of North's assistants, Fawn Hall and Lt. Col. Robert Earl, and Albert Hakim, an Iranian-born businessman who worked with Secord to set up the arms sales to Iran.

55. *Washington Post*, 13 February 1987, p. 1.

56. Memo, Garrett to Wallison, 5 February 1987, in *Report of the President's Special Review Board*, p. G-7.

57. Letter, Wallison to Tower, 6 February 1987, *Report of the President's Special Review Board*, p. G-6.

58. Draft copy of Tower interview, Folder *Ripon Forum* Interview, Box 25, Accn. 92-08-20, JTP-Southwestern University.

59. Lawrence E. Walsh, *Firewall: The Iran-Contra Conspiracy and Cover-up* (New York: W. W. Norton and Company, 1997), pp. 55–56.

60. Tower, *Consequences*, p. 277.

61. Ibid.

62. McFarlane, *Special Trust*, p. 360.

63. Ibid., 91.

64. Ibid.

65. *Report of the President's Special Review Board*, p. D-5.

66. McFarlane, *Special Trust*, p. 328.

67. *Report of the President's Special Review Board*, p. III-7. Michael Ledeen, an NSC consultant involved in the Iranian initiative, agreed with Regan that the Tower Commission's reliance on McFarlane led to inconclusive and suspect findings. See Michael Ledeen, *Perilous Statecraft: An Insider's Account of the Iran-Contra Affair* (New York: Charles Scribner's Sons, 1988), p. 279.

68. Quoted in William S. Cohen and George J. Mitchell, *Men of Zeal* (New York: Viking Press, 1988), p. 233.

69. McFarlane, *Special Trust*, pp. 338–339.

70. Ibid., 339.

71. Tower, *Consequences*, p. 282.

72. Confidential telephone interview.

73. Tower, *Consequences*, p. 283.

74. Wallison diary, quoted in Walsh, *Iran-Contra: The Final Report*, p. 521.

75. In his final report, Independent Counsel Walsh revisited the issue. He charged that the White House had developed a strategy to make McFarlane, North, and Poindexter the "scapegoats whose sacrifice would protect the Reagan Administration in its final two years." See *Iran-Contra: The Final Report,* p. xv.

76. Tower, *Consequences*, p. 283.

77. Confidential telephone interview.

78. Walsh noted that, under federal statute, it is illegal to provide "material false statements to a department or agency of the United States in a matter within its own jurisdiction." See *Iran-Contra: The Final Report*, p. 469.

79. Wallison diary, in Walsh, *Iran-Contra: The Final Report*, p. 522.

80. *Report of the President's Special Review Board*, p. B-19.

81. Folder "Confirmation," Accn. 92-08-31, Box 34, JTP-Southwestern.

82. Muskie made this comment during an appearance on "Face the Nation," 1 March 1987. The quote is taken from O'Connor, *The Iran-Contra Puzzle*, p. 81.

83. Confidential telephone interview.

84. Telephone interview with Muskie.

85. *Report of the President's Special Review Board,* p. B-19.

86. Telephone interview with Clark McFadden, 9 March 1995.

87. Telephone interview with Rhett Dawson, 13 October 1994.

88. Krieg was no stranger to commission-based inquiries. He had worked, along with Rhett Dawson, on the 1985 Packard Commission on defense management procedures.

89. Telephone interview with Rhett Dawson, 13 October 1994.

90. Tower, *Consequences*, p. 285.

91. Ibid., 280.

92. Ibid., 281.

93. Telephone interview with Nicholas Rostow, 21 September 1994.

94. George J. Church, "Tower of Judgment," *Time* 129 (2 March 1987), p. 15.

95. Ledeen, *Perilous Statecraft*, p. 277.

96. Richard Secord and Jay Wurts, *Honored and Betrayed* (New York: John Wiley and Sons, Inc., 1992), p. 282.

97. Regan, *For the Record*, p. 360.

98. Peter J. Boyer, "How the Story of the Commission Report Played on the Networks," *New York Times,* 27 February 1987, p. 13.

99. "Excerpts from the Tower Commission's News Conference," *New York Times,* 27 February 1987, pp. 8–9.

100. *Report of the President's Special Review Board*, p. IV-2.

101. Ibid., III-19.

102. Ibid., IV-3.

103. Ibid., IV-4.

104. Ibid., IV-11.

105. Ibid., V-5.

106. Ibid., IV-10.

107. "The Tower Report," *Wall Street Journal*, 27 February 1987, p. 14.

108. Editorial, *New York Times,* 27 February 1987, p. 26.

109. O'Connor, *The Iran-Contra Puzzle*, p. 79.

110. R. W. Apple Jr., "At a Crossroads," *New York Times*, 27 February 1987, p. 1.

111. Steven V. Roberts, "Tower Panel Portrays the President as Remote and Confused Man," *New York Times*, 27 February 1987, p. 1.

112. Draper, *A Very Thin Line*, p. 571.

113. Ben Bradlee Jr., *Guts and Glory: The Rise and Fall of Oliver North* (New York: Donald I. Fine, Inc., 1988), p. 484.

114. Secord and Wurts, *Honored and Betrayed*, p. 337. See also Arthur L. Liman, *Lawyer: A Life of Counsel and Controversy* (New York: Public Affairs Books, 1998), pp. 306–307.

115. Ledeen, *Perilous Statecraft*, pp. 277–278.

116. Christopher Hitchens, "Minority Report," *Nation* 244 (14 March 1987), p. 314.

117. O'Connor, *The Iran-Contra Puzzle*, p. 78.

118. E. J. Dionne Jr. "Poll Shows Reagan Approval Rating at 4-Year Low," *New York Times,* 3 March 1987, p. 1.

119. "Address to the Nation on the Iran Arms and Contra Aid Controversy," 4 March 1987, *Public Papers of the Presidents*, Ronald Reagan, 1987, pp. 208–210.

120. Colin L. Powell, *My American Journey* (New York: Random House, 1995), pp. 336–337.

121. Draper, *A Very Thin Line*, pp. 536–537.

122. Casey died of cancer in May 1987, just before the start of congressional hearings into Iran-Contra.

123. Richard L. Berke, "Tower Says Hearings Hurt Congress," *New York Times,* 11 August 1987, p. 8.

124. *Atlanta Constitution*, 22 January 1988, in Folder 6–Press Clippings, Accn. 92-08-20, Box 25, JTP-Southwestern. The Tower Commission did not single out Bush for criticism in its report. At the time of its investigation, most of the board's interest in the vice president focused on his meeting with Israeli official Amiram Nir in Tel Aviv on 29 July 1986. Bush told the commission that their discussion focused largely on counterterrorism efforts, with little mention of "specifics related to arms going to the Iranians." However, notes taken at the meeting by Craig Fuller, Bush's chief of staff, told another story. Fuller's account, which appeared in the Tower Report, indicated that the arms sales were discussed in some detail. See *Report of the President's Special Review Board*, p. B-145.

125. The PFIAB varies in size and activity according to the president's wishes. For example, Carter abolished the board, while Reagan revived it and expanded its membership to twenty-one. See Pat M. Holt, *Secret Intelligence and Public Policy* (Washington, DC: Congressional Quarterly, 1995), pp. 203–205.

126. Telephone interview with Thomas.

127. Telephone interview with Rostow.

128. Telephone interview with Muskie.

129. The Hughes-Ryan Amendment to the 1961 Foreign Assistance Act directed the president to inform Congress of any new covert action, though no exact time limit was placed on the notification procedure. In his intelligence finding of 6 January 1986, Reagan determined that prior notice could jeopardize the Iran initiative and thus ordered the CIA to refrain from reporting the operation to Congress. See *Report of the President's Special Review Board*, p. B-60.

6

The Politics of Terror:
Tom Kean and the 9/11 Commission

I want a real investigation. I don't want lip service. I'm angry, and I'm not going away.
— Ellen Mariani, 9/11 widow

This was a commission unlike any other.
— Tom Kean on the 9/11 Investigation

At 8:46 on the morning of 11 September 2001, American Airlines Flight 11, a hijacked Boeing 767 with 233 souls aboard, slammed into the north tower of New York's famed World Trade Center complex. Twenty-two minutes later, United Airlines Flight 175 struck the south tower. Within the hour, two other planes would plunge to earth, one striking the outer ring of the Pentagon and the other crashing into a deserted field outside Shanksville, Pennsylvania. Thus began the war on terror, the focal point of the US national security effort in the early twenty-first century. But like other conflicts before it, both hot and cold, the war on terror turned out to be more than a military and foreign-affairs venture. It also affected domestic politics. Power began to flow to the incumbent president, George W. Bush, who used the new calculus to solidify his standing with the voters and enhance his position with Congress. In so doing he engineered his reelection in November 2004.

In this environment, blue-ribbon inquiry has returned to the center stage of US politics. A host of investigative and advisory commissions have been created to deal with national security concerns. Most were created in the wake of the attacks of 11 September and the subsequent war on terror.

One of the Bush-era panels stands out due to its marquee value and political significance. The 9/11 Commission, headed by Thomas Kean, must be considered one of the most important blue-ribbon inquiries of all time. Although not a "presidential" commission in the traditional sense, the panel's investigation, and indeed its very existence, was inextricably connected with the administration of George W. Bush. When other Bush-era panels are brought into the analytical mix, his presidency becomes an excellent tutorial on blue-ribbon politics in the national security arena. The work of the 9/11 Commission is the focus of this chapter.

Early Calls for an Investigation

Given the obvious comparison with Pearl Harbor, it was inevitable that the call would go out to create a special probe of the circumstances surrounding the attacks of 11 September. Most analysis to date has focused on the eventual creation of a blue-ribbon commission, the subsequent investigation, and the panel's findings as set forth in its final report of July 2004. Almost forgotten is the fact that it took well over a year to get an inquiry going. The reasons for that delay are rooted in partisan politics, squabbling among branches of the US government, and the idiosyncratic nature of the Bush administration.

The first discussion of a commission-based probe of 9/11 came just one day after the horrors in New York, Washington, and Pennsylvania. Robert Torricelli, a New Jersey Democrat, stepped to the floor of the US Senate on 12 September 2001 to urge a declaration of war against "a series of terrorist organizations." Then Torricelli turned his attention to the question of accountability.

> The American people have trusted this Government through our intelligence communities to defend our Nation and its people and our varied interests. This has not occurred. It is my belief that the President of the United States should form a board of general inquiry to review the actions of the U.S. intelligence community and the failures which led to this massive loss of life and compromise of national security.[1]

Two weeks later, Torricelli announced he would pursue the idea as far as needed: "If I have to return to this Chamber every day of every week of every month," he warned, "this Senate is going to vote for some board of inquiry."[2] Torricelli should have added "every year" to his threat, for the road to the 9/11 inquiry would take over fourteen months and would encompass seven separate proposals. Table 6.1 provides an overview of the various plans put forth for an inquiry into the terrorist attacks.

On 26 September 2001, the House Select Committee on Intelligence endorsed H.R. 2883, the Intelligence Authorization Act for 2002, and sent the bill to the full House for action. Embedded in the bill was section 306 to establish a "Commission on Preparedness and Performance of the Federal Government for the September 11 Acts of Terrorism."[3] That provision, which had already survived one internal challenge by Representative Ray Lahood (Republican-Illinois), was the brainchild of committee Democrats led by Representative Nancy Pelosi of California.[4] Pelosi envisioned a panel of ten members—four appointed by the president, with the

Table 6.1   9/11 Commission Proposals

Date of Introduction	Sponsor and Legislation	Name of Proposed Panel	Total Members / Presidential Appointments	Subpoena Power
09/26/01	Pelosi H.R. 2883	Commission on Preparedness and Performance of the Federal Government for the September 11 Acts of Terrorism.	10 / 4	Yes
10/05/01	Goss Amdt to H.R. 2883	Commission on National Security Readiness	8 / 2	No
12/18/01	Torricelli/Grassley S. 1837	Board of Inquiry into the September 11, 2001, Terrorist Attacks	12 / 4	Yes
12/20/01	McCain/Lieberman S. 1867	National Commission on Terrorist Attacks Upon the United States (1)	14 / 4	Yes
05/20/02	Roemer H.R. 4777	National Commission on Terrorist Attacks Upon the United States (2)	10 / 0	Yes
07/25/02	Roemer Amdt to H.R. 4628	National Commission on Terrorist Attacks Upon the United States (3)[a]	10 / 1	Yes
09/18/02	Shays H. Res 537	Presidential Commission on Terrorist Attacks Upon the United States[b]	N/A	N/A

Notes: a. Became Public Law No. 107-306 on 27 November 2002.
b. Resolution to encourage presidential action; no specification for membership or powers.

remaining six named by various congressional leaders. It was a strong commission, complete with subpoena power and the ability to grant immunity for testimony.

Once on the House floor, however, resistance began to build from Republicans concerned that the design of the commission was such that it would invite finger-pointing at administration officials. During debate on 5 October, Representative Porter Goss, a former clandestine-services officer in the CIA and member of the intelligence committee, won approval for an amendment that effectively neutered the commission. Goss's amendment replaced Pelosi's language with a "Commission on National Security Readiness," an eight-member group with the nebulous charge to "identify structural impediments to the effective collection, analysis, and sharing of information on national security threats, particularly terrorism." As approved, the panel would have eight members and would not be able to issue subpoenas. The weakness of Goss's commission was no accident. The Bush administration had already established its opposition to the idea of a blue-ribbon probe, and Goss began to emerge as the president's most loyal and effective enforcer on intelligence issues and related matters.

But even Goss's toothless proposal proved too much for the Senate. None of the upper chamber's versions of the bill included his commission, and House negotiators agreed to drop the provision altogether when the bill went to conference. Thus ended the first attempt to create a blue-ribbon panel to probe the 9/11 attacks.

Round two of the quest began in October 2001 when key senators began to pick up the call for a special investigation. In a 21 October appearance on *Meet the Press*, Senator John McCain (Republican-Arizona) declared his support for a commission.[5] He joined forces with Joseph Lieberman, a Democrat from Connecticut and fellow veteran of the 2000 presidential contest. The two men wrote to President Bush in November asking him to support the creation of a special board of inquiry. They received no response.[6]

The silence from the White House did not deter other senators from pressing the issue. On 18 December, Torricelli and Senator Charles Grassley (Republican-Iowa) sponsored a bill to create a twelve-member "Board of Inquiry into the September 11, 2001, Terrorist Attacks."[7] The Torricelli-Grassley proposal, however, was soon overshadowed by a bill that proved to have more staying power. On 20 December McCain and Lieberman introduced a measure to establish a fourteen-member "National Commission on Terrorist Attacks Upon the United States," with Bush picking the chair and three other members.[8] Although this was not the format that ultimately prevailed, the bill stayed under active consideration well into the spring of 2002.

The McCain-Lieberman bill also sparked another House proposal, this time offered by Representative Timothy Roemer.[9] An Indiana Democrat, Roemer proved to be a man of equally strong conviction on the issue of accountability for the attacks (later he was tapped to serve on the 9/11 Commission). With his emergence, an informal caucus of legislators comprising Roemer, McCain, Torricelli, and Lieberman had begun to take shape. Together, these lawmakers would play an important role in keeping the issue of a blue-ribbon investigation alive during the spring and summer of 2002.

With the commission proposal gaining momentum, the Bush administration began to act more aggressively to thwart the initiative. In late January, Bush and Vice President Richard Cheney prevailed upon Senate majority leader Tom Daschle to help kill the idea.[10] A special investigation, Cheney warned, would divert time and attention from the war on terror. The list of objections began to grow. In addition to being a distraction, the president's advisers pointed out, a blue-ribbon inquiry would also waste resources and would "tie up" key officials.[11] Thus began the creation of a brief against the commission that was used by Bush and his lieutenants throughout the congressional debate.

By May 2002 a new argument had entered the mix in the form of a charge, advanced most vigorously by Cheney, that another investigation would heighten the risk of leaks of sensitive information about US intelligence. In an interview with CNN's Larry King, Cheney expressed his concern that a new investigation would

> multiply potential sources of leaks and disclosures of information we can't disclose. The key to our ability to defend ourselves and to take out the terrorists lies on intelligence. And we're discussing such things as the president's daily brief, which is the most sensitive product, if you will, of the intelligence community; it comes from our most sensitive and secret sources. If there are leaks from that document … we will lose the capacity to defend ourselves against future attacks.[12]

To further underscore the danger, Cheney asserted that the joint House–Senate inquiry into 9/11, under way since February, had already created trouble through unwise disclosures. If veteran members of Congress could not handle secrets with care, how could one expect an ad hoc group of concerned citizens to do any better?

It is easier to describe than to explain the administration's opposition to a blue-ribbon investigation in the months following 9/11. Objectively, one could argue that for purely political reasons Bush should have acted quickly to create a presidential commission soon after the tragedy. That course of action would have taken the issue away from Congress and the Democrats. It would also have been historically defensible. Key Democrats had already invoked the example of Roosevelt and Pearl Harbor, thereby opening the door for Bush to create an executive branch–dominated board of inquiry along the lines of the Roberts Commission.[13] But there is no indication that the administration gave serious consideration to any of the early commission plans. The break with tradition was not lost on everyone. David Rosenbaum of the *New York Times* noted that the president's stance represented a "reversal of normal form … usually, after a calamitous event or a political embarrassment, it is the White House that seeks a commission to investigate."[14]

Sometimes the most obvious explanation for a phenomenon is also the best. And in the weeks and months after 9/11, the defining characteristics of Bush's decisionmaking were (1) a desire for maximum latitude of action, and (2) an unusually strong penchant for secrecy. These two factors combined to create a visceral reaction to the idea that a group of luminaries from outside the government would be permitted to sniff around the executive branch and to question the administration's actions before and on 11 September 2001. Such a development would run counter to the unilateralist philosophy so evident in the administration. It would also cast doubt on the carefully constructed image of Bush as a resolute wartime leader more concerned with meeting the future threat than with agonizing over past failures.

Added to this philosophical resistance was a more practical consideration. In the aftermath of 9/11, political power shifted from Congress and toward the president. Then–White House press secretary Ari Fleischer explained the shift as a natural development: "The way our nation is set up, and the way the Constitution is written, wartime powers rest fundamentally in the hands of the executive branch. It's not uncommon in time of war for a nation's eyes to focus on the executive branch and its ability to conduct the war with strength and speed."[15] Bush and his advisers were attuned to the changing balance of power in Washington. Accordingly, they must have realized that they were uniquely well situated to try to stop the commission from being created.

Fourteen Months and Sixteen Days

Bush's strategy of delay and obstruction worked. None of the commission proposals in the air appeared likely to pass as the summer approached. Then in May 2002, there was a flurry of activity from an unexpected source—interest groups. But these were not typical interest groups. These were clusters of wives, husbands, sons, daughters, mothers, and fathers of 9/11 victims. Dubbed "the families" by the press, they proved to be an important and ultimately irresistible force for accountability in the 9/11 storyline.

The growing organization and muscle of the families coincided with startling new press reports that cast doubt on administration decisions in the days leading up to the attacks. On 15 May 2002, *CBS News* revealed that President Bush had received an intelligence briefing on 6 August 2001: "Bin Laden determined to strike in the U.S."[16] For House minority leader Richard Gephardt this was the final straw. Invoking the language of Watergate, he told the press that he would support the Roemer proposal in an effort to find out "what the White House knew about the events leading up to 9/11, when they knew it and, most importantly, what was done about it."[17]

Major media outlets echoed Gephardt's sentiment. In a 26 May editorial titled "The Past as Prelude," the *New York Times* demanded that the president and Congress "move immediately to establish an independent investigative commission with the authority, expertise and financial support necessary to determine why Washington failed to recognize that Osama bin Laden was on the hunt in America last summer."[18] As for Congress, the *Times* noted that "the committees bear some responsibility for the pre-September 11 record. That complicity ... may explain why the White House favors working with them rather than an independent commission." Conservative commentators also joined the cause. George Will, William Safire, and William Kristol all stepped forward to call on the administration for action.[19]

The cumulative weight of these developments began to take a toll on Bush's political standing. An *NBC News–Wall Street Journal* poll in early June of 2002 revealed that less than half the public thought the administration was being "open and candid" about the facts surrounding 9/11.[20] But for Bush, things were about to get worse. On 11 June the families staged a major rally outside the Capitol to call attention to the need for a blue-ribbon investigation. Ellen Mariani, a 9/11 widow, articulated the group's resolve: "I want a real investigation. I don't want lip service. I'm angry, and I'm not going away."[21]

Although Bush and his congressional allies were able to stall for another month, the movement had at last hit critical mass. Representative Roemer sprang a surprise when he revived the National Commission on Terrorist Attacks Upon the United States, a reconfigured version of his original bill, and submitted it as an amendment to the upcoming Intelligence Authorization Act for 2003. Roemer's amendment sparked intense debate in the House. The fight pitted Republicans loyal to Bush against an odd grouping that included most Democrats plus a handful of Republican lawmakers, many from districts around New York City, who were concerned that further delay could turn into a public-relations disaster. Twenty-five of these Republicans eventually broke ranks, and the Roemer amendment passed by 218 to 189 in the early-morning hours of 25 July.[22] The Senate followed suit after the August recess, and by 10 October all that remained was for House and Senate negotiators to iron out last-minute differences in conference.

But after having fought the proposal for over a year, Bush and Cheney were determined to make one last stand. They took issue with the commission's subpoena power, arguing that six of the ten members should have to agree before issuing a subpoena (Roemer's original language specified that five members would be sufficient). The White House also took a dim view of the proposal that the panel have a co-chair, with Bush picking one of the leaders and congressional Democrats selecting the other. Bush wanted the sole power to select the commission's leader and made it clear to his lieutenants that he would not budge on either issue. "Keep negotiating,"

Cheney told administration stalwart and conferee Porter Goss.[23] House Democratic whip Nancy Pelosi was furious. She charged that "the White House is professing openly to support an independent commission" while operating behind the scenes "to thwart the commission."[24]

There the issue remained throughout October 2002. But the political calculus began to change when, on 5 November, Republicans picked up congressional seats in the midterm election. The victory, an improbable one in light of historical trends for the White House party, improved Bush's negotiating position. Democrats must have feared what would happen if the issue were left for the 108th Congress to settle. There were also rumors that Bush might use the deadlock as an excuse to declare the Roemer proposal dead and to insert a more traditional presidential commission in its place.[25] These were not idle fears. Republican members of Congress had only recently introduced a resolution to endorse a panel that would have featured little legislative input and been directly under White House control.[26]

In the end, Bush did not have to use this option. Just one week after the election Democratic conferees yielded to the administration's demands. Congress approved the revised bill on 15 November and sent it to the White House for action. On 27 November 2002, fourteen months and sixteen days after the terrorist attacks of 9/11, President Bush signed Public Law 107-306, breathing official life into the National Commission on Terrorist Attacks Upon the United States. As shown in Table 6.2, the delay in establishing an active commission was unprecedented. Bush's slowness stands in marked contrast to the other presidents who confronted crises of a similar or lesser magnitude.

A Rough Start

The newly signed legislation called for a commission of ten members. Of these, two would be selected by the Senate majority leader, two by the Senate minority leader, two by the House majority leader, and two by the House minority leader. The vice chair would be chosen through consultation between Democratic leaders in the House and Senate. Last, but not least, the president would appoint the panel's chair.

The commission was charged with examining "the facts and causes relating to the terrorist attacks of September 11, 2001." With regard to the ongoing joint congressional inquiry, the act mandated that the commission "build upon the investigations of other entities, and avoid unnecessary duplication." After offering a "full and complete accounting of the circumstances surrounding the attacks," the commission was also directed to make "recommendations for corrective measures that can be taken to prevent acts of terrorism." The act specified that the commission make a final report to the president and Congress within eighteen months of the bill's signing.

Table 6.2   Time Between Crisis and Commission Appointment

Crisis and Date	Presidential Action	Time Lapse
Japanese Attack 7 December 1941	Roosevelt appoints Roberts Commission 16 December 1941	9 Days
Assassination of JFK 22 November 1963	Johnson appoints Warren Commission 29 November 1963	7 Days
CIA Scandal 22 December 1974	Ford appoints Rockefeller Commission 4 January 1975	13 Days
Iran-Contra 3 November 1986	Reagan appoints Tower Commission 1 December 1986	28 Days
Terrorist Attack 11 September 2001	Bush signs bill for 9/11 Commission 27 November 2002	442 Days

And in keeping with Bush's wishes, the act stipulated that subpoenas could only be issued by agreement of the chair and vice chair or by vote of at least six members. Significantly, the act expressly removed the commission from the scope of the Federal Advisory Committee Act, a move that reduced public-access requirements in order to enhance the protection of classified information.[27]

Standing beside Bush as he signed the commission into law was Henry Kissinger, the president's choice to head the panel. Daschle and Gephardt selected former Senate majority leader George Mitchell as vice chair. Other Democratic slots went to Tim Roemer (recently retired from his House seat), former Department of Justice official Jamie Gorelick, and Washington attorney Richard Ben-Veniste. The final Democratic seat went to Max Cleland, who only one month earlier had lost his Georgia senate seat in a bitterly contested race that saw President Bush use his clout to aid the challenger. On the Republican side, majority leaders Trent Lott and William Frist teamed up to appoint former senator Slade Gorton of Washington, former Nixon aide Fred Fielding, Reagan-era secretary of the navy John Lehman, and former Illinois governor James Thompson.

Two appointments caused considerable controversy. Prior to the public announcement of the members, McCain and Lieberman had mounted a strong campaign to convince Lott to give Senator Warren Rudman a seat on the commission.[28] Rudman had co-chaired the 1999 US Commission on National Security in the 21st Century and was regarded as a tough-minded expert when it came to blue-ribbon investigations. Lott had other ideas, however, and Lehman ended up getting that appointment.

But the real controversy focused on the appointment of Kissinger as chair. To a host of critics, the very idea that a "Kissinger Commission" would get to the bottom of a political issue was laughable. Although the former secretary of state had a long record of public service, he could not escape the shadow cast by his association with Nixon. "Kissinger," wrote one observer, "is the guy you put in charge when you don't want people to find things out, not when you do."[29]

With five Republicans and five Democrats, the commission looked respectably bipartisan. But party allegiance aside, critics found plenty to worry about as they scanned the list of members. In the view of one editorial writer:

> The panel is made up of nine rich white men and one rich white woman. Six of the ten are lawyers; another is a lobbyist. There is no police officer, no firefighter. There is no relative of anyone killed in the attacks.
>
> Five of the ten members are key players at large corporate law firms, virtually all with clients who stand to win or lose depending on the commission's findings. The airline industry, which could lose or gain billions, has its key corporate lawyers on the commission, whose members were appointed by the President and House and Senate leaders, equally from each party.[30]

Each member had also served in government at some point, with some of that service occurring in the immediate run-up to 9/11.

These were not the only issues in the air in the weeks following the creation of the panel. Both Kissinger and Mitchell were embroiled in disputes regarding how much disclosure they would be required to make about contacts and client lists for their respective firms.[31] Neither survived the controversy as commission members. Mitchell chose to leave on 11 December 2002 and Kissinger followed suit two days later. In retrospect, Kissinger's resignation was a godsend for Bush: it denied critics an easy target and a reason to dismiss the commission before it could hold its first hearing.

The resignations of Mitchell and Kissinger left the commission leaderless, if only briefly. Daschle and Gephardt moved quickly to install Lee Hamilton, a former House member and seasoned veteran of Washington politics, as the new vice chair. By 15 December, just two days after Kissinger's resignation, Bush had identified a new chair for the commission: Thomas H. Kean, former governor of New Jersey. Ari Fleischer told reporters that Kean had first been mentioned as a possibility by White House chief of staff Andrew Card in late October. Moreover, it was Card who phoned Kean to pop the question: "Do you want to do it?"[32]

At the time he agreed to head the most important blue-ribbon panel in US history, the sixty-seven-year-old Kean was serving as president of Drew University. As governor of New Jersey from 1982 to 1990, he had won points from many different quarters for his quiet competence, thoughtful manner, and moderate approach to policy issues. The son of a congressman, Kean had inherited his father's sense of public duty. "When the President of the United States asks me … to bring resolution to the greatest crime committed in the history of this nation," he said, "then nothing takes higher precedence."[33] Kean was also no stranger to blue-ribbon service, having worked on various state and federal task forces including the (1997) President's Initiative on Race.

Personal factors also affected Kean's decision to accept the post. He had grown up and established his political career in an area adjacent to New York City, so he was directly and profoundly affected by the events of 9/11. He knew victims and survivors of the attacks. In response to a question during an early press conference, he identified those who had lost loved ones as "the group I care about the most."[34] "He's been very affected by the families," confirmed his friend and political associate Christie Todd Whitman, also a former New Jersey governor.[35] This connection to the tragedy played a role in his selection; Bush cited Kean's ties to New York as the "main reason" for his appointment.[36]

Kean presented a much lower profile than Kissinger and was thus the recipient of fewer attacks in the days following his appointment. But there was some sniping. William Rivers Pitt, author (with recent UN weapons inspector Scott Ritter) of *War on Iraq* and editor of the progressive Internet magazine *Truthout*, found Kean to be a "curious choice … someone who will be easily controlled by the administration. Kean does not possess, by dint of experience, the wherewithal to ask the difficult questions."[37] A spokesman for the group Families of September 11 sounded a similar theme, registering his disappointment with the new chairman's lack of experience in areas the commission would investigate, including aviation, diplomacy, immigration policy, and intelligence.[38] Kean took the criticism in stride. "I am not a Washingtonian," he told reporters,. "I am going to learn."[39]

Upon assuming the job, Kean phoned Kissinger to find out what had been done to get the commission up and running. Much to his surprise, he discovered that virtually nothing had taken place. Kissinger was able to offer little more than his best wishes.[40] Thus the early months of the commission were marked by controversy and delay. All the while, the clock was ticking on the eighteen-month deadline for completion of the investigation.

The first meeting of the National Commission on Terrorist Attacks Upon the United States took place on 27 January 2003. The members agreed to the appointment of Dr. Philip Zelikow, a historian, as the commission's executive director. Over the course of the investigation Zelikow would play an important role. Like other staff directors before him—Walter Howe on the Roberts Commission, David Belin on the Rockefeller

Commission, and Rhett Dawson on the Tower Commission—he would leave an indelible imprint on the inquiry.

As executive director, Zelikow presided over an impressively large staff. Over sixty individuals worked behind the scenes, ranging from public information specialists to attorneys to investigators. The staff was divided into eight work teams, with each given its own assignment: Al Qaeda and the organization of the 9/11 attacks, management of intelligence, counterterrorism policy, terrorist financing, border security, domestic law enforcement, transportation security, and the emergency response to the 9/11 attacks.[41]

Even with the investigation in its infancy, Kean realized that the commission's original budget of $3 million would be utterly inadequate. Responding to his plea for help, a group of senators led by Lieberman asked the administration for an additional $11 million. When the administration balked, Kean moved to settle the issue once and for all. "I believe we can do it for $12 million," he told legislators in late March, "but not a cent less."[42] The White House agreed to the compromise and the additional funds were provided to the commission as part of the National Intelligence Program budget.[43]

The Baggage of a Broken Heart

The board heard its first witnesses on 31 March 2003, nineteen months after the attacks and four months after Bush signed the commission into law. The session took place at the Alexander Hamilton US Customs House in lower Manhattan, near Ground Zero. New York governor George Pataki was the first to appear. Next came Michael Bloomberg, mayor of New York City. Then came the survivors and family members. It was an agonizing experience for all. The testimony of Lee Ielpi, while especially poignant, was indicative of the tone throughout the day:

> I come to you today as an ambassador for the dead and on behalf of the many others who toiled at Ground Zero.... My son Jonathan, a member of Squad Company 288 at the New York City Fire Department, was killed in the South Tower. I am a retired firefighter and a grieving father. I bring no agenda to this hearing. The only baggage I bear is a broken heart and a resolve that the terrible events of September 11th not be repeated.[44]

Widower Stephen Push sounded an angrier tone. He urged the commission to reject the many admonitions against finger pointing. "I think this Commission should point fingers," he told the members, because of the "people in responsible positions who failed us."[45]

The relationship between the administration and the commission began to sour in the weeks following the initial public hearing. Although the specific points of disagreement shifted over time, the fundamental issue was always the same: access to documents and witnesses. It is difficult to overstate the importance of this conflict. It ate up an enormous amount of the commission's time that could have been devoted to the investigation itself. Much of the story of the 9/11 Commission revolves around this conflict with the president, his advisers, and executive-branch agencies.

A pattern began to develop. The commission would request information from an administration that had worked diligently behind the scenes to prevent a blue-ribbon probe, but now presented a facade of public cooperation. In response to these requests, the administration and the executive agencies under its control behaved erratically, granting easy access in some instances and stonewalling in others, all the while professing to support the commission in its important work. The commission's response to this resistance was determined by the particular situation. In some cases the members agreed to negotiate with the White House to resolve the issue amicably. At other times they played hardball.

Round one of the battle over access came in late April 2003 when, as part of the investigation, Commissioner Roemer attempted to review classified transcripts of hearings held by the House Intelligence Committee the previous fall. Roemer was shocked to discover that he could not review the documents. Under the terms of an agreement negotiated by Zelikow, the documents first had to be vetted by administration lawyers to determine if they contained "privileged" information. For Roemer, there was a maddening irony to the whole affair. While a member of the House Intelligence Committee in the previous session of Congress, he had personally participated in the very hearing for which he was now denied access to the record.[46]

The situation continued to deteriorate. As the sixth month of the investigation drew to a close, the commission issued a report card on the level of cooperation from sixteen federal agencies covered by the investigation. Only the State Department was deemed fully cooperative.[47] And for the first time the issue of access to witnesses also entered the mix, albeit with a twist. Over strong objections from the commission, the Justice Department (DOJ) insisted on sending a high-ranking official to sit in on the testimony of any employee. Although this practice became more common over time, it never ceased to rankle critics like Kyle Hence of 9/11 Citizens Watch:

> There are concerns about how the commission is conducting interviews. It appears that it has knuckled under, bowed to demands by the administration to have "minders" sit in on all interviews. The commission said, "Well, if it's a really important point we'll ask the minders to leave the room." How conducive is this for someone to get out and really tell the truth when they know a superior is watching over them? I mean how absurd is that?[48]

Kean was also displeased. "Still got minders, still don't like them," he told an interviewer in September. But he also realized the need to be pragmatic: "You have to accept the conditions, or you may not get the interview."[49]

Brinksmanship

But as tense as things were, the relationship between the commission and the administration had yet to enter its most trying period. That occurred during mid-October when the commission issued two high-profile subpoenas to executive-branch agencies. The first went to the Federal Aviation Administration (FAA) and the second to the Defense Department (DOD)[50] There is little doubt the commission felt that the two agencies had been uncooperative with the investigation, but it is also clear that Kean and company were sending a message. The real issue at play in the fall of 2003 was access to the most sensitive of all pre-9/11 intelligence papers, the president's daily briefings (PDBs). PDBs are documents ten to twelve pages long that summarize for the president the most important intelligence developments in the preceding twenty-four hours. Consequently they could offer key insight into the all-important questions about pre-9/11 intelligence: What did the president know and when did he know it?

Kean had no illusions that a fight lay ahead. He termed the PDBs the "Holy Grail of the nation's secrets" and noted that "no congressional committee has ever seen them."[51] To gain access, he had to overcome the argument that as private communications intended for the president, the briefings were protected from disclosure by executive privilege.

Kean's strategy was twofold. Publicly he began to speak with a force that was unusual for the mild-mannered college president. "Any document that has to do with this investigation cannot be beyond our reach," he told the *New York Times*. "I will not stand for it. That means that we will use every tool at our command to get hold of every document."[52] Kean's threat to use "every tool" was a direct reference to the commission's ultimate option, a subpoena directed at the White House and, by inference, at the president.[53] "You get the feeling," said New Jersey journalist Mike Kelly, "that he is trying to get the White House to pay attention."[54] Kelly was right on the mark. Kean admitted that "the threat of a subpoena is just as important as the subpoena itself."[55]

Behind the scenes, Kean pursued a simultaneous effort to allay White House fears on the use of the PDBs and to educate officials on the unique role of the commission. "We are not the Congress," the chairman argued, thus "these arguments about presidential privilege do not apply."[56] But that was not the only distinction Kean was prepared to make. Because 9/11 was unique in US experience, he believed that precedents set by past blue-ribbon panels were of limited use in charting a course for his investigation. He took it as his mission to "convince the White House that this was a commission unlike any other."[57]

Whether Kean was prepared to actually fire off the White House subpoena is debatable. What is less debatable is that other members of the panel were fed up with the endless foot-dragging by the administration. At a closed meeting on 8 November 2003 there was a discussion about the PDBs. A motion to issue a subpoena to the administration failed, although the vote was reportedly very tight. Despite the defeat, Roemer warned that the panel remained "very serious about getting access to the PDBs and extremely interested in maintaining our credibility." Unnamed commission members also hinted that another meeting could be held "within days" to reconsider the measure if there were no movement by the White House.[58]

A National Scandal

The crisis finally subsided when, on 13 November, negotiators for the two camps reached an accord on the PDBs. Although details of the compromise were supposed to be confidential, journalists began to uncover key parts of the agreement. Two members of the commission would have full access to the briefings but could take no notes. Two other members would have access to only those briefings deemed relevant by the White House. The four members would constitute a subcommittee that would report back to the panel as a whole.[59] Most commission members were satisfied with the compromise and were simply glad to be able to move on after the long and trying delay. But that sentiment was not universal. Commissioners Roemer and Cleland viewed the arrangement as unacceptably restrictive and went public with their unhappiness.[60] "We shouldn't be making deals," said Cleland. "If somebody wants to deal, we issue subpoenas. That's the deal."[61]

The fight over the PDBs proved to be Cleland's last hurrah. The Vietnam veteran and former senator had established himself as a favorite of the families due to his outspoken nature. Openly critical of the administration, he served as the conscience of the commission and was even willing to engage Kean publicly on issues like the briefings. Cleland saved his sharpest comments for an interview published in the online journal *Salon* on 21 November. He spoke of the pressures generated by the administration's obstruction:

> It's all about 9/11. This is not a political witch hunt. This is the most serious independent investigation since the Warren Commission. And after watching History Channel shows on the Warren Commission last night, the Warren Commission blew it. I'm not going to be part of that. I'm not going to be part of looking at information only partially. I'm not going to be part of just coming to quick conclusions. I'm not going to be part of political pressure to do this or not do that. I'm not going to be part of that. This is serious. It is a national scandal.[62]

Later in the interview, he accused the White House of trying to "slow walk" the commission into obscurity.

But Cleland's time on the commission was to come to an abrupt end. On 21 November 2003, the same day that the *Salon* interview appeared, Bush nominated him to the board of directors of the Export-Import Bank.[63] Cleland accepted the nomination and was easily confirmed by the Senate. Commission rules prohibited him from serving in both roles, however, so he had to resign his seat on the panel. For Bush and Rove it was a master-stroke. With a strategic appointment they had effectively silenced the most outspoken critic on the commission. Daschle appointed Bob Kerrey, a former senator and decorated war hero in his own right, to fill the vacancy.

Cleland's departure came as a blow to the families, who shared his disdain for the commission's willingness to compromise on the PDBs. Aside from the obvious objection that the arrangement limited access to key information, the relatives were critical of the manner in which the deal was brokered. Zelikow had acted as the negotiating agent on behalf of the commission. Significantly, he had not insisted that the compromise, which he described as a "series of communications," be codified as a formal, signed agreement.[64]

Zelikow's performance on the issue did little to improve his reputation with the families. He was already under close scrutiny due to his personal ties to administration figures. While a professor at the University of Virginia he had co-authored a book with Condoleezza Rice. He also had served on President Bush's Foreign Intelligence Advisory Board in 2001.[65] Accordingly, the new revelations gave rise to wild speculation regarding the director's real motives. Some rumors even had him coordinating strategy behind the scenes with Bush adviser Karl Rove.[66]

The arrangement engineered by Zelikow failed to bury the controversy surrounding the daily briefings. New questions arose as the investigation progressed. One journalist close to the commission described the evolution of the agreement:

> The deal ... quickly broke down. By the beginning of February this year [2004] it proved merely to have shifted the terrain of negotiations from the abstract (i.e., what access should the commission have) to the concrete (i.e., which of the notes produced by the subcommittees can be seen by other commissioners).[67]

Roemer dismissed the summary he received as a "strained, edited, vetted report."[68]

Press coverage of the commission in the winter and spring of 2004 was dominated by two issues, a fight to extend the commission's deadline and a fight to secure interviews with senior White House officials. The effort to prolong the life of the commission was a direct by-product of the PDB controversy. That issue had consumed an inordinate amount of the commission's time and disrupted the schedule for the investigation.

Panel members began to wonder aloud about their ability to meet the May 2004 deadline. Before his departure, Cleland had speculated that a move might be afoot to "run out the clock" on the investigation.[69] Widower Bill Harvey pointed out, however, that the commission had to accept some responsibility for the delay:

> The lack of urgency on the part of the commission that reaches all the way back into the spring is something we've argued about with them. Now the commissioners see that they're six months away from issuing a report and are becoming frantic. I don't like to be the person who told them so, but I told them. They haven't taken advantage of all the weapons at their disposal to prosecute a vigorous investigation. Yes, they're doing it now, but I wonder if it's too late.[70]

Sympathetic members of Congress began to join the issue. Lieberman served notice that, if necessary, he and John McCain were "prepared to go to the floor of the Senate to extend the life of the commission."[71]

Eventually the commissioners agreed to seek a two-month extension, a move that would push the deadline for the final report back to late July. But the families were unhappy with the plan. Some argued that the commission needed more than a few months of extra time to finish the investigation. Others worried that the proposed extension would push the final report into the middle of the presidential election. The resulting political pressures, warned the Family Steering Committee, would be "an insult to the dead."[72]

Because the commission was a statutory creation, Congress would have to approve any extension of time. But Bush was very active behind the scenes. His party controlled both chambers on the hill and, as with the initial creation of the commission, he had enough political muscle to stop any proposal not to his liking. White House officials sent mixed signals on the extension. Initially they seemed to support extra time, but only if it extended the commission past the November presidential election. At other times they seemed opposed to any change in the original schedule.

Finally, on 4 February 2004 White House spokesman Scott McClellan released a statement saying that the president would support the commission's request for an additional two months.[73] Media pressure might have had something to do with the new spirit of cooperation. Press coverage was overwhelmingly sympathetic to the commission. In a 30 January editorial, the *Washington Post* had argued that it would "be better to lift the deadline entirely."[74] Whatever the source, Bush's change of heart helped break Republican resistance on Capitol Hill, and Congress passed a bill to give the commission the two months it desired. Bush signed the legislation on

16 March 2004, and with that the deadline for the final report was changed from 27 May to 26 July 2004.[75]

A Visit with the President

The other issue that arose involved the testimony of senior administration officials. The commission requested that Condoleezza Rice, the president's national security advisor, appear before the panel to provide sworn testimony in a public hearing. Rice had already participated in a private interview in February. That four-hour discussion had not been recorded, nor had Rice been put under oath.

Bush balked at the request. Rice was in a different position than the cabinet secretaries. A presidential adviser, she had an office in the West Wing and a direct line of authority to the Oval Office. She was also not subject to Senate confirmation. Consequently, Bush argued that her appearance before the commission would violate the most basic principles of separation of powers and would open the door for Congress (as the authorizing agent of the commission) to summon other presidential advisers at will.[76]

Once again, however, the administration showed a remarkable ability to change positions on the fly. On 30 March White House counsel Alberto Gonzales phoned Kean and Hamilton to report that Rice would testify.[77] The reversal occurred exactly one week after the commission heard testimony from Richard Clarke, Bush's former counterterrorism chief. Bob Kerrey, the commission's newest member, was surprised by the White House missteps. "Given their political expertise," he observed, "it's surprising they keep making these kinds of mistakes."[78]

Clarke was the star witness of the entire investigation. He did not hesitate when asked to testify, nor was he put off when Kean asked him to take an oath—(the swearing of witnesses had begun on 26 January).[79] Clarke kicked off his testimony with a startling admission:

> I welcome these hearings because of the opportunity that they provide to the American people to better understand why the tragedy of 9/11 happened, and what we must do to prevent a reoccurrence. I also welcome the hearings because it is finally a forum where I can apologize to the loved ones of the victims of 9/11, to them who are here in the room, to those who are watching on television, your government failed you. Those entrusted with protecting you failed you. And I failed you. We tried hard, but that doesn't matter because we failed. And for that failure, I would ask, once all the facts are out, for your understanding and for your forgiveness.[80]

Clarke's testimony sent the White House damage-control team into high gear. Officials determined that the only thing likely to divert attention from Clarke's damning admission was an appearance by Rice.

But the controversy over Rice's testimony turned out to be the opening act for the real show, which was the commission's attempt to secure
an interview with President Bush. Although some historians noted that
the request to interview the president was highly unusual, it was not
without precedent. As discussed in this book's Chapter 5, President
Reagan met twice with the Tower Commission during the Iran-Contra
probe. President Lyndon Johnson submitted a three-page statement to the
Warren Commission, though he did not personally appear before that
body.[81]

As with Rice's testimony, events began to drive the issue. The pressure
on Bush to appear increased dramatically when former President Clinton
agreed to meet with the panel to discuss his administration's experience
with Al-Qaeda and related issues. Kean and Hamilton did not miss the
opportunity to twit Bush publicly. On 25 February, they released a statement to the press noting that they welcomed "the decision of former
President Clinton and former Vice President Gore to meet privately with all
members of the Commission." As for Bush's reluctance, the statement
expressed the commission's hope that he would reconsider.[82]

For a third time in as many months, Bush flip-flopped. First he
declared that he would meet with Kean and Hamilton only, then he
switched and agreed to meet with the full commission. Finally came a declaration that he would meet with the full commission subject to the following conditions: (1) he would make a joint appearance with Cheney; (2) the
commission could take notes but not record the session, even though the
White House was free to do so; and (3) the commission had to stipulate in
writing that it would forgo additional requests for public testimony.[83] In a
small victory for the commission, the White House agreed to drop its
demand that the president's appearance be limited to one hour.[84]

Kean appreciated the irony that the president himself would have a
"minder" present during his interview. "We recognize that Mr. Bush may
help Mr. Cheney with some of the answers," he quipped.[85] Others were less
amused by the compromise. Bruce Fein, a former Justice Department official from the Reagan administration, charged that "a joint appearance sabo-
tages the idea of a unitary executive—the 'buck stops here' attitude of
Harry Truman—by enabling Bush to shift blame or accountability to
Cheney when politically expedient."[86]

The commission met with Bush in the Oval Office on 29 April 2004.
The session, described by White House spokesman Scott McClellan as
"very cordial," lasted just over three hours.[87] Also present were NSC counsel Bryan Cunningham and presidential aides Alberto Gonzales and Tom
Mannheim. Bush described it as "a good conversation" and boasted that he
"answered every question they asked."[88] Lee Hamilton also characterized
the meeting as cordial and productive. "I don't think there was a single

moment of tension," he said. "We weren't there to challenge him or ask any contentious questions designed to contradict him."[89]

Bush earned points with the members by leading off with an apology to Commissioner Jamie Gorelick. In his appearance before the panel on 13 April Attorney General Ashcroft had hinted that Gorelick herself, while serving as Janet Reno's deputy at the Justice Department, had created the very policies that impeded the necessary sharing of valuable information between law enforcement and intelligence entities. "Someone built this wall," Ashcroft told the commission. Then he made sure his point was not lost: "Although you understand the debilitating impacts of the wall, I cannot imagine that the Commission knew about this memorandum. So I have had it declassified for you and the public to review. Full disclosure compels me to inform you that the author of this memorandum is a member of the Commission."[90]

Ashcroft's appearance dovetailed with the sudden appearance of documents on the department's website that further implicated Gorelick in the pre-9/11 intelligence failure.[91]

The Final Report

The appearance of Bush and Cheney before the commission was the last major controversy before the investigation began to draw to a close. Before the commission lay the Herculean task of taking the vast quantity of material they had acquired, 2.5 million pages of documents plus testimony from more than 1,200 witnesses, and organizing it into a final report.[92] Equally daunting was the task of coming up with findings and recommendations that all ten members would support. Kean characterized his job as overseeing a report "that's not Democratic or Republican. We're about telling a story." Hamilton agreed that the report had to be bipartisan in tone. He told reporters that it was too early to predict a unanimous effort but that he and Kean were doing their "very best to get it."[93]

And get it they did. On 22 July 2004 the commission presented its final report "to the president of the United States, to the United States Congress, and the American people."[94] Over two and a half years had passed since the attacks that had given rise to the commission. Kean spoke first, wasting no time in pointing out that the report represented the unanimous conclusion of the panel.

> Five Republicans and five Democrats have come together today with … unity of purpose. We file no additional views in this report. We have no dissents. We have each decided that we will play no active role in the fall presidential campaign. We will instead devote our time, as we have, to work together in support of the recommendations in this report.[95]

As the press conference progressed, each member had an opportunity to offer comments and to answer questions. Hamilton noted that the commission "does not have all the answers. But we have thought about what to do ... and how to do it." Ben-Veniste reminded the press that the commission "had certain road blocks. We had to push hard for information." Kerrey addressed the frustrations of trying to dig for answers "in the most partisan city in the world." And Gorelick seemed surprised by the enormous attention focused on the commission and its report. "I had thought we would labor away in obscurity for 18 months," she said, "and then beg for attention when the report came out."[96]

She could not have been more wrong. The 567-page report became a national bestseller. Fortunately Kean had anticipated the interest. In addition to the normal print run handled by the Government Printing Office, he had made prior arrangements with publisher W. W. Norton to help distribute the report. The goal, he said, was to "get it in every bookstore."[97] Presidential aides reported that Bush read his copy during a weekend stay at his ranch in Crawford, Texas.[98]

The report was divided into 13 chapters, 11 devoted to description and analysis and 2 focused on the future. Chapters 12 and 13 contained 41 specific recommendations for improving security against the terrorist threat. The suggestions ranged from the specific (supporting a new International Youth Opportunity Fund) to the general (seeking more collaboration with foreign governments), and from the obvious (tracking terrorist financing) to the darkly prophetic (ensuring the humane treatment of prisoners).

The media reaction to the report was decidedly positive. For its sober assessment of pre-9/11 failure, the *New Republic* called it "the Black Book of American Security."[99] Some were impressed with the openness of the investigation and the candor of the report. "Kean, Hamilton, and their colleagues," wrote E. J. Dione Jr., "have shown that open government is the ally, not the enemy, of effectiveness. The process through which the commission's recommendations were produced guarantees that they will be taken seriously."[100] Others were impressed by the report's overall readability and the "novelistically intense" prose.[101] Kean saw the issue in practical terms. "You cannot report to the American people with language that is either dull or obtuse," he observed. "Unless people read the report, they wouldn't understand the problems and support our recommendations." In response to questions about authorship, Zelikow maintained that no outsiders were brought in to help ghostwrite the report.[102]

Richard Clarke was among a minority less enamored of the report. In a 25 July column for the *New York Times*, he praised the panel for its "extensive exposition of the facts" but suggested that it had achieved unanimity at the expense of clear statements of accountability.[103] Two former CIA officers were less circumspect. "The whole name of the game," said Ray McGovern "is to exculpate anyone in the establishment."[104] Michael Scheuer wrote directly to the members to ask why they had pulled punches on CIA Director Tenet and other "bureaucratic cowards."[105] Finally came those who wondered why the commission did not delve more deeply into the war with Iraq. Hamilton explained that the panel's mandate was not broad enough to permit that line of inquiry. But he also alluded to a more basic concern. "If we had gone into the war on Iraq," he told CNN's Wolf Blitzer, "it would have been highly divisive, and we would not have been able to agree on the factual record, not been able to agree on recommendations."[106]

Commission politics did not end with the issuance of the final report. There was intense maneuvering by both executive- and legislative-branch actors in the period between the press conference and the end of the year. And as the families had feared, the commission's report and its recommendations became entangled with the upcoming presidential election. Democratic nominee John Kerry endorsed the board's proposals *en bloc* and even suggested that Congress should skip the August recess in order to get a headstart on new legislation.[107] Although Republicans complained that the move smacked of a cheap attempt to play on an emotional issue, Bush could ill afford to sit by and do nothing. Consequently, he sought to create a perception that the administration was moving decisively on the commission's proposals. He appointed chief of staff Andrew Card to head a task force to examine the individual recommendations.[108] By the middle of August, presidential adviser Frances Fragos Townsend was bragging that the administration's quick action on the recommendations had "enabled us to get in front of it."[109]

But for all the posturing, work on the most important piece of reform legislation, the Intelligence Overhaul Bill, almost died for want of presidential backing. It was a repeat of Bush's performance during the investigation. Outwardly he professed to concur with the need for the legislation and promised to use the resources at his disposal to ensure its passage; privately, however, he was not enamored of the bill and did little to drum up support among congressional Republicans. Roemer sensed Bush's reluctance and mocked the administration's efforts. "It's going to take more than two phone calls," he said, "you have to use the bully pulpit."[110]

A key sticking point was the provision that a new post be created, the Director of National Intelligence (DNI), to supervise the collective effort of the intelligence community. Critics on the right feared that the move would weaken the Pentagon's historically strong role in intelligence matters. Secretary of Defense Rumsfeld was openly critical of the measure.[111] Critics on the left worried that the DNI would become "an intelligence czar in the hip pocket of the president."[112] With opposition from both ends of the ideological spectrum the bill appeared headed for failure.

Kean was determined not to let that happen. With the commission set to expire as an officially sanctioned government entity on 21 August 2004, he announced that he was looking for private funding to continue the lobbying effort. "We want to be part of the debate," he declared. Toward that end he and Hamilton appeared before congressional panels, hosted public meetings, and became regular fixtures on television news programs.[113] In the end their efforts succeeded. On 17 December 2004 Bush signed the Intelligence Reform Bill into law. Standing by his side at the ceremony were Kean and Hamilton, both of whom were rumored to be under consideration for the new intelligence position.[114] The job eventually went to Ambassador John Negroponte in April 2005.

The members of the 9/11 commission succeeded in finding a new life for the panel, albeit under a slightly different title. The ten formed the nucleus of a 501(c)(3) organization, the 9/11 Public Discourse Project (PDP). According to the project's website, the group was created to "educate the public on the issue of terrorism and what can be done to make the country safer" as well as to guard against "insufficient public examination of how the lessons learned from the terrorist attacks can be used to shape public policy."[115] The PDP remained an important voice in the national dialogue over security priorities for the remainder of 2004 and much of 2005.

Evaluation

In the modern era of blue-ribbon politics, the Roberts Commission on Pearl Harbor stands as one bookend and the Kean Commission on 9/11 stands as the other. But these two panels do more than bracket a specific period of time. They also serve as excellent markers with which to trace the maturation of commission inquiry. The Roberts Commission was most notable for what it did not have. The panel suffered from a curiously configured mandate, insufficient staff support, and inadequate protection from political pressure. Other complicating factors included a rushed investigation and a chairman who at times seemed bewildered by the task at hand.

The 9/11 Commission offers a radically different perspective on blue-ribbon investigation. By all accounts Kean was an alert, involved, and politically astute leader. Although the former governor's actions failed to please all parties, the critics nonetheless found much to like about him. Kristen Breitweiser, a 9/11 widow who followed the commission from start to finish, wished that Kean had been "more aggressive" with the administration. Even so, she gave him high marks for accessibility, noting his willingness to return calls and to listen to the families' concerns.[116] "I respect him," said Mary Fatchet of the Family Steering Committee. "He has high integrity, high values. He is diplomatic. And he was able to solidify the group through the process."[117]

Kean also demonstrated good internal capacity as a leader. He never let differences of opinion interfere with the work of the commission. Roemer, who inherited the title of the commission's most outspoken member following Cleland's departure, noted that "disagreement with Tom Kean does not result in division or personal animosity ... he doesn't burn bridges."[118] Commissioner Ben-Veniste, another Democratic appointee, characterized Kean as a "national icon." "I did not know Kean before," he said, "but I learned this was a steel fist in a velvet glove."[119] The chairman was tough when he needed to be. He repeatedly warned the members that the commission's credibility rested on presenting a defiantly nonpartisan face to the public. And behind closed doors, he could be quite direct, especially if he felt that a member's conduct had violated the rule of strict neutrality.[120]

The 9/11 Commission also did much to institutionalize blue-ribbon inquiry. It set a new standard by which future panels will be judged. In sharp contrast to the Pearl Harbor investigation, Kean's group benefited from a well-defined mandate, an impressively large support staff, and sufficient resources. To make good on its promise of maximum transparency, the commission maintained a well-organized website (<www.9-11commission.gov>) that provided a wealth of information on the members, staff, issues, and events. It also featured an extensive archive of public hearings and press conferences. Finally, the twenty-month investigation was longer than the blue-ribbon average by any objective measure.

To be sure, the commission had its share of internal problems. The decision to begin taking sworn testimony from witnesses began halfway through the investigation. The abruptness of the decision was at odds with the smoothness with which Kean and Hamilton had handled other procedural questions. In addition, there were plenty of small missteps that aggravated already tense situations. The controversy over the PDBs flowed in part from the administration's stubbornness, but it also reflected distrust in the secrecy with which the executive director negotiated the agreement

The 9/11 Commission will be remembered for having had the strongest interest-group following of any blue-ribbon probe in history. The families were a constant presence before, during, and even after the investigation. Their passion and attentiveness turned out to be a double-edged sword for the commission. On one hand, Kean and the members must have been frustrated at having their every move scrutinized by groups of individuals who followed each development with an intensity born of loss. As chairman, Kean believed in the virtue of patience and pragmatism as they applied to the issues confronting the commission. But the families approached those same issues from a perspective that was decidedly more emotional: to them, patience meant delay and pragmatism meant surrender. Although the survivors and relatives became more politically sophisticated over time, they never wavered in their insistence that the inquiry leave no stone unturned in its search for the truth.

The political weight of the families was not always unwelcome. When the commission encountered obstacles, Kean and company recognized the advantages of having a powerful, well-organized lobby on their side. "We've got the family members," one panel member observed in response to Bush's threat to invoke executive privilege on classified documents.[121] In Congress, sympathetic lawmakers also knew how much clout the families had. At one point Breitweiser urged McCain to provide "a list of the people who are giving you problems and we'll knock on doors."[122]

Finally, no evaluation of the 9/11 Commission can overlook the structural contrast between this, a national commission with heavy congressional involvement, and the more traditional presidential commissions of the past. Bush's failure to preempt Congress by establishing an executive-dominated board of inquiry in the immediate aftermath of 9/11 stands as one of the great political mysteries of recent times. He certainly had every opportunity to do so: Democrats stood on the Senate floor in the fall of 2001 and called repeatedly for a Pearl Harbor-style inquiry (following the Roberts Commission example). Alternatively, he could have embraced the Pelosi bill reported out of the House Intelligence Committee on 26 September 2001. In so doing he would have received credit for acting quickly and in a bipartisan fashion. Moreover, that legislation would have given him the ability to select four of the panel's ten members, including the chair—a far more advantageous configuration than he ultimately got one year later.

These were strategic blunders of the first order. Had Bush been a little more open-minded, a little more savvy, he could have ended up with a far more compliant panel. He also could have avoided the suspicion and ill will caused by his yearlong fight to prevent a blue-ribbon probe. Once the investigation was under way, Bush's attitude ranged from indifferent to defiant. He risked any number of political confrontations with the commission. Conversely, the commission did not hesitate to take on the White House in public. That level of confrontation would have been highly improbable had the 9/11 Commission been more presidential in nature.

Other Panels of the Bush Administration

Blue-ribbon politics in the Bush administration did not end with the 9/11 Commission. In fact there has been a resurgence of commission activity in recent years. The war in Iraq has given rise to a particularly ugly prisoner-abuse scandal at the Abu Ghraib facility west of Baghdad. On 7 May 2004, Secretary of Defense Rumsfeld appointed a four-member panel under DOD authority to follow up on administrative reviews that had already taken place.[123] James Schlesinger, a cabinet official from the Nixon and Ford administrations, chaired the panel. Other members included retired Air Force Gen. Charles Horner, former congresswoman Tillie Fowler, and former secretary of defense Harold Brown.

Critics found plenty to complain about. Wayne Downing, a retired four-star army general, pointed out an inherent conflict of interest in Rumsfeld's response: "I really doubt whether the Defense Department can investigate itself, because there's a possibility the secretary himself authorized certain actions. This cries out for an outside commission to investigate."[124]

Former navy judge advocate John Huston echoed the sentiment, calling for a new "umbrella or overarching investigation that has the power to go wherever it leads."[125]

While its membership was certainly of blue-ribbon quality, the Schlesinger panel did not rise to the level of a national or presidential commission. Organizationally speaking, the board was of the Pentagon, by the Pentagon, and for the Pentagon. The members had no subpoena power and were given only two months to conduct the entire investigation. Bush's decision to forgo a higher profile investigation reflected a determination to keep the ugliness of Abu Ghraib at arm's length. It also reflected his belief that the Schlesinger panel, while not universally accepted, would nonetheless suffice to ward off any attempt by Congress to create another 9/11-style probe.

The Schlesinger panel issued its report to Rumsfeld on 24 August 2004. Although the panel found "institutional and personal responsibility right up the chain of command," it attributed most of the blame to a failure of leadership at the Abu Ghraib prison facility. It faulted the local commanders for failing to adequately monitor the troops assigned to guard the Iraqi prisoners of war. "The night shift was off on its own," Schlesinger said at a news conference. "It was an abhorrent and horrifying crowd ... there is no policy that encourages this kind of behavior." Then came the most memorable line of all: "It was a kind of animal house on the night shift."[126]

Other than the vague mention of institutional responsibility, however, the panel did not lay blame at Rumsfeld's feet. In fact it went out of its way to absolve him of responsibility. Schlesinger deemed the secretary's conduct on the issue "exemplary," and warned that his "resignation would be a boon to all of America's enemies."[127] Given the circumstances of the panel's creation, this endorsement did little to quiet the critics. "Rumsfeld's Torture Panel Clears Rumsfeld," joked one columnist.[128] Even so, the report helped to defuse some of the national anger over the events at Abu

Ghraib, proving once again that an investigation need not be perfect to hold political value.

The war in Iraq was the source of another issue that generated blue-ribbon attention. This time the controversy involved prewar intelligence estimates of Iraqi weapons of mass destruction. Specifically, by late 2003 critics were demanding to know why prewar assurances that weapons of mass destruction (WMD) would be found in Iraq had turned out to be false. Most speculation about the disconnection between assertion and fact focused on one of three possibilities: (1) the intelligence community had simply erred; (2) the intelligence product had been tainted by interference from administration officials; or (3) the administration had "cherry-picked" its way through good intelligence to construct a pretense for going to war.

As issues go, the WMD controversy was more important than the prisoner-abuse scandal since it cast doubt on the president's integrity and decisionmaking. The administration's response reflected this higher order of concern. On 6 February 2004, President Bush signed Executive Order 13328 establishing a Commission on the Intelligence Capabilities of the United States Regarding Weapons of Mass Destruction.[129] Among other particulars, the panel was asked to examine the intelligence community's response to the "threats of the 21st century." But there would be no confusion about the main focus of the investigation. The commission's web address said it all (www.wmd.gov).[130]

Everything about the WMD panel suggested that Bush and his advisers had learned a hard lesson from the 9/11 investigation. This time the White House would draft the mandate. This time there would be no public hearings. This time there would be no subpoenas.[131] Moreover, Bush granted the panel a generous period of thirteen months to conduct its investigation. Critics noted that the schedule was politically convenient since the commission would not issue its report until well after the 2004 presidential election.[132]

The executive character of the commission was best exemplified by the membership. Bush reserved *all* the membership appointments for himself. He named federal judge Laurence Silberman and former senator and governor Charles Robb as co-chairs. The other seven seats went to Senator John McCain; Walter Slocombe, a DOD official who had worked as a senior advisor to the provisional authority in Iraq; Richard Levin, president of Yale University; Adm. William Studeman, former deputy director of the CIA; Judge Patricia Wald of the Washington, DC, Circuit Court; Charles Vest, president of MIT; and Henry Rowen, chairman of the National Intelligence Council under President Reagan. Former Clinton aide Lloyd Cutler joined in the role of counsel.

The Silberman-Robb Commission delivered its final report to the president on 31 March 2005. The report was harshly critical of the intelligence community. It determined that the spies had been "simply wrong" on the question of the Iraqi WMD program.[133] Conversely, the commission found little fault with the president and his inner circle. The investigation uncovered "no evidence" that intelligence assessments had been manipulated to meet political objectives.[134] Even so, a footnote at the end of the report's Chapter 1 offered this disclaimer:

> Our review has been limited by our charter to the question of alleged policymaker pressure on the Intelligence Community to shape its conclusions to conform to the policy preferences of the Administration. There is a separate issue of how policymakers used the intelligence they were given and how they reflected it in their presentations to Congress and the public. That issue is not within our charter and we therefore did not consider it nor do we express a view on it.[135]

Columnist, and former Nixon administration counsel, John Dean had anticipated this dodge. At the time of the commission's appointment he had warned that

> Bush's Executive Order only *pretends* to look at the issue of pre-war Iraqi WMD intelligence. In fact, it does not look at what is really the issue: *the use of that intelligence by policy makers* [emphasis in the original]. The questions of what the intelligence said, and how it was used—specifically, was it exploited or distorted?—are quite separate. Bush's Commission will answer only the first question. And it may not be able to answer even that in a prompt fashion.[136]

Maureen Dowd found it "laughable that the report offers its most scorching criticism of the CIA when the CIA was doing what the White House and Pentagon wanted."[137] David Corn of *The Nation* opined that the commission had "served Bush well, but not the public."[138]

In May 2005 new charges arose that cast doubt on the reliability of the commission's findings. The "Downing Street Memos," a series of secret British communications dating to 2002, offered a damning indictment of US decisionmaking in the months leading up to the attack on Iraq. Once again, the Bush administration found itself scrambling to respond to allegations that intelligence had been "fixed" to support the case for war.[139]

Conclusion

The return of the blue-ribbon option is a commentary on the state of presidential power in the US political system. National security commissions were the order of the day when the Cold War dominated US politics. But the demise of the Soviet Union and its empire caused national security concerns to lose their hold on the public imagination. Domestic issues heated up, and the US Congress began to challenge the president for political primacy. Talk of the imperial presidency had all but stopped by the beginning of the 1990s, and the scandals of the Clinton years accelerated the erosion of executive power.

Then came 9/11. The war on terror has breathed new life into the national security establishment, refocused the electorate's attention, and forced a reevaluation of budgetary priorities. All signs point to a stronger role for the president, a development that is consistent with the governing philosophy of President Bush. In this context, the return of commission politics stands as a by-product of the times and a commentary on the state of executive power.

Notes

1. *Congressional Record–Senate*, 107th Congress, 1st session, 12 September 2001, S9311-S9312 [THOMAS Legislative Information System].

2. *Congressional Record–Senate*, 107th Congress, 1st session, 26 September 2001, S9846 [THOMAS Legislative Information System].

3. Permanent Select Committee on Intelligence, Report 107-219 for H.R. 2883, 107th Congress, 1st session, 26 September 2001 [THOMAS Legislative Information System].

4. Ibid.

5. Alison Mitchell and Todd S. Purdum, "Lawmakers Seek Inquiry into Intelligence Failures," *New York Times*, 22 October 2001, p. A1.

6. *Congressional Record - Senate*, 107th Congress, 1st session, 24 September 2002, S9086, [THOMAS Legislative Information System].

7. Bill Summary, S. 1837, 107th Congress, 1st session, 18 December 2001 [THOMAS Legislative Information System].

8. Ibid.

9. Bill Summary, H.R. 4777, 107th Congress, 2d session, 20 May 2002 [THOMAS Legislative Information System].

10. Susan Cornwell, "Daschle: Bush, Cheney Urged No Sept. 11 Inquiry," *Reuters News Service*, 26 May 2002 [Lexis-Nexis Academic].

11. Andrew Jacobs, "Traces of Terror," *New York Times*, 12 June 2002, p. A25.

12. "Cheney Blasts 9-11 Critics," *CNN Access* < http://archives.cnn.com/2002/ ALLPOLITICS/ 05/23/cheney.king.cnna/>.

13. Robert Torricelli, "For a Pearl Harbor Inquiry," *Washington Post*, 17 February 2002, p. B7.

14. David E. Rosenbaum, "Bush Bucks Tradition on Investigation," *New York Times*, 26 May 2002, p. 18.

15. Dana Milbank, "In War, It's Power to the President," *Washington Post*, 20 November 2001, p. A1.

16. Declassified Memo, "Bin Laden Determined to Strike Inside U.S," *CBSNews Online* <http://www.cbsnews.com/htdocs/pdf/pdb_080601.pdf>.

17. Andrew Miga, "Bush Bashed; Dems Slam President on Terror Warnings," *Boston Herald*, 17 May 2002, p. 1.

18. Editorial, "The Past as Prelude," *New York Times*, 26 May 2002, p. 10.

19. See, for example, William Kristol and Robert Kagan, "Still Time for an Investigation," *Weekly Standard* 7:38 (31 May 2002), <http://www.weeklystandard.com/Content/ Public/Articles/000/000/001/306rvawx.asp>.

20. *NBC News–Wall Street Journal* Poll, 8 June 2002, *Pollingreport.com* <http://www.pollingreport.com/terror.htm >.

21. Andrew Jacobs, "Traces of Terror."

22. Among the group of twenty-five were four representatives from New Jersey, one from New York, and one from Connecticut. Roll Call 347 on H.R. 4628, 107th Congress, 2d session, 25 July 2002, U.S. House of Representatives [THOMAS Legislative Information System].

23. Michael Isikoff and Tamara Lipper, "Cheney: Investigators, Keep Out," *Newsweek*, 21 October 2003 [Infotrac One File].

24. Helen Dewar, "Bush Doubted on 9/11 Panel," *Washington Post*, 12 October 2002, p. A6.

25. Helen Dewar, "Deal Reached on 9/11 Commission," *Washington Post*, 15 November 2002, p. A6.

26. House Resolution 537, 107th Congress, 2d session, 18 September 2002 [THOMAS Legislative Information System].

27. See Section 606 of Public Law 107-306, 107th Congress, 2d session, 27 November 2002 [THOMAS Legislative Information System].

28. Amy Goldstein, "9/11 Panel Gets New Chairman," *Washington Post*, 17 December 2002, p. A1.

29. Gene Collier, "How Much Is the Truth About 9/11 Worth?" *Pittsburgh Post-Gazette*, 2 April 2003, p. E2.

30. "Who Represents Whom on 9/11 Commission?" *Washingtonian*, June 2004, pp. 18–19.

31. Dan Eggen, "Kissinger Quits Post As Head of 9/11 Panel," *Washington Post*, 14 December 2002, p. A1.

32. Amy Goldstein, "9/11 Panel Gets New Chairman."

33. Philip Shenon, "Bush Names Former New Jersey Governor to 9/11 Panel," *New York Times*, 17 December 2002, p. 21.

34. Ibid.

35. Linton Weeks, "An Indelible Day," *Washington Post*, 16 June 2004, p. C1.

36. Amy Goldstein, "9/11 Panel Gets New Chairman."

37. William Rivers Pitt, "Bush Nominates Himself to Chair 9/11 Investigation," *Truthout.com*, 19 December 2002 <http://www.truthout.org/docs_02/ 12.20A.wrp.kean.htm>.

38. Amy Goldstein, "9/11 Panel Gets New Chairman."

39. Philip Shenon, "Bush Names Former New Jersey Governor to 9/11 Panel."

40. Linton Weeks, "An Indelible Day," *Washington Post*, 16 June 2004, p. C1.

41. Commission Staff Organization, National Commission on Terrorist Attacks Upon the United States (hereafter NCTA), <http://www. 9-11commission.gov/about/faq.htm>.

42. Dan Eggen, "9/11 Panel to Receive More Money," *Washington Post*, 29 March 2003, p. A4.

43. Ibid.

44. Public Hearing of 31 March 2003, NCTA <http://www. 9-11commission.gov/ hearings/hearing1.htm>.

45. Ibid.

46. Michael Isikoff and Mark Hosenball, "Terror Watch: September 11 Showdown," *Newsweek*, 7 May 2003.

47. Bryan Bender, "Roadblocks Seen in September 11 Inquiry," *Boston Globe*, 9 July 2003, p. A2 [Lexis-Nexis Academic].

48. Kelly Patricia O'Meara, "A Historical Whitewash?" *Insight on the News*, 22 December 2003, p. 18 [Lexis-Nexis Academic].

49. Mike Kelly, "Kean's 9/11 Panel Sets Deadline for Access to Federal Officials," *The Record* (Bergen County, NJ), 24 September 2003 [Lexis-Nexis Academic].

50. The commission later issued a third subpoena to the city of New York.

51. Weeks, "An Indelible Day."

52. Philip Shenon, "9/11 Commission Could Subpoena Oval Office Files," *New York Times*, 26 October 2003, p. 1.

53. Technically, the subpoena would have been issued to the CIA as the originator of the briefs. But the very name of the document in question—the PDB—ensured that the subpoena's most direct impact would be on the White House itself.

54. Mike Kelly, "How Tough Is Tom Kean? We'll Soon Know," *The Record* (Bergen County, NJ), 6 November 2003 [Lexis-Nexis Academic].

55. Mike Kelly, "Tom Kean's Small Victory," *The Record* (Bergen County, NJ), 16 November 2003 [Lexis-Nexis Academic].

56. Shenon, "9/11 Commission Could Subpoena Oval Office Files."

57. Weeks, "An Indelible Day."

58. Philip Shenon, "9/11 Panel Issues Subpoena to Pentagon," *New York Times*, 8 November 2003, p. 13.

59. Philip Shenon, "Panel Reaches Deal on Access to 9/11 Papers," *New York Times*, 13 November 2003, p. 1.

60. Ibid.

61. Max Cleland, Interview by Eric Boehlert, "The President Ought to Be Ashamed," *Salon.com*, 21 November 2003, <http://www.salon.com/news/feature/2003/ 11/21/cleland/index_np.html>.

62. Ibid.

63. Nominations Sent to the Senate, 21 November 2003, White House <http://www.whitehouse.gov/news/releases/2003/11/20031121-18.html>.

64. Shaun Waterman, "Truth Squad," *The American Prospect* (April 2004), 45 [Lexis-Nexis Academic: 3].

65. Dan Eggen, "Sept. 11 Panel Defends Director's Impartiality," *Washington Post*, 14 October 2003, p. A2.

66. Waterman, "Truth Squad."

67. Ibid.

68. Ibid.

69. Shenon, "9/11 Commission Could Subpoena Oval Office Files."

70. O'Meara, "A Historical Whitewash?"

71. Ceci Connolly, "Senators Call on White House to Share Records with 9/11 Panel," *Washington Post*, 27 October 2003, p. A3.

72. "A Citizen's Critique: The 9/11 Commission Process," 9/11 Citizens Watch, <http://www.911citizenswatch.org>.

73. Press Briefing by Scott McClellan, 4 February 2004, White House <http://www.whitehouse.gov/news/releases/2004/02/20040204-7.html#1>.

74. Editorial, "Lift the Deadline," *Washington Post*, 30 January 2004, p. A20.

75. Statement on S. 2136," 16 March 2004, White House <http://www.whitehouse.gov/ news/releases/2004/03/20040316-9.html>.

76. Press Briefing by Scott McClellan, 9 March 2004, White House <http://www.whitehouse.gov/news/releases/2004/03/20040309-5.html>.

77. Press Briefing by Scott McClellan, 30 March 2004, White House <http://www.whitehouse.gov/ news/releases/2004/03/20040330-4.html#2>.

78. Mike Allen and Dan Eggen, "President to Let Rice Testify About 9/11," *Washington Post*, 31 March 2004, p. A1.

79. Public Hearing of 26 January 2004, NCTA <http://www. 9-11commission.gov/ hearings/hearing7.htm>.

80. Public Hearing of 24 March 2004, NCTA <http://www. 9-11commission.gov/ archive/hearing8/9-11Commission>.

81. Dan Eggen, "Bush, Clinton Agree to Testify Privately to Panel Probing 9/11," *Washington Post*, 14 February 2004, p. A12.

82. Statement by Kean and Hamilton, 25 February 2004, NCTA <http://www.9-11commission.gov/press/pr_2004-02-25.pdf>.

83. Allen and Eggen, "President to Let Rice Testify About 9/11."

84. Dana Milbank, "Speculation About Joint Appearance," *Washington Post*, 25 April 2004, p. A1.

85. Ibid.

86. Ibid.

87. White House Press Briefing, 29 April 2004, White House <http://www. whitehouse.gov/news/releases/2004/04/20040429-4.html>.

88. Remarks by the President, 29 April 2004, White House < http://www .whitehouse. gov/news/releases/2004/04/20040429-1.html>.

89. Michael Isikoff, "9/11 Commission: The Panel Tones It Down," *Newsweek* (10 May 2004), p. 6 [Infotrac One File].

90. Public Hearing, 13 April 2004, NCTA <http://www.9-11commission.gov/ archive/hearing10/9-11Commission_Hearing_2004-04-13.htm>.

91. White House Press Briefing, 29 April 2004, The White House <http://www.whitehouse.gov/ news/releases/2004/04/20040429-4.html>.

92. *The 9/11 Commission Report,* authorized edition (New York: W. W. Norton, 2004), p. xv.

93. Weeks, "An Indelible Day."

94. Transcript, "9/11 Panel Releases Final Report," *Washington Post*, 22 July 2004.

95. Ibid.

96. Ibid.

97. Weeks, "An Indelible Day." A similar distribution pattern occurred when Bantam Books printed the Warren Commission report. See David Flitner Jr., *The Politics of Presidential Commissions* (Dobbs Ferry, NY: Transnational Publishers, 1986), p. 101.

98. Dan Eggen and Helen Dewar, "Hill, Bush React to 9/11 Report," *Washington Post*, 25 July 2004, p. A6.

99. Editorial, "The Black Book," *The New Republic*, 9 August 2004, p. 7 [Lexis-Nexis Academic].

100. E. J. Dionne Jr., "A Lesson from 9/11: Openness," *Washington Post*, 23 July 2004, p. A29.

101. Editorial, "The Black Book."

102. Jeff Baenen, "9/11 Report Leads Finalists for National Book Awards," Associated Press, 13 October 2004 [Lexis-Nexis Academic].

103. Richard A. Clarke, "Honorable Commission, Toothless Report," *New York Times*, 25 July 2004, pp. 4–11.

104. William Raspberry, "Failures of the Sept. 11 Commission," *Washington Post*, 26 July 2004, p. A11.

105. Eric Lichtblau, "CIA Officer Denounces Agency and Sept. 11 Report," *New York Times*, 17 August 2004, p. A14.

106. Transcript, CNN Late Edition with Wolf Blitzer, 25 July 2004, Cable News Network [Lexis-Nexis Academic].

107. Jim VandeHei, "9/11 Panel Roiling Campaign Platforms," *Washington Post*, 9 August 2004, p. A1.

108. Eggen and Dewar, "Hill, Bush React to 9/11 Report."

109. VandeHei, "9/11 Panel Roiling Campaign Platforms."

110. Michael Isikoff and Eleanor Clift, "Intel Reform: Did Bush Push Hard?" *Newsweek*, 6 December 2004, p. 6 [Infotrac One File].

111. Wire Report, "Bush Wants New Chief of Intelligence," *St. Petersburg Times*, 3 August 2004, p. 1A [Lexis-Nexis Academic].

112. Dan Eggen and Walter Pincus, "White House, Senators Object to Key Proposal of 9/11 Panel," *Washington Post*, 1 August 2004, p. A11.

113. VandeHei, "9/11 Panel Roiling Campaign Platforms."

114. Peter Baker and Walter Pincus, "Bush Signs Intelligence Reform Bill," *Washington Post*, 18 December 2004, p. A1.

115. Overview, 9/11 Public Discourse Project < http://www.9-11pdp.org/about/index.htm>.

116. Weeks, "An Indelible Day."

117. Editorial, "The Inquirer's Citizen of the Year," *Philadelphia Inquirer Online*, 2 January 2005, <http://www.philly.com/mld/inquirer/editorial/10545713.htm>.

118. Mike Kelly, "Kean Feels Weight of Past, Present, and Future, Too," *The Record* (Bergen County, NJ), 15 February 2004, p. A1 [Lexis-Nexis Academic].

119. Editorial, "The Inquirer's Citizen of the Year."

120. Isikoff, "9/11 Commission: The Panel Tones It Down."

121. Isikoff and Hosenball, "Terror Watch: September 11 Showdown."

122. Andrew Jacobs, "Trade Center Widows Lobby for Independent Inquiry," *New York Times*, 12 June 2002, p. A25.

123. DOD Press Release No. 433-04, 7 May 2004, U.S. Department of Defense, <http://www.dod.gov/ releases/2004/nr20040507-0744.html>. For a discussion of the army probes that preceded the appointment of the Schlesinger panel, see Steven Strasser, ed. *The Abu Ghraib Investigations* (New York: Public Affairs Books, 2004), pp. xii–xviii.

124. Bradley Graham, "Some Seek Broad, External Inquiry on Prisoner Abuse," *Washington Post*, 27 May 2004, p. A14.

125. Steven Lee Meyers and Eric Schmitt, "Wide Gaps Seen in U.S. Inquiries on Prison Abuse," *New York Times*, 6 June 2004, p. 1.

126. Transcript of News Conference, "Independent Panel Finds No Policy of Abuse at Abu Ghraib," International Information Programs, 24 August 2004 [Lexis-Nexis Academic].

127. Ibid.

128. Chris Shumway, "Rumsfeld's Torture Panel Clears Rumsfeld," *New Standard*, 26 August 2004 <http://www.antiwar.com/orig/shumway.php?articleid=3450>.

129. Executive Order 13328, Commission on the Intelligence Capabilities of the United States Regarding Weapons of Mass Destruction, 6 February 2004, White House, <http://www.whitehouse.gov/news/ releases/2004/02/20040206-10.html>.

130. Commission on the Intelligence Capabilities of the United States Regarding Weapons of Mass Destruction, <http://www.wmd.gov>.

131. Editorial, "Muscle for the Intelligence Commission," *New York Times*, 9 March 2004, p. 24.

132. Mike Allen, "Bush Names Panel on Iraq Data," *Washington Post*, 8 February 2004, p. A1.

133. *Report to the President of the United States*, Commission on the Intelligence Capabilities of the United States Regarding Weapons of Mass Destruction (Washington, DC: Government Printing Office, 2005), Letter of Transmittal.

134. Ibid., 188.

135. Ibid., 247.

136. John W. Dean, "President Bush's New Iraq Commission Won't Be Investigating the Key WMD Issue: How the Executive Order Fatally Limits Their Agenda," *Findlaw: Writ*, 13 February 2004, <http://writ.news.findlaw.com/dean/20040213.html>.

137. Maureen Dowd, "I Spy a Screw-Up," *New York Times*, 31 March 2005, p. 27.

138. David Corn, "WMD Commission Stonewalls," Capital Games Blog, *Nation* 1 April 2005, <http://www.thenation.com/blogs/capitalgames>.

139. Walter Pincus, "British Intelligence Warned Blair of War; Prime Minister Was Told of White House's Resolve to Use Military Against Hussein," *Washington Post*, 13 May 2005, p. A18.

7

Conclusion:
The Politics of Damage Control

*The processes of government are very like an iceberg: what appears on
the surface may be but a small part of the reality beneath.*
  —Harold Laski, *The American Presidency*

The preceding chapters have provided a behind-the-scenes look at some
of the most important blue-ribbon security panels ever appointed. The
cases presented span six decades, cover four presidential administrations,
and incorporate a "who's who" of key players in the national security
establishment. Given the details of each case, attention may shift from the
particular to the general. We begin with a discussion of two currents that
run throughout the five cases.

First, there is more to national security commissions than meets the
eye. Some of the hidden activity is purely administrative in nature. No
commission could function without the support of a loyal staff and a dedi-
cated executive director. Indeed, the commissioners encountered in this
study were rightly awed by the enormous investment of time and effort by
those who organize the investigation, carry out the research, and write the
report. More than one beleaguered staffer was observed to be "chained to"
a typewriter or word processor as a deadline approached. The fact that
these individuals carry such a burden without public acclaim is a testament
to their level of commitment.

But other types of activity are also concealed. This is true of political
interaction both within a commission as well as between the commission
and external actors. As a case in point, all five of the commissions generated final reports that ostensibly enjoyed the support of each of the commissioners. But to term them "unanimous," while technically correct, obscures
important detail.

In the Pearl Harbor investigation, Admiral Standley threatened to go
public with his concern about the tenor of the Roberts report. In the CIA
investigation, Erwin Griswold agreed only at the last minute to forgo a formal dissent and to condense his objections into a footnote. And in the case
of the 9/11 Commission, Vice Chairman Lee Hamilton admitted that one
reason the panel did not address the war in Iraq was fear that the members

would be unable to agree and would openly break ranks. In most cases this maneuvering was not reported, if at all, until after the investigation was over. Laski's iceberg analogy, then, should be taken as a cautionary note for future commission scholars. What is visible at first represents only a portion of the story.

Another general observation is that the late Aaron Wildavsky had it right all along. There might be one president in the United States but there are two presidencies, one for domestic affairs and the other for national security.[1] Each of these policy areas has its own actors and unwritten rules of conduct. In the arena of national security the president enjoys the advantage. Congress is more compliant, the media are more deferential, and the public is more supportive. In addition, the president is constitutionally well equipped to deal with security issues by virtue of his roles as commander in chief and chief diplomat. The leader who uses his political capital wisely can play to these strengths and reap the attendant political benefits.

The presidents featured in these case studies (Franklin D. Roosevelt, Ford, Reagan, and George W. Bush) behaved exactly as Wildavsky would have predicted. For starters, they were attentive. One wonders if inquiries dealing with social issues would have commanded the same amount of White House interest. They were also highly protective of their position atop the national security establishment; they acted decisively when they sensed others encroaching on executive authority. A recurring theme in the five cases was a push on the part of presidents and other executive-branch officials to keep Congress away from foreign and defense policy.

Damage Control

At the heart of this book is the question of the true nature of presidential commissions. Are they appointed to serve as legitimate fact-finding agents, as most of the literature suggests, or do they exist merely to protect the president and make the "bad thing" go away?[2] Some scholars have suggested that this is a false dichotomy, that commissions can serve more than one end.[3]

Maybe. But whatever commensurability exists is tenuous. A more defensible proposition is that no two presidents are the same and no two commissions are alike, so the degree to which the latter are politicized depends on the situation. Along these lines, Thomas Wolanin cautions against simplistic explanations that fail to acknowledge that a commission might serve "multiple and interrelated purposes" for a president. Only detailed case studies, he argues, can reveal if a "dominant purpose" was at work in the decision to create a commission.[4] For this reason it is difficult to make general statements regarding presidential intent and the blue-ribbon option.

This study, however, does not focus on the larger universe of federal advisory bodies or even on the subset of bodieŝ classified as presidential commissions. Instead it concerns itself with an even narrower substratum of advisory body, the national security commission. As discussed in Chapter 1, there are good reasons to believe these panels are qualitatively different from other types of commissions. National security is a unique policy area, and presidents behave differently when the focus turns to defense or foreign affairs.

The preceding chapters have illuminated the interplay among presidents, commissions, and other actors in the national security apparatus. Each case serves a dual purpose, standing both as a story unto itself as well as contributing to a more general understanding of the dynamics that shape security commissions. With regard to the latter, Robert Yin argues that studies based on multiple cases, such as this one, can produce "analytical generalizability."[5] Simply put, when the same dynamics appear in case after case, there is more than coincidence at work.

Certainly one of the most important dynamics seen in the commissions examined was a concerted effort by presidents to protect their prerogative on matters of national security. As an objective, it appeared in each of the five cases and transcended time, party, and ideology. White House officials worked tirelessly to keep Congress at bay and allay public concerns. Ultimately, the search for a device to facilitate that effort led presidents to the blue-ribbon option.

This finding casts doubt on the claim that blue-ribbon commissions exist primarily as fact-finding agents. In those instances where the commission emanated from the White House (the 9/11 panel being the lone exception here), the push to launch such an investigation was driven more by political considerations than by any real desire to get to the bottom of things.

Consider these excerpts from the five cases. Each represents a contemporaneous observation from someone at or near the center of decisionmaking as the commission took shape:

Roberts Commission:
- Secretary of the Navy Frank Knox: On the eve of commission's creation, he wrote to a friend that he feared a "nasty congressional investigation."
- Secretary of War Henry Stimson: On 11 December, he noted in his diary that he and Knox were looking for a way to avoid an "interdepartmental scrap" over responsibility for Pearl Harbor.
- President Franklin Roosevelt: As the commission got under way, he used press outlets to urge "no back seat drivers" in the war effort.

Rockefeller Commission:
- President Gerald Ford: He privately expressed his concern that "unnecessary disclosures would result from an investigation dominated by Congress."
- Presidential assistant Jack Marsh: He told Ford that "the panel's efforts would take the initiative rather than finding ourselves whipsawed by prolonged congressional hearings."
- CIA Director William Colby: He was informed by White House aides that a commission would be created "to still the outcry and thus prevent a full investigation of intelligence from getting started."

Scowcroft Commission:
- Deputy National Security Advisor Robert McFarlane: He argued for a commission "to overcome Cap Weinberger's inability to ... promote our defense policy successfully."
- McFarlane: In setting up commission, he cites his conviction that "the administration just has to win" upcoming MX vote in Congress.
- Commissioner Thomas Reed: He stated his belief that commission's purpose was "to get around the fact that Congress had defeated the measure to fund the MX."

Tower Commission:
- Presidential assistant Dennis Thomas: He conceived of the commission as a means of "pulling the pin on political pressure."
- White House Chief of Staff Donald Regan: He supported commission as part of damage-control effort: He argued that "blame must be put at NSC's door—rogue operation, going on without President's knowledge or sanction."
- Commission counsel Nicholas Rostow: He viewed commission as an attempt to "take the steam out of a very nasty political episode."

It is difficult to reconcile these comments with the traditional academic view that presidents appoint commissions to provide objective fact finding and analysis. These were not the main concerns of the officials responsible for creating these panels. As priorities go, damage control was demonstrably more important.

In a general sense damage control means protecting the president's political interests. Beyond that, however, the concept becomes a bit more slippery. Sometimes damage control involves a strategy of preemption. That is, the president appoints a commission to prevent congressional action. Preemption was the main objective at work in the appointment of the Roberts and the Rockefeller commissions. For Roosevelt, the blue-ribbon option worked beautifully: congressional Democrats used the existence of the Roberts Commission to argue against special legislative hearings. Congress did not begin its own inquiry into the attack via the Joint Committee until November 1945, three months after the end of the war. Ford had less luck. The CIA scandal, coming as it did on the heels of Watergate, was simply too tempting a target for Congress to ignore. Even so, the Rockefeller report provided Ford with an early, and politically safe, set of findings on which to base his intelligence reform proposal.

Damage control can also take the form of political spin. This was the case with the Tower Commission. The Iran-Contra story dominated the headlines in late 1986 and early 1987, and Reagan's advisers knew that congressional hearings were unavoidable. The objective in appointing the Tower Commission, then, was to generate an early set of findings that could compete with the product taking shape on Capitol Hill. Reagan got what he needed. For although the Tower board criticized him, it did so in ways that were far less damning than the later investigations by Congress and Independent Counsel Walsh. Reagan's commission faulted him for sins of omission rather than commission. At worst, Reagan was portrayed as a detached leader poorly served by his top lieutenants. The Tower board also focused heavily on the arms sales to Iran and gave less attention to the diversion of funds to the contras. That emphasis was of great importance since, at least for a time, it diverted the public's attention from the most scandalous and impeachable part of the controversy.

In the case of the Scowcroft Commission, damage control meant *rapprochement* with Congress. The Reagan presidency was in its early stages when lawmakers drew a line in the sand with the vote to deny funding for the MX missile. It was a humiliating defeat for a president who had made restoration of national defense the centerpiece of his campaign. To make matters worse, Reagan's brain trust was divided on the issue, and there was a good deal of sniping about Secretary of Defense Weinberger's inability to work with Congress. With two outs in the bottom of the ninth, Reagan called on a trusted group of security gurus to save the day.

The Scowcroft panel's success in convincing Congress to fund the MX was an impressive political feat. Even more impressive was the fact that they were able to sway Congress with a missile-deployment scheme that Reagan himself had previously dismissed as unworkable. It was a remarkable sales job.[6]

Damage control took a very different form in the context of the Kean Commission. George W. Bush missed an early opportunity to get ahead of the curve on the 9/11 investigation. He continued to misjudge the situation badly and, consequently, found himself watching as Congress began to assume ownership of the blue-ribbon inquiry. Once the commission was working, however, the president found his cadence and began to practice damage control. Publicly he lauded the work of the commission he had signed into law. Behind the scenes things were different: Bush and his advisers showed remarkable determination to keep the investigation in check. They fought hard to get the exact subpoena proviso they wanted, a move that turned out to be important, given the closeness of the vote on the PDBs. They slowed the pace of the inquiry through administrative foot-dragging on requests for access to documents and key officials. They neutralized the most outspoken member of the commission by luring him off the panel with a plum appointment. They watched as one of their own cabinet officers sat in the witness chair and deftly turned the tables on one of his questioners.

In short, Bush played hardball when it mattered and tried to keep the commission off balance. Had Kean been a less skillful leader, and had the 9/11 families not emerged as such a potent political force, Bush might have succeeded in derailing the whole investigation, an outcome that would have caused a gigantic sigh of relief from the White House.

The Mechanisms of Control

As a strategy, damage control suggests that an overarching political imperative is at work behind the scenes. Presidents have a preferred outcome and are willing to use the blue-ribbon option to help achieve that end. But that represents only the first part of the political equation. For once an inquiry is established, presidents often take steps to ensure that the commission performs as expected. Previous commission scholars have given little credence to this possibility. "The White House," Wolanin argued, "lacks the time and manpower to closely monitor or to try to influence a commission."[7] But time and manpower did not hinder Roosevelt, Ford, Reagan, or Bush from acting decisively to influence the investigations presented in this book.

The political pressure on commissions comes in different forms. In the five cases examined, political activity ran the gamut from careful screening of members to censored reports, from curiously defined mandates to secretive phone calls. From a president's perspective it is clear that a little planning goes a long way. As was demonstrated most clearly with the Scowcroft Commission, the president who does a careful job constructing a commission—picking the right members, fashioning the right mandate, and stipulating the right deadline—will have little need to exert overt pressure as the inquiry progresses.

Sometimes, though, the stakes are just too high for a president to remain detached. In those instances presidents can be quite heavy-handed in their conduct. The behavior of executive-branch officials during the Pearl Harbor probe was so bold as to be shameless. Roosevelt had the panel wired from the start. As the investigation progressed, he was arguably more aware of developments than was the bewildered Roberts. Secretary Stimson kept close tabs on the deliberations through his friend Frank McCoy, a commission member, and through the timely efforts of Roberts's fellow jurist Felix Frankfurter. General Marshall had the Hawaii testimony in hand before the commission ever arrived back in Washington.

The case studies also underscore the importance of mandate, membership, and time on an investigation. These factors have been identified and explored in previous studies, yet each is deceptively complex.[8] For example, it is a given that a narrowly drawn mandate can prevent a panel from asking the right questions. The Rockefeller and Tower commissions both labored under such limitations. The award for the worst mandate, however, goes to the Roberts Commission. In tasking the commission to determine whether army or navy personnel were guilty of dereliction of duty, Roosevelt made it clear that his blue-ribbon panel was *not* at liberty to follow the evidence wherever it went. Washington decisionmakers would not, and could not, be held accountable for the disaster.

But the ability to fulfill any mandate, narrow or otherwise, depends upon adequate material resources, staff support, and legal authority. *All* of these elements must be in place for an investigation to succeed. The Roberts Commission had subpoena power but was hampered by a small and inadequate staff. In contrast, the Tower Commission had a larger and more capable staff but did not have subpoena power. The 9/11 Commission had both, yet it almost dissolved during the first six months for want of sufficient funding.

Membership is also a key concern. The size of a commission is important, as is its partisan balance and diversity. But one of the most underappreciated aspects of blue-ribbon inquiry is the *absolute importance of the commission's chair*. The chair's influence is amplified by the ad hoc nature of the inquiry. Unlike standing committees or judicial bodies, a commission must chart its own course amid partisan fights, personal disagreements, and institutional rivalries. There is no playbook to guide the investigation. In this context the values, vision, and leadership of the chair take on added importance. Find the right leader and the inquiry has a good chance of success. Find the wrong leader and the outcome is likely to be far less satisfactory.

Of the commission chairs covered in this book, Kean, and to a lesser degree Tower, stand out as the top performers. They resisted political pressure, yet worked to keep the lines of communication open with the White House and executive-branch agencies. As a result, they presided over investigations and reports that contributed to a healthy dialogue on the means and ends of US security. Other chairs were less impressive. Vice President Rockefeller was disinterested in a real investigation of the CIA

and even moved to discourage witnesses from providing too much information. In the Pearl Harbor probe Justice Roberts appeared to have good
intentions. He had few resources at his disposal, however, and seemed
completely overwhelmed by the enormity of the task given him.

Finally, the cases demonstrate that time pressures are a chronic afflic-
tion of commission-based inquiries. Of the five commissions featured in
this book, only the Roberts Commission avoided the indignity of having to
beg for more time. Ironically, at just over a month, it was also the shortest
of the investigations and it had no formally prescribed deadline. The other
panels received extensions ranging from one month (Tower) to two months
(Rockefeller, Kean) to eight months (Scowcroft).

Usually a commission makes its own case for extending an investigation. A reluctant president, after some prodding, may be induced to offer
extra time. But even this equation is subject to political maneuvering. The
Scowcroft Commission was not the driving force in the two extensions it
received. The first came courtesy of Representative Les Aspin and the second from President Reagan. Both were meant to maximize the effect of the
report and to reassure a doubtful Congress on the MX missile. Still another
twist on this issue was seen with the 9/11 Commission's decision to unoffi-
cially extend its own life, reconfigured as the 9/11 Public Discourse
Project, in order to monitor Bush's promise to pursue the panel's recommendations.

Aside from this question of the length of the investigation, there is a
second consideration that has been ignored in the literature: the amount of
time between the precipitating event and the establishment of an inquiry.
Presidents have wide latitude to control this function. As a case in point,
President Bush could have launched an investigation into 9/11 at any point
during the first year after the attack. He chose not to do so, and instead
waited fourteen months and sixteen days before Congress finally cajoled
him into signing the bill to create the 9/11 Commission. If Bush's slowness
represents one extreme, then Roosevelt's haste to get the Pearl Harbor
Commission going represents the other. Prange argues that Roberts's investigation was in fact too close to the attack. Kimmel and Short appeared
before the commission while the recovery of bodies from the harbor was
still under way.[9] The key here is balance. An investigation should be far
enough removed from the event to permit objectivity, while not being so far
away as to produce cold trails or other obstacles to the investigation.

Looking to the Future

Organizationally, the most important development surrounding commissions is the expanding role of Congress. Legislative attempts to make presidential commissions a little less presidential date to the 1980s. Democratic

lawmakers, tired of being excluded from the blue-ribbon panels of the Reagan era, began to press for a more meaningful role in the process of selecting commission members. Their insistence was rewarded. In 1985, House and Senate leaders were given the opportunity to select four of the seven members of the President's Blue Ribbon Task Group on Nuclear Weapons Program Management.[10] President George H. W. Bush continued the tradition, consulting closely with Congress on the selection of fifteen members for the 1991 Commission on the Assignment of Women in the Armed Forces.[11] And of the seventeen members who sat on the 1994 Commission on the Roles and Capabilities of the US Intelligence Community, President Clinton selected only nine.[12]

The clearest demonstration of Congress's determination to play a more important role in sanctioning blue-ribbon inquiry came in 2002 with the creation of the National Commission on Terrorist Attacks Upon the United States. As detailed in Chapter 6, there would have been no commission-based inquiry into the attacks had it not been for the persistence of key lawmakers and pressure from the 9/11 families. Bush reluctantly joined the proposal only when public opinion compelled him to do so.

Despite Bush's initial obstinacy, this sharing of responsibility by the executive and legislative branches of government is a healthy development. The manipulation of commission inquiry should become less pronounced as advisory panels move outside the president's immediate sphere of influence. But the story of the 9/11 Commission also sounds a cautionary note. For although Kean's panel enjoyed some protection from presidential influence, Bush and his advisers still managed to play the game of commission politics. To paraphrase Wildavsky, just because panels have become more congressionalized does not mean that presidents cannot win; it just means that they must win differently. Future commission scholars would be well advised to remember that a panel need not be "heavily presidential" in organization to feel the weight of White House pressure.

There is no guarantee that the trend toward joint presidential-congressional commissions will continue. In response to criticism of US decisionmaking leading up to the war with Iraq, Bush established the 2004 Commission on the Intelligence Capabilities of the United States Regarding Weapons of Mass Destruction. The commission was a throwback to the days of the imperial presidency. Structurally it was much more closely akin to the Roberts Commission than to the 9/11 Commission. The panel was created by executive order, composed solely of presidential appointees, had no subpoena power, and was completely beholden to the White House for its authority. Whether the Silberman-Robb Commission turns out to be the last of a dying breed or the harbinger of a return to the traditional presidential commission remains to be seen.

Another set of questions surrounds the trend toward more standardized and transparent investigations. Gone are the days when the Roberts Commission could operate outside of the public eye with no time limit, no investigative protocol, and no real interaction with Congress or the media. Commissions have matured as political actors in the decades since Pearl Harbor, with the 9/11 panel offering the most striking commentary on how far things have come. Kean realized at the outset that his commission would be judged as much for its public relations skill, political savvy, and procedural correctness as for its investigative competence. Moreover, the reach of the Internet and the electronic media meant that the panel's every move would be scrutinized and debated. And as discussed in Chapter 6, the presence of the 9/11 families brought interest groups into the blue-ribbon equation in a way never seen before.

One could argue these dynamics were specific to a panel that was historically unique. Topically that might be true, but the 9/11 Commission seems destined to cast a long shadow over the executive advisory system. A new set of expectations is emerging that will make it increasingly difficult for commissions to continue to function as closely held investigations answering only to the president. When panels fail to meet these new expectations (as happened with the WMD inquiry in 2005), they risk alienating key constituencies or undermining their own legitimacy.

It is difficult to predict the long-term impact of these pressures. Transparency and administrative sophistication are positive developments, but they nonetheless represent a challenge to blue-ribbon tradition. As political actors go, commissions have always been unique. They have operated in a political limbo of sorts, separated from normal bureaucratic processes and functioning with minimal attention. It thus seems fair to ask how they will adapt to the new order. Will there come a point at which commissions become so standardized that they lose their distinctive character and become just another type of government committee?

Whatever the outcome of these questions, presidents will continue to use commissions for damage control. The blue-ribbon option is simply too seductive to resist. Injected into the right situation, a panel can help quiet a furor and deflect criticism. It can also keep the president in the driver's seat when conflicts arise in the national security arena.

But the political imperative does not account for other priorities. Damage control is a strategy, not a policy, just as commission politics addresses the means rather than the ends of power. A well-designed commission can protect the president's influence over national security affairs, but it cannot dictate how that influence is ultimately used. In short, what is good for the president might *not* be good for the body politic. Only an alert and knowledgeable citizenry can see to it that the president acts for the larger good. Consequently, it is essential to have a realistic understanding of the pressures that shape blue-ribbon inquiry.

Notes

1. Aaron Wildavsky, "The Two Presidencies," *Transaction* 4 (December 1966), 7–14.

2. William Powers, "Oh My!" *New Republic* 216 (11 August 1997), 9.

3. Thomas R. Wolanin, *Presidential Advisory Commissions: Truman to Nixon* (Madison: University of Wisconsin Press, 1975), p. 26.

4. Ibid.

5. Robert K. Yin, *Case Study Research: Design and Methods* (Beverly Hills, CA: Sage Publications, 1984), pp. 37-39.

6. For a discussion of the use of a commission to enhance credibility, see Wolanin, *Presidential Advisory Commissions*, p. 17.

7. Ibid., 91.

8. This finding is supported by other studies of commissions. See Terrence R. Tutchings, *Rhetoric and Reality: Presidential Commissions and the Making of Public Policy* (Boulder, CO: Westview Press, 1979), Ch. 3; David Flitner Jr., *The Politics of Presidential Commissions* (Dobbs Ferry, NY: Transnational Publishers, 1986), Ch. 3; Wolanin, *Presidential Advisory Commissions*, Ch. 5.

9. Gordon W. Prange, *At Dawn We Slept: The Untold Story of Pearl Harbor* (New York: Penguin Books, 1981), p. 602.

10. Executive Order 12499, 18 January 1985, Ronald Reagan Presidential Library <http://www.reagan.utexas.edu/resource/speeches/1985/11885b.htm>.

11. Public Law 102-190, 102d Congress, 1st session, 5 December 1991 [THOMAS Legislative Information System].

12. Public Law 103-359, 103d Congress, 2d session, 14 October 1994 [THOMAS Legislative Information System].

Bibliography

Abraham, Henry J. *Justices and Presidents: A Political History of Appointments to the Supreme Court.* 2d ed. New York: Oxford University Press, 1985.

Abshire, David, ed. *Triumphs and Tragedies of the Modern Presidency: Seventy-Six Case Studies in Presidential Leadership.* Westport, CT: Praeger, 2001.

Ackerman, Wendy E. "Separation of Powers and Judicial Service on Presidential Commissions." *University of Chicago Law Review* 53 (1986): 993–1,025.

Annual Report of the President on Federal Advisory Committees. Washington, DC: General Services Administration, 1972–2005.

Aspin, Les. "The MX Bargain." *Bulletin of the Atomic Scientists* 39 (November 1983): 52–54.

Bacevich, A. J. *Diplomat in Khaki: Major General Frank Ross McCoy and American Foreign Policy 1898–1949.* Lawrence, KS: University Press of Kansas, 1989.

Batten, Donna, ed. *The Encyclopedia of Governmental Advisory Organizations.* 16th ed. Detroit: Gale Research, 2002.

Beach, Edward L. *Scapegoats: A Defense of Kimmel and Short at Pearl Harbor.* Annapolis: Naval Institute Press, 1995.

Beckman, Peter R., Larry Campbell, Paul W. Crumlish, Michael N. Doblowski, and Steven P. Lee. *The Nuclear Predicament: Nuclear Weapons in the Cold War and Beyond.* 2d ed. Englewood Cliffs, NJ: Prentice Hall, 1992.

Belin, David W. Executive Director, Rockefeller Commission. Telephone interview by author, 18 February 1994.

———. *Final Disclosure: The Full Truth About the Assassination of President Kennedy.* New York: Charles Scribner's Sons, 1988.

———. *You Are the Jury.* New York: Quadrangle Books, 1973.

Beyers, R. B., ed. *Deterrence in the 1980s.* New York: St. Martin's, 1985.

Bland, Larry I., ed. *The Papers of George Catlett Marshall.* Baltimore: The Johns Hopkins University Press, 1991.

Bledsoe, W. Craig, Harrison Donnelly, Richard A. Karno, Steven L. Robertson, and Margaret C. Thompson. *Cabinets and Counselors: The President and the Executive Branch.* Washington, DC: *Congressional Quarterly,* 1989.

Boston Herald. Selected articles on the 9/11 investigation, 2001–2004.

Bradlee, Ben Jr. *Guts and Glory: The Rise and Fall of Oliver North.* New York: Donald I. Fine, Inc., 1988.

Breckinridge, Scott C. *The CIA and the Cold War.* Westport, CT: Praeger, 1993.

Brown, Harold. Senior Counselor, Scowcroft Commission. Telephone interview by author, 9 March 1995.

Brownlow, Donald Grey. *The Accused: The Ordeal of Rear Admiral Husband Edward Kimmel, U.S.N.* New York: Vantage Press, 1968.
Bundy, McGeorge. *Danger and Survival.* New York: Random House, 1988.
Campbell, Colton C. *Discharging Congress: Government by Commission.* Westport, CT: Praeger, 2002.
Cartwright, T. J. *Royal Commissions and Departmental Committees in Britain.* London: Hodder and Stoughton, 1975.
Chapman, Richard A., ed., *The Role of Commissions in Policy-Making.* London: George Allen and Unwin, 1973.
Charlton, Michael. *From Deterrence to Defense.* Cambridge: Harvard University Press, 1987.
Cimbala, Stephen J. *First Strike Stability: Deterrence After Containment.* Westport, CT: Greenwood, 1990.
————. "Midgetman: Major Problems." *Bulletin of the Atomic Scientists* 40 (February 1984): 7–8.
Clausen, Henry C. and Bruce Lee, *Pearl Harbor: Final Judgement.* New York: HarperCollins, 2001.
Cleland, Max. Interview by Eric Boehlert. "The President Ought to Be Ashamed." *Salon.com*, 21 November 2003, <http://www.salon.com/news/feature/2003/11/21/cleland/index_np.html>.
Cohen, William S. and George J. *Men of Zeal.* New York: Viking, 1988.
Colby, William and Peter Forbath. *Honorable Men: My Life in the CIA.* New York: Simon and Schuster, 1978.
Commission on CIA Activities Within the United States 1975. *Report of the Commission on CIA Activities Within the United States* (Rockefeller Commission Report). Washington, DC: Government Printing Office, 1975.
Commission on the Japanese Attack of December 7, 1941. In *Pearl Harbor Attack: Hearings Before the Joint Committee on the Investigation of the Pearl Harbor Attack*, 79th Congress, 1st session, 1946.
Cronin, Thomas E. and Sanford D. Greenberg, eds. *The Presidential Advisory System.* New York: Harper and Row, 1969.
Dawson, Rhett. Executive Director, Tower Commission. Telephone interview by author, 13 October 1994.
Dean, John W. "President Bush's New Iraq Commission Won't Be Investigating the Key WMD Issue: How the Executive Order Fatally Limits Their Agenda." *Findlaw: Writ*, 13 February 2004, <http://writ.news.findlaw.com/dean/20040213.html>.
Dexter, Lewis Anthony. *Elite and Specialized Interviewing.* Evanston, IL: Northwestern University Press, 1970.
Donovan, John C. *The Cold Warriors: A Policy-Making Elite.* Lexington, MA: D.C. Heath and Company, 1974.
Douglas, William O. *The Court Years, 1939–1975.* New York: Random House, 1980.
Draper, Theodore. *A Very Thin Line: The Iran-Contra Affairs.* New York: Hill and Wang, 1991.
Drew, Elizabeth. "A Political Journal." *New Yorker* (20 June 1983): 39–75.
————. "On Giving Oneself a Hotfoot: Government by Commission." *Atlantic Monthly* (May 1968): 45–49.
Eckstein, Harry. *Regarding Politics: Essays on Political Theory, Stability, and Change.* Berkeley: University of California Press, 1992.

Edwards, George C. and Alec M. Gallup. *Presidential Approval: A Sourcebook.* Baltimore: The Johns Hopkins University Press, 1990.

Edwards, John. *Super Weapon: The Making of MX.* New York: W. W. Norton and Company, 1982.

Epstein, Edward Jay. *Inquest: The Warren Commission and the Establishment of Truth.* New York: Viking, 1966.

Firestone, Bernard J. and Alex Ugrinsky, eds. *Gerald R. Ford and the Politics of Post-Watergate America.* Westport, CT: Greenwood, 1993.

Fitzpatrick, J. C., ed. *The Writings of George Washington from the Original Manuscript Sources, 1745–1799,* vol. 34. Washington, DC: Government Printing Office, 1938.

Flitner, David Jr. *The Politics of Presidential Commissions: A Public Policy Perspective.* Dobbs Ferry, NY: Transnational Publishers, 1986.

———. "Why the Cynics Are Wrong About Presidential Commissions." *History News Network,* 9 February 2004, <http://hnn.us/articles/3439.html>.

Ford, Gerald R. *A Time to Heal.* New York: Harper and Row, 1979.

———. Materials on the Commission on CIA Activities Within the United States (Rockefeller Commission). Gerald R. Ford Library, Ann Arbor, MI.

———. *Portrait of the Assassin.* New York: Simon and Schuster, 1965.

———. *Public Papers of the Presidents of the United States: Gerald R. Ford, 1974–77.* Washington, DC: Government Printing Office, 1975–1978.

Frankfurter, Felix. Papers. Library of Congress. Washington, DC.

———. Papers. Harvard Law School Collection.

Freedman, Max, ed. *Roosevelt and Frankfurter: Their Correspondence 1928–1945.* Boston: Little, Brown and Company, 1967.

Gannon, Michael. *Pearl Harbor Betrayed: The True Story of a Man and a Nation Under Attack.* New York: Owl Books, 2001.

Garson, Brett. "Clandestine Operations in the CIA: When Secrecy Becomes Overextended." *Michigan Journal of History* (Winter 2004) <http://www.umich.edu/ ~historyj/papers/winter2004/garsonart.htm>.

Gellhorn, Ernest. Senior Counsel, Rockefeller Commission. Telephone interview by author, 7 September 1993.

Gore, Albert Jr. "A Bipartisan Approach to Arms Control." *Bulletin of the Atomic Scientists* 40 (October 1984): 7–8.

Graham, Hugh Davis. "The Ambiguous Legacy of American Presidential Commissions." *Public Historian* 7 (Spring 1985): 5–25.

Gray, Marvin. Counsel, Rockefeller Commission. Telephone interview by author, 31 August 1993.

Greene, Ronald. Special Counsel, Rockefeller Commission. Telephone interview by author, 17 September 1993.

Griswold, Erwin. Member, Rockefeller Commission. Telephone interview by author, 27 September 1993.

———. *Ould Fields, New Corn.* St. Paul: West Publishing, 1992.

Hadley, Stephen. Counsel, Tower Commision. Telephone interview by author, 21 September 1994.

Halperin, Morton H. "The Gaither Committee and the Policy Process." *World Politics* 3 (April 1961): 360–384.

Hanser, Charles J. *Guide to Decision: The Royal Commission.* Totowa, NJ: The Bedminster Press, 1965.

Helms, Richard, with William Hood. *A Look over My Shoulder: A Life in the Central Intelligence Agency.* New York: Random House, 2003.

Herken, Gregg. *Counsels of War.* New York: Alfred A. Knopf, 1985.

Hitchens, Christopher. "Minority Report." *The Nation* (14 March 1987): 314.

Holt, Pat M. *Secret Intelligence and Public Policy.* Washington, DC: *Congressional Quarterly,* 1995.

Howe, Bruce. Son of Recorder on Roberts Commission. Telephone interview by author, 6 August 2004.

Howe, Walter Bruce. Papers. Naval Historical Collection. Naval War College. Newport, RI.

Inglis, Fred. *The Cruel Peace.* New York: Basic Books, 1991.

Jeffreys-Jones, Rhodri. *The CIA and American Democracy.* New Haven: Yale University Press, 1989.

Johnson, Loch. *A Season of Inquiry: Congress and Intelligence.* Chicago: The Dorsey Press, 1988.

———. "The Aspin-Brown Intelligence Inquiry: Behind the Closed Doors of a Blue Ribbon Commission." *Studies in Intelligence* 48:3 (2004) <http://www.cia. gov/csi/ studies/vol48no3/article01.html>.

Jordan, Amos A., William J. Taylor, and Lawrence J. Korb. *American National Security: Policy and Process.* 4th ed. Baltimore: The Johns Hopkins University Press, 1993.

Kimmel, Husband E. *Admiral Kimmel's Story.* Chicago: Henry Regnery Company, 1955.

Kitts, Kenneth. "Commission Politics and National Security: Gerald Ford's Response to the CIA Controversy of 1975." *Presidential Studies Quarterly* 26:4 (Fall 1996): 1,081–1,098.

Knox, Frank. Papers. Library of Congress. Washington, DC.

Kornbluh, Peter and Malcolm Byrne, eds. *The Iran-Contra Scandal: The Declassified History.* New York: The New Press, 1993.

Kristol, William and Robert Kagan. "Still Time for an Investigation." *Weekly Standard* 7:38 (10 June 2002).

Landau, Saul. *The Dangerous Doctrine: National Security and U.S. Foreign Policy.* Boulder, CO: Westview, 1988.

Lane, Mark. *Rush to Judgment.* New York: Holt, Rinehart, and Winston, 1966.

Lash, Joseph P. *From the Diaries of Felix Frankfurter.* New York: W. W. Norton and Co., 1974.

Layton, Edwin T., Roger Pineau, and John Costello. *And I Was There: Pearl Harbor and Midway—Breaking the Secrets.* New York: William Morrow and Co., 1985.

Ledeen, Michael A. *Perilous Statecraft.* New York: Charles Scribner's Sons, 1988.

Lens, Sidney. "Partners: Labor and the CIA." *The Progressive* 39 (February 1975): 35–39.

Leonard, Charles A. "A Revolution Runs Wild: Mr. Justice Roberts' Last Four Years on the Supreme Court." *Supreme Court Historical Society 1980 Yearbook.*

———. *A Search for a Judicial Philosophy: Mr. Justice Roberts and the Constitutional Revolution of 1937.* Port Washington, NY: Kennikat Press, 1971.

Lettow, Paul. *Ronald Reagan and His Quest to Abolish Nuclear Weapons.* New York: Random House, 2005.

Lifton, Robert Jay and Eric Markusen. *The Genocidal Mentality: Nazi Holocaust and Nuclear Threat.* New York: Basic Books, 1990.

Liman, Arthur L. *Lawyer: A Life of Counsel and Controversy.* New York: Public Affairs Books, 1998.

Linowes, David E. *Creating Public Policy: The Chairman's Memoirs of Four Presidential Commissions*. Westport, CT: Praeger, 1998.

Lipsky, Michael and David J. Olson. *Commission Politics: The Processing of Racial Crisis in America*. New Brunswick, NJ: Transaction Publishers, 1977.

———. "Riot Commission Politics." *Transaction* 6 (July/August 1969): 9–21.

———. "Sins of Commission." *American Prospect* 12:11 (18 June 2001): 16.

Little, Daniel. *Varieties of Social Explanation*. Boulder, CO: Westview Press, 1991.

Lowi, Theodore J. *The Personal President: Power Invested, Promise Unfulfilled*. Ithaca: Cornell University Press, 1985.

Mahajani, Usha. "Kennedy and the Strategy of AID: The Clay Report and After." *Western Political Quarterly* 18 (September 1965): 656–668.

Marcy, Carl. *Presidential Commissions*. New York: King's Crown Press, 1945.

Marsh, Gerald E. "Is Smaller Better?" *Bulletin of the Atomic Scientists* 40 (February 1984): 9–10.

Mason, Alpheus Thomas. *Harlan Fiske Stone: Pillar of the Law*. Hamden, CT: Archon Books, 1968.

Matthews, Chris. *Hardball: How Politics Is Played—Told by One Who Knows the Game*. Revised edition. New York: Simon and Schuster/Touchstone, 1999.

Mayer, Jane and Doyle McManus. *Landslide: The Unmaking of the President, 1984–1988*. Boston: Houghton Mifflin Company, 1988.

McCain, Morris. *Understanding Arms Control: The Options*. New York: W. W. Norton and Company, 1989.

McCoy, Frank Ross. Papers. Library of Congress. Washington, DC.

McFadden, Clark. Counsel, Tower Commission. Telephone interview by author, 9 March 1995.

McFarlane, Robert C. *Special Trust*. New York: Cadell and Davies, 1994.

———. National Security Advisor, Reagan Administration. Telephone interview by author, 30 March 1995.

Melosi, Martin V. *The Shadow of Pearl Harbor*. College Station: Texas A&M Press, 1977.

Miller, Steven E. "The Politics of Saving the MX." *New Leader* 66 (2 May 1983): 5–7.

Muskie, Edmund. Member, Tower Commission. Telephone interview by author, 14 February 1995.

National Archives. Files of the Pearl Harbor Liaison Office. General Records of the Department of the Navy. RG 80.

National Commission on Terrorist Attacks Upon the United States. *The 9/11 Commission Report*. Authorized edition. New York: W. W. Norton, 2004.

———. Online archive of public hearings and press releases. <www.9-11commission. gov>.

Nessen, Ron. *It Sure Looks Different from the Inside*. Chicago: Playboy Press, 1979.

Newmann, William W. "The Structures of National Security Decision Making: Leadership, Institutions, and Politics in the Carter, Reagan, and G. H. W. Bush Years." *Presidential Studies Quarterly* 34:2 (June 2004): 272–306.

Newsweek. Selected articles on the Roberts (1941–1942), Rockefeller (1974–1975), Scowcroft (1982–1983), Tower (1986–1987), and 9/11 (2001–2004) commissions.

New York Times. Selected articles on the Roberts (1941–1942), Rockefeller (1974–1975), Scowcroft (1982–1983), Tower (1986–1987), and 9/11 (2001–2004) commissions.

O'Connor, Patricia Ann, ed. *The Iran-Contra Puzzle.* Washington, DC: Congressional Quarterly, Inc., 1987.

O'Reilly, James T. "Advisers and Secrets: The Role of Agency Confidentiality in the Federal Advisory Committee Act." *Northern Kentucky Law Review* 13 (1986): 27–49.

Oseth, John M. *Regulating U.S. Intelligence Operations.* Lexington: University of Kentucky Press, 1979.

Parenti, Michael. *The Sword and the Dollar: Imperialism, Revolution, and the Arms Race.* New York: St. Martin's, 1989.

Persico, Joseph E. *The Imperial Rockefeller.* New York: Simon and Schuster, 1982.

Pfaltzgraff, Robert L., Jr. and Uri Ra'anan, eds. *National Security Policy: The Decision-Making Process.* Hamden, CT: Archon Books, 1984.

Philadelphia Inquirer. Selected articles on the 9/11 Commission, 2004–2005.

Pittsburgh Post-Gazette. Selected articles on the 9/11 Commission, 2003.

Popper, Frank. *The President's Commissions.* New York: Twentieth Century Fund, 1970.

Powaski, Ronald E. *March to Armageddon: The United States and the Nuclear Arms Race, 1939 to the Present.* New York: Oxford University Press, 1987.

Powell, Colin L. with Joseph E. Persico. *My American Journey.* New York: Random House, 1995.

Powers, Thomas. *The Man Who Kept the Secrets.* New York: Alfred A. Knopf, 1979.

Powers, William. "Oh My!" *New Republic* 216:6–7 (11 August 1997): 9.

Prange, Gordon W. *At Dawn We Slept: The Untold Story of Pearl Harbor.* New York: Penguin Books, 1981.

———. *Pearl Harbor: The Verdict of History.* New York: Penguin Books, 1986, 204.

President's Commission on Strategic Forces 1983. *Report of the President's Commission on Strategic Forces* (Scowcroft Commission Report). Washington, DC: Government Printing Office, 1983.

President's Special Review Board 1987. *Report of the President's Special Review Board* (Tower Commission Report). Washington, DC: Government Printing Office, 1987.

Principles of Federal Appropriations Law, 2d edition, vol. 1. Washington, DC: U.S. General Accounting Office, 1991.

Probert, Edwin N. II. Archivist, Germantown Academy. Email correspondence with author. May-July 2004.

———. "Owen Josephus Roberts: A Short Retrospective on a Favorite Son," *The Patriot,* 1990-2000 edition, Germantown Academy, PA, <http://www.germantownacademy.org/ aboutga/history_traditions/profiles/Roberts/portrait.shtml>;

Puddington, Arch. *Lane Kirkland: Champion of American Labor.* Hoboken, NJ: John Wiley and Sons, 2005.

Ranelagh, John. *The Agency: The Rise and Decline of the CIA.* New York: Simon and Schuster, 1987.

Reagan, Ronald. *An American Life* New York: Simon and Schuster, 1990.

———. *Public Papers Of The Presidents Of The United States: Ronald W. Reagan, 1981–89.* Washington, DC: Government Printing Office, 1982–1990.

Record (Bergen County, NJ). Selected articles by Mike Kelly on the 9/11 investigation, 2001–2005.

Reed, Thomas C. *At the Abyss: An Insider's History of the Cold War.* New York: Presidio Press, 2004.

————. Member, Scowcroft Commission. Telephone interview by author, 9 March 1995.

Reeves, Richard. *A Ford Not a Lincoln*. New York: Harcourt Brace Jovanovich, 1975.

Regan, Donald T. *For the Record: From Wall Street to Washington*. New York: Harcourt Brace Jovanovich, 1988.

"Remarks at the Meeting of the Office of the Secretary of Defense and Members of the Kimmel Family." 27 April 1995. Transcription by Patricia A. LaMonica Riverton, NJ: LBS, Inc., 1995.

Reuters News Service. Selected articles on the 9/11 investigation, 2001–2004.

Rhodes, Gerald. *Committees of Inquiry*. London: George Allen and Unwin, 1975.

Richardson, James O. and George C. Dyer. *On the Treadmill to Pearl Harbor: The Memoirs of Admiral James O. Richardson*. Washington, DC: Department of the Navy—Naval History Division, 1973.

Roberts, Owen J. "Now Is the Time: Fortifying the Supreme Court's Independence." *American Bar Association Journal* 35:1 (January 1949): 1–5.

Roosevelt, Elliott, ed. *F.D.R.: His Personal Letters 1928–1945*. New York: Duell, Sloan and Pearce, 1947.

Roosevelt, Franklin D. Materials on the Commission to Investigate the Japanese Attack of December 7, 1941 (Roberts Commission). Franklin D. Roosevelt Library, Hyde Park, NY.

Rosenman, Samuel I., ed. *The Public Papers and Addresses of Franklin D. Roosevelt*. New York: Harper and Brothers, 1950.

Rostow, Nicholas. Counsel, Tower Commission. Telephone interview by author, 21 September 1994.

Rumsfeld, Donald. Senior Counselor, Scowcroft Commission. Letter to author, 19 April 1995.

Russell, Henry Dozier. *Pearl Harbor Story*. Macon, GA: Mercer University Press, 2001.

Schlesinger, Arthur Jr. *The Imperial Presidency*. New York: Popular Library, 1974.

Schlesinger, James. Senior Counselor, Scowcroft Commission. Telephone interview by author, 7 April 1995.

Schwartz, Michael, ed. *The Structure of Power in America*. New York: Holmes and Meier, 1987.

Scowcroft, Brent. Chair, Scowcroft Commission and Member, Tower Commission. Telephone interview by author, 24 April 1994.

Secord, Richard and Jay Wurts. *Honored and Betrayed*. New York: John Wiley and Sons, 1992.

Shull, Stephen A., ed. *The Two Presidencies: A Quarter Century Assessment*. Chicago: Nelson-Hall, 1991.

Skinner, Kiron K., Annelise Anderson, and Martin Anderson, eds. *Reagan: A Life in Letters*. New York: Free Press, 2003.

Smist, Frank J. *Congress Oversees the United States Intelligence Community*. Knoxville: University of Tennessee Press, 1990.

Snow, Donald M. *National Security: Enduring Problems in a Changing Defense Environment*. 2d ed. New York: St. Martin's, 1991.

Standley, William H. Papers. Library of Congress. Washington, DC.

Standley, William H. and Arthur A. Ageton. *Admiral Ambassador to Russia*. Chicago: Henry Regnery Company, 1955.

Stimson, Henry L. *Diaries of Henry L. Stimson*. New Haven: Yale University Collection.

St. Petersburg Times. Selected articles on 9/11 Commission recommendations, 2004.

Strasser, Steven, ed. *The Abu Ghraib Investigations: The Official Independent Panel and Pentagon Reports on the Shocking Prisoner Abuse in Iraq*. New York: Public Affairs Books, 2004.

————, ed. *The 9/11 Investigations: Staff Reports of the 9/11 Commission: Excerpts from the House-Senate Joint Inquiry Report on 9/11*. New York: Public Affairs Books, 2004.

Sulzner, George T. "The Policy Process and the Uses of National Government Study Commissions." *Western Political Quarterly* 24 (September 1971): 438–448.

Theobald, Robert A. *The Final Secret of Pearl Harbor*. New York: Devin-Adair Company, 1954.

Thomas, Dennis. Deputy White House Chief of Staff, Reagan Administration. Telephone interview by author, 14 December 1994.

Thomas, Evan. *The Man to See: Edward Bennett Williams—Ultimate Insider; Legendary Trial Lawyer.* New York: Simon and Schuster, 1991.

Time. Selected articles on the Rockefeller (1974–1975), Scowcroft (1982–1983), and Tower (1986–1987) commissions.

Toland, John. *Infamy: Pearl Harbor and Its Aftermath*. New York: Berkley Books, 1982.

Tower, John G. *Consequences: A Personal and Political Memoir*. Boston: Little, Brown and Company, 1991.

————. Materials on the President's Special Review Board. John G. Tower Papers. Southwestern University, Georgetown, TX.

Truman, Louis W. Oral History. Harry S. Truman Library, Independence, MO.

Turner, Michael. *The Vice-President as Policy Maker*. Westport, CT: Greenwood Press, 1982.

Tutchings, Terrence R. *Rhetoric and Reality: Presidential Commissions and the Making of Public Policy.* Boulder, CO: Westview Press, 1979.

U.S. Congress. House. Select Committee to Investigate Covert Arms Transactions with Iran, and U.S. Congress. Senate. Select Committee on Secret Military Assistance to Iran and the Nicaraguan Opposition. *Joint Hearings on the Iran-Contra Investigation*. 12 vols. 100th Congress, 1st session, 1987.

————. House. Select Committee to Investigate Covert Arms Transactions with Iran, and U.S. Congress. Senate. Select Committee on Secret Military Assistance to Iran and the Nicaraguan Opposition. *Report of the Congressional Committees Investigating the Iran-Contra Affair with Supplemental, Minority, and Additional Views*. 100th Congress, 1st session, 1987.

————. Joint Committee on the Investigation of the Pearl Harbor Attack. *Pearl Harbor Attack: Hearings Before the Joint Committee on the Investigation of the Pearl Harbor Attack*. 79th Congress, 1st session, 1946.

————. Senate. Committee on Armed Services. *Hearings on the MX Missile Basing System and Related Issues*. 98th Congress, 1st session, 1983.

————. Senate. Committee on Foreign Relations. *Hearings on the Arms Control and Foreign Policy Implications of the Scowcroft Commission Report*. 98th Congress, 1st session, 1983.

————. Senate. Committee on Foreign Relations. *The Role of Advisory Committees in U.S. Foreign Policy*. 94th Congress, 1st session, 1975.

————. Senate. Committee on Governmental Affairs. *The Federal Advisory Committee Act: A Sourcebook*. 95th Congress, 2d session, 1978.

————. Senate. *Resolution to Approve the Obligation and Expenditure of Funds for Full-Scale Engineering Development of a Basing Mode for the MX Missile.* Senate Report 98-95 to Accompany S. Con. Resolution 26. 98th Congress, 1st session, 1983.

————. Senate. Select Committee on Government Operations with Respect to Intelligence Activities. *Final Report.* 95th Congress, 1st session, 1976.

Wall Street Journal. Selected articles on the Rockefeller (1974–1975), Tower (1986–1987), and 9/11 (2001–2004) commissions.

Walsh, Lawrence E. *Firewall: The Iran-Contra Conspiracy and Cover-up.* New York: W. W. Norton and Company, 1997.

————. *Iran-Contra: The Final Report.* New York: Times Books, 1994.

Washington Post. Selected articles on the Roberts (1941–1942), Rockefeller (1974–1975), Scowcroft (1982–1983), Tower (1986–1987), and 9/11 (2001–2004) commissions.

Waterman, Shaun. "Truth Squad." *American Prospect* (April 2004): 45.

Wecht, Cyril H. "Why Is the Rockefeller Commission So Single-Minded About a Lone Assassin in the Kennedy Case?" *Journal of Legal Medicine* 3 (1975): 22–25.

Weinberger, Caspar. Secretary of Defense, Reagan Administration. Telephone interview by author, 14 December 1994.

Werner, M. R. and John Starr. *Teapot Dome.* New York: Viking Press, 1959.

Wicker, Tom. *On Press.* New York: Viking Press, 1978.

Wildavsky, Aaron. "The Two Presidencies." *Transaction* 4 (December 1966): 7–14.

Wildenberg, Thomas. *All the Factors of Victory: Admiral Joseph Mason Reeves and the Origins of Carrier Airpower.* Washington, DC: Brassey's, 2003.

Wise, David and Thomas B. Ross. *The Invisible Government.* New York: Vintage Books, 1974.

Wolanin, Thomas R. *Presidential Advisory Commissions: Truman to Nixon.* Madison: University of Wisconsin Press, 1975.

Woolsey, R. James. Member, Scowcroft Commission. Telephone interview by author, 7 April 1995.

Woolsey, R. James, ed. *Nuclear Arms: Ethics, Strategy, Politics.* San Francisco: Institute for Contemporary Studies, 1984.

Wunderlin, Clarence E., ed. *Papers of Robert A. Taft 1939–1944.* Kent, OH: Kent State University Press, 2001.

Yin, Robert K. *Case Study Research: Design and Methods.* Beverly Hills: Sage Publications, 1984.

Zegart, Amy B. "Blue Ribbons, Black Boxes: Toward a Better Understanding of Presidential Commissions." *Presidential Studies Quarterly* 34:2 (June 2004): 366–394.

Zink, Stephen D. *Guide to the Presidential Advisory Commissions, 1973–1984.* Alexandria, VA: Chawyck-Healey, 1987.

Index

About the Book

Kenneth Kitts offers entry into the highly political, behind-closed-doors world of blue-ribbon investigative commissions convened in the aftermath of national security crises.

Ranging from Pearl Harbor to the September 11 terrorist attacks, Kitts takes the reader into the "backroom" to watch as presidents, their advisers, and commission members confront an armory of pressures. With rich detail and accounts of political intrigue, he reveals just how and when presidents reach for the blue-ribbon option to try to defuse crises, deflect criticism, and maintain control of national security policy—and how presidential expectations are sometimes unmet, as commissions issue damning reports with unforeseen and explosive consequences.

Kenneth Kitts is associate provost and professor of political science at Francis Marion University.